National Governments and Control of the Internet

Over the last decade, the Internet has transformed how information can be made available – it is now used to transfer information about things as varied as financial transactions and celebrity gossip and to link and coordinate activities between otherwise isolated people, from protest groups to lonely hearts. This unprecedented ease of access to a wealth of information and contacts presents a challenge to national governments who wish to control and restrain some of this activity.

In recent years, Internet control has become one of the major indicators to assess the balance between freedom and security in democracies. This book explores and compares how, why, and to what extent, national governments decide to control the Internet and how this impacts on crucial socio-economic activities and fundamental civil rights. The author provides detailed studies on the US, Germany, and Italy and further case studies on Japan, Canada, Australia, the Netherlands, France, Austria, Israel, Spain, Finland, and Switzerland to address topics such as cyberterrorism, the protection of information infrastructures, and the impact on individual privacy and freedom of speech.

This is the first cross-country, comparative study on the issue of Internet control. It will be of interest to international relations scholars and students, and particularly to those with an interest in the Internet.

Giampiero Giacomello is a post doctoral associate at the Peace Studies Program, Cornell University, and a visiting professor of international relations in the Department of Politics, University of Bologna. His research interests include international relations and security, and computer networks and cyberterrorism.

Routledge research in information technology and society

Reinventing government in the information age
International practice in IT-enabled public sector reform
Edited by Richard Heeks

Information technology in government
Britain and America
Helen Margetts

Information society studies
Alistair S. Duff

National electronic government
Building an institutional framework for joined up government –
a comparative study
Edited by Martin Eifert and Jan Ole Püschel

Local electronic government
A comparative study
Edited by Helmut Drüke

National Governments and Control of the Internet
A digital challenge
Giampiero Giacomello

National Governments and Control of the Internet

A digital challenge

Giampiero Giacomello

NEW YORK AND LONDON

First published 2005
by Routledge
2 Park Square, Milton Park, Abingdon, Oxon OX14 4RN

Simultaneously published in the USA and Canada
by Routledge
270 Madison Ave, New York, NY10016

Routledge is an imprint of the Taylor & Francis Group

Typeset in Times Roman by Keyword Publishing Services Ltd
Printed and bound in Great Britain by MPG Books Ltd, Bodmin

British Library Cataloguing in Publication Data
A catalogue record for this book available from the British Library

Library of Congress Cataloging-in-Publication Data
Giacomello, Giampiero, 1959- National governments and control
  of the Internet : a digital challenge / Giampiero Giacomello.
    p. cm.
  Includes bibliographical references and index.
  ISBN 0-415-33136-6 (hardback)
  1. Internet–Social aspects–Cross-cultural studies. 2. Internet–
  Government policy–Cross-cultural studies. 3. Internet–Access
  control–Cross-cultural studies 4. Telecommunication policy–
  Cross-cultural studies. 5. Internet industry-Government policy–
  Cross-cultural studies. 6. Information superhighway–Social
  aspects–Cross-cultural studies. I. Title.

  HM851.G5 2005
  303.48'33–dc22   2004016885

  ISBN 0-415-33136-6

To my parents and to Emma Michela

"Quis custodiet ipsos custodies?"

Decimus Junius Juvenalis

Contents

Illustrations

Figures

Table

Foreword

Before I comment on the substantive content of this book, let me just tell readers how it all began. Imagine a very nice sunny afternoon on the terrace of the "Convento," an old monastery converted into offices, at the European University Institute (EUI) in San Domenico di Fiesole overlooking Florence in Italy. Giampiero Giacomello had just been accepted as a doctoral researcher into the EUI and he wanted to have a first chat about his project with his future supervisor. We started talking about his academic background and then came to his dissertation proposal, which focused on the war in Bosnia-Herzegovina. We talked for about half an hour when Giampiero suddenly shifted gears and explained with some exasperation in his otherwise calm voice: "You know, Professor Risse, I am not really interested in studying the Bosnian war. Do you actually think that one could do some research on the Internet, or is this completely nonsensical for a political scientist?" This book results from a journey that began with that question in the early summer of 1997.

Indeed, this study is still among the few that deal with the Internet from a political science perspective. Yet, it tackles a research question of interest to both academic scholars and practitioners alike: is the Internet beyond the control of nation-states, and how can we explain the differences in the degree to which national governments try to exert authority over the Web? During the early Internet hype, few people thought that this question actually made sense. The Internet was seen as a "wired world" beyond the control of nation-states, as part and parcel of globalization's relentless attack on national sovereignty and autonomy. Well, the crash of the dot.com industry and September 11, 2001, have changed this perception considerably. The Internet quickly entered the realm of national security.

As Giampiero Giacomello shows in this important book, politics entered the Web long before 9/11. From the beginning, governments attempted to control access to the Web and to ensure that it would not interfere with national security concerns. As the fascinating story about the fight over encryption in Chapter 2 documents, governments failed to control encryption software, but not because of technical difficulties. Rather, national authorities faced a formidable coalition – an "accidental alliance," as Giacomello calls it – between information technology companies on the one hand, and civil liberties NGOs on the other. NGOs and companies joined forces – and won.

As the book documents, it is not particularly interesting to study why autocratic governments would want to exert control over the Internet concerning both access by users and content. The more liberal ideas are diffused over the Web, the more dictators all over the world should worry. Moreover, the Internet serves as a powerful connectivity tool among transnational social movements and NGOs which should also be of concern for autocratic states. In this context, the Internet is probably the one symbol of globalization that is not controversial between transnational activists and Wall Street bankers, as Giacomello implies.

But why would democratic governments want to control the Internet? As Giacomello points out, we need to distinguish between information as content and information as infrastructure. On the one hand, information as content should not be of concern to democracies, since it is protected by the freedom of speech (within certain limits, as the controversies over child pornography and hate speech reveal). Protecting the information infra-structure and preventing criminals as well as terrorists from using it, on the other hand, are of legitimate security concerns to national governments. Yet, there are trade-offs between protecting the information infrastructure as well as preventing criminal usage and non-interference in content. The more states care about the Internet infrastructure from a national security perspective, the more likely they are to interfere with content. This book is about how different governments deal with these challenges.

The study compares the United States – the information superpower – with Germany and Italy, three democracies that nevertheless show different approaches to the Internet. Giacomello argues that two factors determine the interaction patterns between national governments, the ICT industry, and civil liberties NGOs. First, the structure of interest aggregation in the country is crucial, namely whether it follows a more pluralist or a more corporatist pattern. The United States exhibits a more pluralist way of interest aggregation, while Germany and Italy can be viewed as more consensus-oriented democracies. Second, it matters a great deal whether governments succeed in "securitizing" the Internet, i.e., whether they can convincingly link policies toward the Internet to national security concerns. Here, of course, 9/11 was crucial for the United States, but securitizing efforts began long before the terrorist attacks on the World Trade Center. Compared to the United States, national security concerns were of little interest in Germany and Italy, even after 9/11.

So, why do you have to read this book? First, it constitutes a fascinating case study on the crucial question of how globalization affects the ability of governments to conduct policies. The book shows that globalization is not the end of politics, but its transformation. It puts yet another nail in the coffin of "globalists" of all kinds who have argued that globalization is the end of the nation-state as we knew it. If the Internet has so far survived control efforts by governments, it has done so because of political struggles, not because of some technological dynamics outside human control.

Second, the book is of immediate concern to those of us interested in the information age. Giampiero Giacomello tells about the trade-offs between civil liberties and national security, both of central and legitimate concern to liberal democracies in the age of transnational terrorism. The book shows that total protection of a country's information infrastructure is impossible without seriously hampering democratic freedom and free speech. These are trade-offs that have to be dealt with politically. The book demonstrates how different democracies deal with these challenges in various ways.

Thus, the Internet indeed presents a "digital challenge" to all of us. In this well-researched book, Giampiero Giacomello does a terrific job in making us all much better informed participants and users of the information age.

Thomas Risse
Professor of International Politics,
Freie Universität Berlin

Acknowledgments

The theme of Internet control accompanied me for almost eight years, from the European University Institute in Florence to the University of Bologna, to the Peace Studies Program at Cornell University. When I started, the "Net" was a very different phenomenon and I thought that it would be fascinating to witness how the Internet would slowly change my field of study. International relations is a discipline that changes very slowly but I thought I might contribute to that change. It all happened very quickly then, and "Internet" is now a common word (albeit not a well-understood concept) for the general public. In these years the number of friends and colleagues who have influenced my thinking about this topic (and international relations in general) is simply mind-boggling. I want to express my appreciation to at least a few of them.

Thomas Risse and Craig Nation have been true mentors and friends. During the outstanding time I spent in Ithaca, NY, with the Peace Studies Program, Matthew Evangelista, Kathleen Vogel, Judith Reppy, Allan Dafoe, Peter Katzenstein, Sid Tarrow, and Makiko Nishiyama read various chapters, offered sharp remarks, and always encouraged me. In Bologna, Piero Ignazi and Lucio Picci never failed to point out inconsistencies in my arguments and ways to correct them. Ralf Bendrath, Myriam Dunn, and Lorenzo Valeri were insightful sources of facts, amazing details, and stories, while Johan Eriksson provided strong (albeit indirect) intellectual stimuli. I want to thank Lee Miller who was present at the difficult start of this project. Chiara Strozzi, who weathered the "dreadful Chapter 3," was glad to see how it all ended.

This book is dedicated to my parents and to my daughter Emma Michela. My father was a true visionary of electronic commerce and was amazingly correct in what he predicted. Emma had not been born when I started this long path and she was not even a toddler when she sat in front of a computer for the first time (to play a game). I hope that one day she will be genuinely amused to read how computers, networks, and governments used to be, way, way back then.

Giampiero Giacomello
Ithaca, NY
June 2004

Abbreviations

ACLU	American Civil Liberties Union
AG KRITIS	Arbeit Gruppe für Kritische Infrastrukturen
AKSIS	Arbeitskreis Schutz von Infrastrukturen
ALCEI	Associazione per la Libera Communicazionione Elettronica
ARPA	Advanced Research Projects Agency
ARPANET	ARPA Network
BDSG	Bundesdatenschutzgesetz
BfV	Bundesamt für Verfassungsschutz
BND	Bundesnachrichtendienst
BKA	Bundeskriminalamt
BSI	Bundesamt für Sicherheit in der Informationtechnik
CALEA	Communications Assistance for Law Enforcement Act
CCC	Chaos Computer Club
CDA	Communication Decency Act
CDT	Center for Democracy and Technology
CERT	Computer Emergency Response Team
CIAO	Critical Infrastructure Assurance Office
CNIPA	Centro Nazionale per l'Informatica nella Pubblica Amministrazione
CNR	Consiglio Nazionale delle Ricerche
COE	Council of Europe
COPA	Children On-line Protection Act
COPPA	Children On-line Privacy Protection Act
CSA	Computer Security Act
CYTEX	Cyber Terror Exercise
D21	Deutschland 21st Century Initiative
DARPA	*See* ARPA
DES	Data Encryption Standard
DNS	Domain name system
DHS	Department of Homeland Security (US)
DOC	Department of Commerce (US)
DOD	Department of Defense (US)

DOJ	Department of Justice (US)
DoS	Denial of service
DTAG	Deutsche Telekom
EFF	Electronic Frontier Foundation
ENISA	European Network and Information Agency
EPIC	Electronic Privacy Information Center
Europol	European Police
FBI	Federal Bureau of Investigation
FCC	Federal Communications Commission
GdF	Guardia di Finanza
GILC	Global Internet Liberties Campaign
ICANN	Internet Corporation for Assigned Names and Numbers
ICT	Information and communication technologies
ISOC	Internet Society
ISP	Internet service provider
ITAR	International Traffic in Arms Regulations
ITU	International Telecommunication Union
MOD	Ministry of Defense
NBS	National Bureau of Standards
NGO	Non-governmental organization
NII	National information infrastructure
NIPC	National Infrastructure Protection Center
NIST	National Institute of Standards and Technology
NPD	Nationaldemokratische Partei Deutschlands
NSA	National Security Agency
NSDD	National Security Decision Directive
NSFNET	National Science Foundation Network
NTIA	National Telecommunications and Information Administration
OECD	Organization for Economic Cooperation and Development
OSI	Open Systems Interconnection
PA	Public administration
PCCIP	Presidential Commission on Critical Infrastructure Protection
PDD	Presidential Decision Directive
PGP	Pretty Good Privacy
PKC	Public key cryptography
RFC	Request for comments
RSA	Rivest, Shamir, and Adleman
SigG	Digitale Signatur Gesetz
SIGINT	Signal Intelligence
SPD	Sozialedemokratiche Partei Deutschlands
TCP/IP	Transmission Control Protocol/Internet Protocol
TKG	Telekommunikation Gesetz

TIM	Telecom Italia Mobile
USA Patriot (Act)	Uniting and Strengthening America by Providing Appropriate Tools Required to Intercept and Obstruct Terrorism
WA	Wassenaar Agreement
WIPO	World Intellectual Property Organization
WTO	World Trade Organization
W3C	World Wide Web Consortium
Y2K	Year 2000 (also known as the Millennium bug)

1 Introduction

Everyone has the right to freedom of opinion and expression.
(Universal Declaration of Human Rights, Article 19, 1948)

The Internet is for everyone, but it won't be if governments restrict access to it.
(Vint Cerf, co-founder, Internet Society, and co-inventor of TCP/IP, April 7, 1999)

"On the Net, nobody knows you're a dog"

In 1993, a popular cartoon in the *The New Yorker* pictured a dog in front of a computer, describing the Internet (or, more familiarly, "the Net") to a fellow dog with this wry but appropriate punch-line.[1] It was an early attempt to lighten up a stodgy, though brand-new, piece of technology: the "network of computer networks." The joke summarized well one of the features of the Net that many users already treasured at that early date: on the Internet, one's identity could be concealed, or altered, or falsified at will. This important feature, however, like many aspects of the Internet, had not been an explicit part of the network's original concept.

The birth and expansion of the Internet have been riddled with contra-dictions and surprises.[2] Originally a communication network designed to connect the many different machines of the US Department of Defense (DOD), the Internet had its roots "in the darkness of the Cold War" (Rosenzweig, 1998: 1533). DOD planners and engineers thought it might further be useful in a nuclear war. Otherwise "the Defense Department would never have committed funds to projects like ARPANET without the beliefs that they would ultimately serve specific military objectives and larger Cold War goals" (Rosenzweig, 1998: 1533). Indeed, it was the Soviet success with the Sputnik satellite that prompted the DOD Advanced Research Projects Agency (ARPA) to start pouring money into what would become, in the mid-1990s, the "accidental superhighway" as *The Economist* correctly labeled it (Anderson, 1995). Concepts and ideas such as packet-switching, distributed networks, and TCP/IP (the "Internet" protocol) slowly but steadily built on each other thanks to the dedication and ingenuity of several engineers and technicians.[3] Ironically, "anarchy" (that is, the lack of effective control by a superior authority, despite the origins in the US government ARPANET) is the one feature that the early Internet shared with the "international system."

Despite those murky origins, almost by accident the Internet then developed into a "network of networks" to disseminate knowledge among universities. There was no need to build the information highways because the Internet was already there. It now carries news, data, encrypted financial transactions, and impressive sex-related material. It has, ultimately (again by coincidence), revolutionized the way private companies do business. As it expanded in both size and scope, the computer network was seen simultaneously as a threat to, a tool for, or the object of statutory control (Mulgan, 1991: 5). National governments grew "schizophrenic" about it, because they found its "libertarian culture and contempt for national borders subversive and frankly terrifying" (*The Economist*, 1998: 18). The growing importance of economic liberalization has also led to substantial changes in the way that state control is exercised. By the late 1980s and early 1990s, Mulgan (1991: 137) noted, "deregulations coincided with an ever more active role for governments and state agencies in creating what they believed to be the best climate for the communications economy." What happened was not the end of state control, but rather a change in its forms.

These remarks trigger some puzzling questions. Why do national governments want to control what is, apparently, so difficult to control?[4] Why bother to put resources into monitoring a network that may route around control points the way it was designed to do around interruptions after a nuclear exchange? And if governments press on with their control programs, what levels of control would be reasonable to attain, since countries and their governments tend to be socially, culturally, and economically very different from one another? Answering these dilemmas is the central goal of this book.

Control, with its many variants, is a much studied theme in the social sciences. The form of control examined in this work is statutory control, that is, control exercised by the "state" and, in its place, by its material counterpart, the government. In the classification of international relations, this means that this work focuses on the *unit* level of analysis. Control often goes hand in hand with "power," although the two concepts do not coincide (Lukes, 1974; Horowitz, 1990; McMahon, 2002). Indeed, power is often identified with a property, an ability or mechanical energy, that can be directed or stored. But control carries with it "the sense of information environment" (Mulgan, 1991: 52). This is the reason why so many authors have analyzed information (and communications) and control, whether social or political, together (Pool, 1983, 1990; Beniger, 1986; Buchner,

1988; Horowitz, 1990; Chomsky, 1997; Pound, 1997; Shapiro, 1999; Wright, 2000; McMahon, 2002; Mueller, 2002; Zittrain, 2004). Information, communications (conveyed information), and control are all functions in the same equation (Mowlana, 1997).[5] Given these conditions, one would hardly fail in summoning the broad class of "media" to explain Internet control.

Radio, television, and one-to-many broadcasting in general in twentieth-century Europe were born under state structures with centralized control. This centralized control was what made (and makes, according to Chomsky, 1997) propaganda possible. The identification of the Internet as the newest communication medium would therefore explain why it is controlled. After all, "governments, fearful of a loss of control over sovereignty and culture, would continue to resist opening new communication channels" (Noam, 1990: vii), despite the century-old, self-defeating experience of that restrictiveness.[6] The answer "the Internet is controlled because it is a new communication medium" is an incomplete and very partial answer.

A most striking feature of the Internet is its complexity. Engineers and computer scientists have long lost track of how the "whole" works. They know and understand the single parts, but nobody can comprehend the whole structure. This complexity is the outcome of three crucial sets of factors. First, there is dual nature of the Internet that makes it, *at the same time*, an infrastructure (that is, the actual computer network) and a communication medium. The Internet "as infrastructure" allows the functioning of other distribution networks such as water, gas, or energy.[7] In the case of telecommunications (telecom) the Internet is so embedded into the overall structure that it is simply impossible to make any distinction at all. Despite using the same wires and software, the Internet communication medium is a substantially different phenomenon from the Internet infrastructure. Unlike radio and television, the former is a many-to-many broadcasting system in which users are, at the same time, audience and producers of information, data, knowledge, outright lies, and propaganda.[8]

The crucial point here is that information and data about the utilities travel on the Internet as packets that are exactly the same as the packets that carry the bytes of an e-mail to a friend, a newspaper article, my travel plans, or the request for a Web server to open the weather Web page. The bytes of financial transactions are usually encrypted, thus the information cannot be easily read. But even those packets are not any different for the router computer that is sending them to their destination. Hence, the disruption of that router would also affect the encrypted packets of a multimillion-dollar financial transaction. Information and data on the utilities are hardly ever encrypted. All the packets travel together along the same wires and routes and are indistinguishable, but the information they carry does not have equal value. The loss of an e-mail to a friend, the reservation for a car rental, or a bank transfer have different consequences and meaning for their senders and receivers.

Second, there is the paradoxical multiple jurisdiction of the Internet. What authorities, domestic as well as international, are institutionally competent for regulating, monitoring, and maintaining the "two Internets?" The answer to this question is simple but with complicated implications: multiple authorities that have different goals and different tools at their disposal. Therefore, if there is a threat, domestically originated, to the Internet as infrastructure, then law enforcement officers should have jurisdiction. If the origin of the threat is not domestic but international, then a mix of law enforcement agencies and the national security agencies could be the solution. A further distinction is whether the cause of an international menace is a state or a non-state actor, which would influence the proportion of military/police personnel necessary. On the other hand, if the threat is not to the Internet as infrastructure *per se*, but it uses the Internet as communication medium, then it becomes a crime. In these circumstances, regardless of whether the source is domestic or international, the proper answer would be domestic and, if necessary, international law enforcement agencies. A further distinction is that the gravity of the crime depends on the domestic criminal legislation: an offense that would be dealt with through lawyers in a democracy might imply capital punishment in an autocratic country. The series of distinctions could continue.

The third set of factors is the multiplicity of stakeholders (Keohane and Nye, 2000; Herrera, 2002; Giacomello, 2003). There are three main sets of stakeholders on the Internet: national governments (and their agencies), the information and communication technology (ICT) business sector, and non-governmental organizations (NGOs). The NGO set may include a vast (and loose) array of individual users' groups, civil liberties advocates, and consumers' organizations, which operate to advance their specific interests. NGOs and ICT firms may or may not be transnational. NGOs are non-state actors that may pursue perfectly legal ends such as protecting human rights, the environment, or privacy. A minority of NGOs, however, namely terrorist groups or organized crime, are involved in assassination, destruction, or illegal trafficking (Josselin and Wallace, 2001). These NGOs use the Internet mostly as a communication medium, exactly as the "legal" NGOs do. At different stages, the diverse, individual actors that constitute the three stakeholders have formed alliances to increase or to resist control on the Internet. In this respect, September 11, 2001, was the watershed. Before that date, especially in the United States, civil liberties NGOs and private industry joined forces to resist the US government's attempts at increasing control on the Internet. As Chapter 2 shows, that "odd alliance" was successful. After September 2001, however, the US government was apparently able to convince the ICT industry to privilege security, even if at the expense of civil liberties.

So, why do governments want to control the Internet? The more advanced a country is, the more dependent on computer networks (like the Internet) it will be. Governments want to control the Internet to protect their information infrastructure networks that are so crucial to the survival and well-being of their countries. As early as the 1970s, the new information technologies were thought to be likely to increase states' vulnerability. A report to the Swedish government, the Tengelin Report (Tengelin, 1981), emphasized the main risks of a networked society (including dependence on foreign vendors and the threat of hackers' raids). Once national governments realized the actual extension of the Internet and the potential reach of individual users, they started to consider increasing their control over the network. After all, controls over inflows and outflows of people, goods, and information have been vital for states to assert their authority, and thus their sovereignty.

These viewpoints require some further specifications. There are two distinctive faces to the problem of "control to protect": (a) controlling the national information infrastructure (NII), of which the Internet is an integral part, and (b) controlling on-line content. In case (a), the NII should be controlled for protection in the same way as governments control and try to protect their sea-lanes or railways. In case (b) that control may easily turn into abuse, censorship, and violation of privacy. It is not accidental that some less developed countries such as China, which are less dependable on computer networks, tend to focus on controlling content first and securing the NII second. For most countries, (a) and (b) cases are placed on a security continuum that goes from national security to law enforcement and public order. On that continuum, advanced countries (which happen to be, in most cases, democracies) have a propensity to see (a) and (b) within the domain of law enforcement and public order rather than of national security. For these democratic countries, cybercrime, perhaps cyberterrorism, is what they perceive as Internet threats more than hostile governments trying to wage cyberwar on their NII. Law enforcement agencies should primarily deal with those threats. The majority of case studies presented in this volume support these findings.

Protecting the NII is hence one of the principal reasons why national governments want to control the Internet, and it is also an integral part of the national security policy of most countries (national security can be seen as a counterpart of social control, according to McMahon, 2002). But states are now substantially different institutions from what they were when international trade (and the business sector) was considered to be subordinate to national security (Strange, 1988). Today, the mission of national security, particularly in the area of ICT, cannot be fulfilled without close cooperation between the public and the private sector (Bendrath, 2001; Rathmell, 2001; Bruno, 2002; Dunn and Wigert, 2004a). The largest portion of the NII is owned by private enterprises and the necessary software and communication tools are also produced by companies. This growing (and indispensable) presence of the private sector in the most exclusive government function, namely national security policy, represents an epochal change. One may object that the defense industry has always been crucial to national security or that mercenaries, as a form of private enterprise, have been offering their services for centuries.[9] Most importantly, this new role for ICT firms in the shaping of national security policy implies that the private sector would yield an influence on national governments never before seen in history.

It is common that private interests of firms collide with the requirements of national security. In the current circumstances, however, national governments cannot simply overrule whatever opposition the ICT sector may have with reference to protecting the NII. Ironically, countries that have experience with telecommunications and utilities (traditional government monopolies) should be better off to some extent. If push comes to shove, these governments would have some expertise on how to take most of the NII under their direct jurisdiction and control. For example, small, neutral countries such as Sweden or Switzerland adopted a "total defense" model during the Cold War that required a very close partnership between the public and private sector. In Israel, this integration is even further advanced. Although the United States has always cherished pragmatic, business-like approaches to problem-solving, close cooperation between the public and private sector is not the rule. Some large industries, such as automobiles or steel, have undoubtedly benefited from strong government support, but the American business culture has traditionally been wary of government intervention.

National governments of advanced countries then have a new "partner" in the decision-making process of national security policy. But if the *sancta sanctorum* of national governments (the national security policy) is necessarily open to non-governmental actors like software and telecom companies, it also becomes more accessible to other non-governmental actors. In the 1990s, Internet users and consumers, independent software developers, and civil liberties advocates created a network of NGOs. These organizations are mostly concerned with content control and free access to the Internet, but with computer networks it is often quite difficult to keep content separated from the infrastructure. As the case of cryptowars[10] presented in Chapter 2 shows, this state of affairs may have considerable implications for the policy-making of national security.

National governments want to control the Internet because they need to protect their NII and they need the active contribution of the private sector. The difficult distinction between content and infrastructure makes it somehow easier for autocracies to control the Internet. Autocracies all over the world have a long-standing praxis of monitoring content on radio and television networks. The literature on how autocratic countries control the Internet no less than other media is now abundant (Saich, 2001; Chase and Mulvenon, 2002; Kalathil and Boas, 2003; Reporters Sans Frontières, 2003; Kurlantzick, 2004).[11] Indeed, Kurlantzick (2004: 21) notes how easy "authoritarian regimes have controlled and, in some cases, subverted it." If, for all autocracies, controlling Internet content is a sort of "second nature" (Gibbs, 2004), China has been (thanks to Western technology) the most efficient controller (Saich, 2001; Chase and Mulvenon, 2002; Kalathil and Boas, 2003; Kurlantzick, 2004).[12]

Autocratic governments claim that, in this era of terrorism, they need to control the Internet (with no distinction between content and infrastructure) to protect their NII and to fight the (greatly exaggerated) "cyberterrorists." The national security communities have also a powerful voice with those autocratic leaders. For autocratic governments, controlling Internet content is still far more important than protecting the NII. In fact, with the exception of Singapore, their dependence on computer networks is still very limited. Despite the impressive economic growth of China, for instance, its information infrastructure is far behind that of most advanced economies (United Nations Development Program, 2001; Kirkman *et al.*, 2002a; Mingers, 2003). The emphasis on the global "war on terror" has simply made the argument of protecting the NII for national security reasons more compelling.

To sum up, autocracies do not need reasons to control the Internet (perhaps only "justifications"). They do it by default (Chase and Mulvenon, 2002; Kalathil and Boas, 2003; cf. Gibbs, 2004). What about democracies? They need to explain to their voters/taxpayers why they want to do that. National governments in open democratic countries face the "hardest" digital challenge. They have to balance exploiting the economic potentialities of the new technology while protecting citizens' privacy, freedom, and health, and protecting the NII. They have more access points through which outsiders may influence government decisions (Risse-Kappen, 1995b). Interest aggregations, whether of entrepreneurs, consumers, Internet users, human rights activists, or environmentalists, are the norm in democracies. Hence, the other Internet stakeholders, namely businesses and the non-governmental community, have ample opportunities to influence the highly complex and articulated (and sometime even contradictory) policy-making process. As Risse-Kappen (1995b: 188) correctly puts it, "ideas do not float freely" and decision-makers are always exposed to several and often contradictory policy concepts.

The model

To sum up, national governments want to control the Internet to protect the NII, but while for autocracies control on the Internet as infrastructure or content medium is the same, democracies, because of their "checks and balances," are required to differentiate. Furthermore, autocratic states and governments can more easily coerce the private sector (both domestic and foreign) to actively participate in their control policies. Finally, these governments do not have to struggle with the third stakeholders (civil liberties NGOs) because the domestic political structures of their states simply allow them to do so. Figure 1.1 shows the causal flows for autocracies

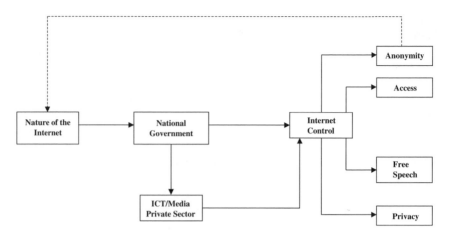

Figure 1.1 Autocracies and Internet control.

The dual, technical nature of the Internet obliges autocratic governments to take notice. Autocracies exercise direct control on the network and compel (or buy out) the private sector to support that control. Issue linkage is extremely prominent here, since Internet control then affects personal privacy, free speech, universal access (not everybody is allowed to go online),[13] and anonymity (users are linked to their acts). Why does anonymity feed back onto the "nature of the Internet"? Because anonymity is the single most crucial factor of Internet and computer network technology. Anonymity is the one feature of the Internet that has worried governments the most. It is clearly possible to trace the IP address of a given machine on the network, but there is no guarantee of the individual's identity behind the computer. Taking away anonymity (as Bill Gates recommended for instance)[14] would drastically change the network (for example making spam almost impossible) and, ultimately, make Internet control more efficient.

Democracies cannot follow the same path, of course. Hence, the domestic political structure of the country considered is the first important variable to explain the difference among autocratic and democratic countries. When it comes to the global information infrastructure, however, democracies, for the reasons presented above, are more important than autocracies. In fact, they possess, rule, and influence a larger portion of the global ICT sector than autocratic states. For the time being, democracies are more dependent and have more at stake in the evolution of global computer networks. Therefore, it is important to explain the different behaviors and diverse levels of control on the Internet that democracies have. Figure 1.2 summarizes the causal flows for democracies.

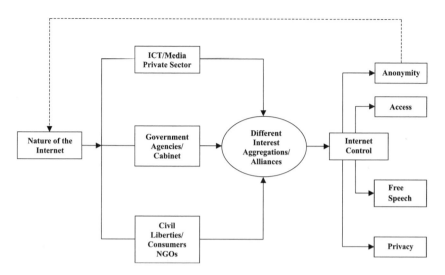

Figure 1.2 Democracies and Internet control.

Again, the dual nature of the Internet prompts the three stakeholders into action to pursue different interests. How the three stakeholders (or subgroups of them) combine their forces, have access points to, or oppose one another determines different interest aggregations and assorted alliances. For example, in the case of control on encryption software (the "cryptowars" examined in the next chapter), civil liberties NGOs and most of the ICT private sector favored liberalization and individual use. Recognizing the importance of the private sector for their battles, NGOs have developed fine diplomatic skills to win over the sympathy and support of the private sector (Doh and Teegen, 2003). The NGOs have been so successful in this strategy that a growing number of companies now integrate the viewpoints of the non-governmental sector in their business plans (*The Economist*, 2003b). This pattern has unmistakably worked also in the ICT/media sector.

Internet control in democracies is justified on the basis of protecting the NII and prosecuting those acts (and only those) that the majority of the public and society's traditions deem as illegal or criminal, such as Internet fraud or child pornography. Free speech cannot cross into libel, access should be non-discriminatory, and individual privacy guaranteed until a judge issues a warrant on reasonable suspicion. But function creep is an irresistible force even for democratic governments. It appears that several of the democracies studied here have exceeded that "normal" level of Internet control described above. September 11 and the war on terror that followed acted as catalysts for the many "solutions in search of a problem"[15] that had appeared in the first phase of development of the Internet. Observations that "governmental controls are ineffective today and in danger of becoming irrelevant tomorrow" (Barth and Smith, 1997: 295) are harder to believe today. Nonetheless, some authors still conclude that "global internet usage famously eludes control" (Zittrain, 2004: 203). Democratic governments decided to adopt worst-case scenario policies for Internet control, without any hard evidence that these policies have made their NII (and their countries) more secure (Schneier, 2003).

The distinction between autocratic or democratic states is simplistic. In fact, there are different types of democracies and their domestic political structure determines what attitude that country's government will have on Internet control. Furthermore, it is essential to comprehend why a democratic government has a certain level of Internet control instead of another. The multiplicity of access points to the executive and legislative branches, and the aggregation of interests and different alliances among stakeholders, shape that outcome. The degree of pluralism of a democratic society is therefore of great consequence to establish how NGOs (and, to some extent, the private sector as well) can interact with the government and influence the policy-making process.[16] Lijphart (1999) provides the most comprehensive recent analysis of pluralism among democracies.

In the countries with lower pluralism, such as Austria and Germany, interest groups are relatively few in number but large in size. The same conditions apply to Italy and Spain, but there, with the exception of traditional trade unions, interest groups are still not well skilled in interacting with the government. Pluralism is at the top in the United States and Canada, but while the latter has adopted Europe's ideology of social partnership, in the United States interest groups define their identities by emphasizing differences with each other and with their counterparts in the government.

Internet control and relevant international relations theories: a brief overview

Bull (1995: 264) noted that the growth of private and international violence, the role of transnational organizations, and the opportunities for global integration provided by the technological unification of the world were "awkward facts for the classical theory of world politics." The end of the Cold War simply reinforced Bull's conclusions. Agnew and Corbrige (1995) observed that the blending of computer technologies with the new systems of telecommunications was leading towards extraordinary changes from the point of view of international relations. Scholars have made several attempts at applying existing international relations theories to understand the impact of computer networks and modern telecommunications on international politics. The record has been one of mixed success. One major drawback of studying the Internet and computer networks from the perspective of international relations is that it is problematical to properly define and frame the issue. Everard (2000) is archetypal in this respect. While challenging "the idea that the nation-state is dead," he explores the systemic inequalities brought about by globalization, covering *en passant* issues such as war, censorship, and the philosophical implications of hypertext, with hardly any causal logic.

For a long time, the two main schools to explain the behavior of states (and governments) have been realism (with all its variants) and liberalism (with all its variants).[17] The former theory emphasizes states' security concerns, power distribution, and the anarchic nature of the international system (and a Hobbesian world-view). The latter stresses international cooperation and interdependence among state actors, and the significance of domestic structures and interest configuration in the making of international politics (a Lockean world-view). Realism basically asserts that when a country's security is at stake, all other matters (including a country's economic well-being) should be of secondary importance for national governments. Liberalism argues that democracies should not feel threatened by other democracies (since democracies do not fight each other), and that economic interdependence and international trade would reduce the risks of war and make the world a safer place. Finally, while realists tend to view states as unitary actors and study their interactions on this premise, liberals consider states (and governments) complex and fragmented organizations, which function as a conglomeration of diverse interests.[18]

These two schools have produced a wealth of other theories that trace their roots back to these schools. More recently, social constructivism has emerged as a new meta-theory to challenge the rational choice meta-theory which comprehends both realism and liberalism (Katzenstein *et al.*, 1998). There are substantial epistemological differences between meta-theories (and schools). But when it comes to finding the empirical causes of important social phenomena, Fearon and Wendt (2002) agued that a synthesis is not only commendable but necessary. This work follows that pathway. The long intellectual tradition of international relations has provided plenty of stimuli and insights to explain why national governments want to control the Internet. To evaluate the contribution of international relations theories to the further understanding of the reasons why states want to control the Internet should start with the need to protect the NII. The technical nature of the Internet (and of computer networks in general) obliges governments to be concerned about that problem. This point of view would present an explanation consistent with realist theory. Indeed, when security is at stake, all other matters must take a back seat. For example, in the United States the information infrastructure can become a target for domestic and foreign enemies, and the United States has been openly identified as the main foe by several countries and non-state actors. In this respect, September 11 is the ultimate proof. But this would be a very incomplete answer to the question of why governments want to control the

Internet and it would not say anything about the reason why there are different levels and types of Internet control.

Few other acts are more representative of states' authority than deciding what national security consists of. This adaptive tool allows states' leaders to identify, often rather subjectively, what can endanger national security, whether another superpower, malicious hackers or, as autocratic states do, unarmed human rights activists. All individuals working in defense departments, intelligence and counterintelligence agencies, and, to some extent, all enforcement officials belong to the "national security community." National security implies the survival of the state. Therefore, realist scholars claim, it should be taken extremely seriously and prevail over any other considerations. Before September 2001, in the United States the national security community was large, most vociferous, and most able to advocate its arguments with other government branches as well as Congress.

Nevertheless, the other alliance (pro-freedom/consumers' organizations and the private sector) made a good case for resisting those demands. Indeed, in the case of the "cryptowars", the "accidental alliance" managed to gain the support of part the government and the general public at the expense of the national security party. As far as the Internet and the NII are concerned, even after September 11, the national security argument has not become uncontroversial at all (Bronner, 2004). Moreover, the private sector has only recently become convinced that "security" is an item worth paying for. The overall level of control on the NII has increased in all countries after September 2001, but less than in the United States. Although the magnitude was different, almost all other countries considered in this work have been threatened or hit by terrorists (as in Spain in March 2004) and are as much dependent on their NII as the United States. A strictly realist explanation would thus be superficial because it would not explicate the differences between autocratic and democratic countries. Nor would it clarify why democracies have different levels of Internet control with most of the computer-dependent countries focusing on threats like malicious hackers or cybercriminals rather than cyberterrorists.

Buzan *et al.* (1998) have proposed an innovative approach to the study of security, which could be seen as the synthesis that Fearon and Wendt (2002) have proposed. The approach of "securitization" is part of the constructivist (or reflectivist) theory of international relations and emphasizes integrating different types of actors interacting through two or more social levels.[19] Securitization is akin to politicization. Whenever an issue becomes politicized, it becomes intensely emotional and often highly controversial. There are two important elements in the process of securitization. The first is the securitization move, that is, a form of discourse of "presenting something as an existential threat" (Buzan *et al.*, 1998: 25). The second element is the implicit acceptance by an audience (public) that the issue is securitized. The two elements are necessary and sufficient.

Several governments' agencies undertook plenty of securitization moves with reference to the NII and the Internet. Since organized crime is hardly perceived as a security threat, the new category of "cyberterrorists" emerged, which would be amenable to securitize the Internet and the NII. The most convincing evidence that this process occurred is the struggle to control encryption software by several national governments, known as the "cryptowars." In the cryptowars (which are examined in Chapter 2) national security agencies, predominantly in the United States but also in Europe (France and the United Kingdom, especially) and in several autocratic countries (China, Singapore, etc.) argued that individual access to strong encryption software would bring about disaster for intelligence. Moreover, cyberterrorists would make their communications impregnable and malicious hackers would rampage thought the Internet and the NII in total anonymity and wreck havoc with impunity. The pessimistic views did not prevail because the alliance of NGOs and ICT firms resisted them and thus the public remained unconvinced. Most European governments as well as Japan remained unconvinced too, and remained focused on cybercrime as the major threat to the electronic economy and the Internet. As further proof that was the correct interpretation, nothing even remotely similar to the apocalyptic consequences depicted by many national security agencies has happened, although strong encryption software is now widely available for individual use.

If the securitization process is accepted as valid, then it is important to investigate in detail not only the domestic struggle among different stakeholders (governments, ICT companies, and NGOs), but also inter-bureaucratic turfs and how ICT companies and NGOs pursue their specific interests. Theories that look at the domestic dimension are thus needed. There is little disagreement among scholars now that the international and the domestic levels influence each other and that it is necessary to study both to comprehend fully how governments behave (Werner *et al.*, 2003). Within liberal theory literature, domestic politics approaches focus on domestic structures (for example, Risse-Kappen, 1995a, 1995b; Katzenstein, 1996) and on domestic interest configurations (for example, Evans *et al.*, 1993; Milner, 1997). Both approaches are extremely useful as they account for the differences among autocracies and democracies and why alliances among stakeholders vary in democracies. In the former occurrence, while both types of governments apparently have incentives to protect the NII, autocracies do not really separate that from controlling Internet content. Democracies, on the other hand, are obliged to keep them separate and cannot appear to exceed with controlling content. The domestic interest approach helps to understand why democracies as diverse as the United States, Canada, Germany, Italy, Japan, Israel, and Switzerland have witnessed such diversity of alliances among Internet stakeholders.

The seminal work of Allison (with Zelikow, 1999) on the bureaucratic model is particularly valuable in this case. Allison and Zelikow noted how, during the Cuban missile crisis, several US government officials, including President Kennedy, were pursuing their specific (and often diverging) political agendas. Furthermore, their beliefs, ideas, functions, and hopes shaped the way they behaved and acted during the crisis. If the mechanisms identified by Allison and Zelikow were at work during that crisis, which had been a paramount watershed in the history of US national security, presumably they have been working in many other situations.

Kozak and Keagle (1988: 258) pointed out that, as with any bureaucracy, "the national security community is penetrated by outside groups and interests." The key factor in setting the agenda for national security and defense is what political leaders *perceive*, in a specific moment, to be a threat. In this respect, national security and defense are just part of "politics." The justification for Internet control based on "national security" conditions has presented civil liberties NGOs, ordinary users, and also private business with considerable complications, since, in many countries, national security cannot even be argued against. In fact, appeals to the exigencies of security take "priority over all other claims on state policy" (Strange, 1984: 184–5). Nonetheless, in the latter, individuals and NGOs are in a position where they can use their "voice options." They can access policy-makers in various parts of government as well as legislators and try to persuade some of them to revise the cabinet's previous position on a given issue or create difference of opinions within the government itself. For instance, before September 11, 2001, the prevailing attitude in the United States and several other countries (like Australia or the United Kingdom) was "let's see what develops" (Kahin and Nesson, 1997: viii) or "hands-off" (*The Economist*, 1997: 13). Despite the opposition of intelligence and law enforcement agencies, the ICT sector and civil liberties NGOs always made sure that some sections of the government apparatus shared their views on key issues such as encryption software or the need to protect privacy so as to foster confidence in electronic commerce. Democratic governments, hardly identifiable with monolithic, homogeneous "black boxes," were particularly susceptible to those tactics. Even in the aftermath of September 11, they still are.[20]

Another crucial element to understand the evolution of Internet control is to observe the distribution (and control) of technical and legal information about computer networks and the NII. Information asymmetries are decisive for maintaining social control and thus societal cohesion. In general, Milner, (1997: 21) notes, "asymmetries of information domestically work in favor of the executive," and her work has indeed called attention to the importance of information distribution among political actors in accomplishing their goals. In this respect, the case of Internet control and the protection of the NII are unique. In fact, unlike other social issues, the pro-control stakeholders (mostly in the national security community) were confronted by the anti-control stakeholders (private business, and users' and consumers' NGOs, etc.) that had the same (and sometimes even better) technical and legal knowledge as their counterparts in the government. Therefore, in the case of the Internet, the information was (and is) scattered among the different actors in interesting ways.

Governments, law enforcement, and intelligence agencies have access to large collections of information on security flaws, social engineering skills,[21] fraudulent techniques, privacy breaks, encryption software keys, and the like. But ICT firms, consumer organizations, civil liberties NGOS, and ordinary users have access to the same information as government agencies themselves. As a matter of fact, the ICT sector owns most of the NII in many countries. This condition denies the usual information advantage that the national security community has in making the case for other defense and security policies, like nuclear weapons for example, in front of parliaments (especially Congress) and public opinion. In that instance, the general public had little or no opportunity to critically evaluate what governments said about national security, since all the relevant information was classified by the government itself.

The distinction between autocracies and democracies is also relevant within this framework. Information asymmetries are present in any society and in any country. They tend to balance out, however, in democracies. There, few would argue that an unrestricted television or un-censored press is a "threat to national security," or that too much control of the radio may endanger the expected returns of a new economic paradigm. If many do support those views, plenty of civil liberties groups, consumers' organizations, political parties, and opposition leaders are ready to stand up and argue against them. These circumstances have all materialized with regard to Internet control and the protection of the NII. Providing information that would otherwise not be available is, according to Keck and Sikkink (1998), one of the key features of international NGOs. Non-state actors gain influence by serving as "alternate sources of information" (Keck and Sikkink, 1998: 19). At the international level, however, the activity of NGOs to dispute government's control on the Internet has been limited. Most international initiatives are in the areas of human rights protection and censorship, but it is rather surprising that, given the international impact of the Internet in particular and ICT in general, NGOs are not even more engaged. For example, personal privacy has become internationalized but few NGOs have brought that up before public opinion in various countries.[22]

In assessing the impact of the Internet on the field of international relations, one aspect is finally worth considering. Mayer-Schönberger and Foster (1997: 243) remarked that international regulatory measures to restrict the content of Internet communications would fail because states "differ dramatically in the kinds of content they prefer to regulate." Governments and users alike know that the most efficient way to manage (and control) the Internet would be through an international regime. Success in this area, however, has been scarce. Several top-down approaches simply failed. For instance, as early as September 1996, ASEAN members apparently agreed to police the Internet and block sites that run counter to Asian values but could not reach an agreement on what to block, or how. Between 1997 and 1998, the EU Commission launched a proposal for an "international charter" for cooperation and greater consistency of rules in the area of the on-line economy. International organizations, Internet non-profit groups, as well as national governments would have roles in this international charter.[23] The United States, which has never favored the intrusion of international institutions into a matter that it considers primarily the competence of the private sector's self-governance, never supported the initiative, which died out. This outcome is hardly surprising, since, as Bessette and Haufler (2001) argued, American commercial interests have consistently lobbied against a common regime for information regulation. One of the few exceptions is the Council of Europe (COE) Convention on Cybercrime.

The United States long supported the COE convention and sought to have non-member countries (including Canada, South Africa, and Japan) sign the convention. Experts considered the Convention a valuable document, but believed that it would also be hard to implement nationally.[24] In the aftermath of September 2001, EU countries, the United States, Japan, Canada, and South Africa signed the Convention in November 2001, but it took almost three years to ratify it so that it could enter into force (July 2004). Nevertheless, when it comes to controversial economic problems such as intellectual property rights or domain names, the United States (and, to a lesser extent, also Australia, Canada, and the United Kingdom) remains strongly in favor of business governance, whereas most EU countries, Japan, and most developing countries would prefer the United Nations to have a more active role.[25] Business matters do allow some room for international settlements. Cultural issues, on the other hand, make it extremely difficult to find enough common ground for needed international agreements.

As long as national governments insisted upon strictly intergovernmental approaches, forcing aside pro-liberties NGOs and users' groups, they had to take into account that these actors put up a very skilled resistance. NGOs working on ICT and Internet issues could display their impressive knowledge of technical and legal details, as well as their ability to use access to legislature and government to effectively oppose national governments. When those NGOs managed to secure support for their views from the private sector, governments' efforts were likely to succeed only at a high price. The governments' attitude has begun to change. For the United Nations World Summit on the Information Society of December 2003, NGOs played a very active role, before the event (helping the organization), during it, and in the follow-up that should lead to a second summit in Tunisia in 2005 (Cogburn, 2004).

To different extents, all the countries have to decide what level of control they can impose on the Internet to foster electronic commerce, protect their citizens' privacy and civil liberties, and assure the security of infra-structures (externally and internally). These goals often require conflicting solutions. But autocratic governments can exclude individuals and cajole the private sector into supporting government-led plans to develop e-business and the Internet economy. For autocracies, preserving the social fabric and control over society are more important than allowing businesses as well as users to take full advantage of an uncontrolled Internet. It is rather different when the debate on and the opposition to Internet control takes place in a democracy or not.

Democracies can take more information, as Keohane and Nye argue (1998), but they also face the hardest digital challenge. Not only do they have to safeguard the state while respecting individual liberties, but, because of their predominance in the networked world, they also set an example of countries such as the United States, Canada, Germany, Japan, and many others, which, rightly or wrongly, are regarded by many as true instances of democratic behavior, do activate restrictive legislation about Internet content or access, what then will happen in countries such as Iran, Saudi Arabia, or China? Their political leaders might comfort-ably claim that even the "advanced" democracies that constantly lecture other governments about their human rights records and lack of personal liberties could not withstand an "uncontrolled" Internet. September 11 altered the balance between security and freedom in the United States and in several other democracies, but it has also robbed democratic countries of the "high moral ground." Just as during the Cold War, autocratic states will be able to increase control on Internet content (that is, on the Internet as communication medium) on the justification that the "war on terror" required such decisions and that democratic countries had the same. It would then be difficult for democratic countries to argue that their increased control was only to raise the level of protection of the NII.

A summary of conclusions and structure of the book

Bennett (1992: 2) noted that "one way to break away from the con-fines of sectorization is to study a completely new policy problem, one not subject to either established wisdom within the political science literature or to a long and institutionalized legacy of political development." Innovative policy problems can contribute to expanding the field of study of the political science discipline, and injecting originality into it. This remains an extremely stimulating policy problem to tackle.

Chapter 2 introduces the "cryptowars," that is, the long battle between national governments and the accidental alliances of civil liberties NGOs and ICT companies to liberalize export and individual use of encryption software. With Internet communications inherently insecure, encryption software became an indispensable commodity. But much as it could help legitimate users like banks or financial firms, it would also help criminals and hinder the activity of intelligence (especially the American National Security Agency) and law enforcement agencies. Hence, these "national security" communities in several countries moved to securitize the issue. Civil liberties NGOs challenged that interpretation, claiming that individuals also had the right to protect their privacy of communication. ICT companies that wanted to benefit from the growing demand for secure communications were also opposed. Moreover, encryption software was the key factor for electronic commerce to finally take off. Because of their sheer technical and legal knowledge and because several actors within governments themselves supported those views, the opposition of national security communities was overridden and almost all limits to individual use of encryption software in most democracies – which, incidentally, produce most of that software – were lifted. The cryptowars are also one eminent example of how securitization moves could be reversed.

Chapter 3 summarizes ten short case studies of democracies. Cases were selected on availability and richness of data from various sources (Van Evera, 1997). Furthermore, these countries together with the United States, Germany, and Italy (the three in-depth cases) are in essence a sort of "board of directors" (or a governing council) of the Internet and the global information infrastructure. These countries own most of the world's information infrastructures and all of them have a more or less developed ICT sector. As OECD members, these countries are all very dependent on information infrastructures and the Internet for their economies and societies. They tend to be consistent with OECD guidelines in various areas such as protection of personal data. They diverge in the level of pluralism (Lijphart, 1999), that is, the number of active interest groups (trade unions, civil liberties NGOs, consumers' organizations). Pluralism is one of the necessary elements to determine the type of domestic structure of a democracy. The number of interest groups is important but so is their efficiency in influencing the government and cooperating with ICT firms. When it comes to protecting the NII, small countries like Israel, Switzerland, or the Scandinavians follow their tradition of a "total defense," in which not only government agencies but also the private sector and possibly the public participate. Other large countries (such as France or Japan) perceive cybercrime as the main Internet risk and are also keen to preserve their cultural individuality.

Chapter 4 considers the United States. With its highly pluralistic, society-dominated structure, the United States was, for all of the 1990s, the only information superpower. Still highly dependent on the Internet for its economy and the functioning of its infrastructures, the United States has seen other countries emerging as strong competitors in the ICT sector. In several measures of technological prowess the Scandinavian countries are far more advanced, while Europe as a whole and Japan are more advanced in certain segments of the telecommunication industry such as mobile phones. China seems determined to replace English with Chinese as the primary language of the network. All in all, the United States is still in a forceful position to steer future structural development of the Internet and of global information infrastructure networks. The federal government saw the world-wide diffusion of the Internet as a positive outcome, despite the recurring requests for increasing Internet control by its intelligence and law enforcement personnel. The stalemate that followed lasted until September 2001. Before that date, the United States had maintained a "hands-off" policy and actively supported the creation of governance structure for the network while protecting its predominant position. The US Department of Commerce oversaw the creation of the Internet Corporation for Assigned Names and Numbers (ICANN), but under Californian state law was unable to maintain direct influence over it.

In the aftermath of September 11 the United States has induced other allies and friendly countries, as well as well-known autocracies, to step up their level of Internet control. The accidental but highly effective alliance between pro-freedom consumers' and users' NGOs and the ICT industry that characterized the late 1990s is largely gone. Nevertheless, the high degree of pluralism of the country means that interest groups and civil liberties NGOs still have ample access to federal and local governments, legislatures, and bureaucracy. These organizations are still able to reasonably influence policies, at least in the short term. If in terms of both soft and hard power the United States remains a *primus inter pares* among all democracies, its attitude toward Internet control is likely to influence the behavior of other countries, not all of them democratic. Indeed, several autocracies used "the war on terror" as an excellent justification to increase their Internet control. The United States is thus a crucial case to assess the complicated relationship between national governments and other stakeholders about Internet control and the protection of NII.

Chapter 5 presents Germany as the corporatist model of democracy, as its level of pluralism is moderate. Institutional actors (business associations, trade unions, consumers' organizations, some NGOs) have excellent access to the federal and local governments and legislatures. All these elements are involved in the consensus-building process, which always takes considerable time. However, once consensus is reached, it lasts. Thus policies resulting from this process are likely to be maintained for a lengthy period of time. Germany welcomed the Internet and the German government did not intend to miss out on the economic benefits that many expect from Internet diffusion. The spreading of information is of high quality, mostly among the institutional actors, but individuals and less institutionalized groups (such as hackers for instance) can benefit from a profusion of independent sources.

The Internet issues that mostly concern the German public are, in order, child pornography, the presence of racist and hatred propaganda, and the protection of privacy. The German federal government is concerned with the protection of the NII, but sees organized crime (cybercrime), as do many other European partners, as the main threat to it, with cyberterrorism seen as a distant second. In the 1990s, the German federal government made the development of the Internet a strategic goal. E-government became a priority, with more and more information available through the government's websites. Newspapers and other media have done the same, thus qualifying Germany as a data-rich case. It would simply be impossible to envision a European plan for the Internet's future without the strong involvement of Germany's government and business.[26] These circumstances make Germany the crucial case for Europe.

While the United States and Germany, along with other "typical" countries such as China, and Singapore, have normally been the topic of investigation in many other Internet studies (Kizza, 1998; Saich, 2001; Chase and Mulvenon, 2002; Kalathil and Boas, 2003; Kurlantzick, 2004), thus far, extremely few comparative studies have been conducted of the Italian situation by Italian or foreign scholars. Chapter 6 seeks to fill that gap by studying Italy, the Internet late-comer case. Unlike the United States, Japan, Canada, Germany, and most other European countries, Italy has rarely enjoyed stable governments and the chapter investigates how a "weak" government tried to spread the Internet in the society. The Berlusconi cabinet of 2001 came into office with grand ideas about the network and its supposed role in the Italian economy. Moreover, the Italian premier had personal interests in the linkage between the media industry and the Internet.

Italy is the "volatile government" model, with a long tradition of intervention in the economy. Because of Italy's political system, the government can hardly enjoy unquestionable confidence from the coalition parties supporting it in Parliament. At periodic intervals, the cabinet had to devote time and resources to negotiate with all the majority parties about how to move, which is a far cry from the mandate that the US President or even the German Chancellor could expect from their electorates. The Berlusconi government was no exception to this rule. Under such conditions, Italian cabinets remain unstable. Parties continue to dominate politics and access to local and national governments. Access to legislatures and bureaucracy is still heavily filtered by middle-men and intermediaries linked to those parties. Policies are the result of exchange of favors and promises among the parties, and thus they are often subject to turnaround and reconsideration. The degree of pluralism is high according to Lijphart (1999), which is counterintuitive for Italy. The reason for that is that there are plenty of interest groups, but (with the exception of trade unions) they tend to be ineffectual in their actions and poor at coordinating. Strong inter-party cooperation is the method to compensate for those weaknesses by interest groups.

Finally, since Italy was a late-comer to the Internet, the delay in setting up the proper legislative framework (still quite underdeveloped) and the postponement of political and social recognition that users' and consumers' NGOs had to endure, could have meant that law enforcement officers and intelligence and defense agencies gained the upper hand in controlling the network.[27] This event did not occur. On the contrary, Italy developed a similar profile to Germany, which had "embraced" the Internet earlier and faster, and the Italian national security community was mostly concerned with cybercrime (child pornography, hatred speech, and electronic fraud), with cyberterrorism a distant threat. Hence, neither Germany nor Italy has put particular emphasis on the Internet as a threat to national security, even after September 11 – the most notable exception being a certain attention to cybercrime, which was also a great concern for electronic business. A realist reading for this variation might be that these two countries do not share the "high risk" position of the United States; therefore they can afford to overlook national security. This explanation is unconvincing. Germany and Italy are advanced economies, and would be vulnerable to attacks on their infrastructures. Both countries have taken seriously the only instance of the Internet dangers that has proved to be at least credible, namely cybercrime. On the other hand, they have disregarded the Internet as an "external" menace or a matter for defense ministries or national security agencies, because there is almost no evidence that such a threat is convincing and probable.

A possible account for the reason why, in many of the cases examined here, the interests of the alliance between civil liberties NGOs and the ICT private sector prevailed, could be that those countries (Germany, Italy, Canada, or Japan) were not vulnerable and did not risk anything. That is why business and social motives could be put at a premium. Such conclusions, however, are incorrect on two accounts. First, logically, the more economically advanced a country is, the more dependent on computer networks it is. Hence, the more dependent on computer networks a country is, the more vulnerable to cyber-attacks it is. As developed economies, Germany, Italy, Japan, or Switzerland are almost as vulnerable as the United States. Second, all these democracies tend to perceive cyber-threats differently. Katzenstein (2003: 733) aptly summarized the different attitudes of big democracies such as the United States, Germany, and Japan, noting that for them fighting terrorism was, respectively, "a war, a crime [or] a crisis." The same deduction applies to cyber-threats, with, for example, the Europeans privileging a law enforcement response and the Americans a national security one.

Among the various cyber-threats, cybercrime (organized crime and other technically savvy criminals) is currently considered by many – including law enforcement officials in the United States and the EU – as the most probable menace. If cybercrime were to become significant enough to constitute a clear and present "national security" crisis, then Germany, France, Finland, and Italy, as computer-dependent, advanced economies, should worry as well. The reason why they have not done so, thus far, is because they think that cybercrime is a believable threat but that it can be dealt with by law enforcement officers. Chapter 7, finally, summarizes the main conclusions of this research, outlining its significance for the field of international relations and offering some clues about what the directions of future research on this topic may be.

In the contest over Internet control, all the stakeholders are assumed to be rational. Policy-makers want to secure economic growth, defend the NII, and protect public order so as to increase their chances of being reelected. Interest groups have their own goals, like enhancing safeguards for personal privacy or fostering intellectual property. Consumers want cheaper prices for Internet access and better services. Individuals and groups, including terrorist organizations, previously excluded from more traditional media, have been offered an "amplifier" to voice their opinions, disagreement, and anger at very affordable prices. Their websites now coexist along with government and private business sites. ICT companies have rejected the "hands-off" attitude of the Internet's early years and plan to privilege security over adding new features, but want consumers to bear the costs. At the same time, they want to protect their investments in the NII (which they mostly own), but do not want to share information about their vulnerabilities and weaknesses with other stakeholders.

The rational assumption is a useful tool for inquiry in the social sciences, but, to paraphrase Milner (1997: 248), it is not "a miracle cure." That rationality is, at best, bounded rationality. Political elites, firms' bosses, civil liberties advocates, and individual consumers all make decisions in tightly constrained social environments and the explanation of the causes of their actions is often unsatisfactory and, in many circumstances, never complete. The world has grown into a complicated place, with a plurality of actors, and "powers", and interacting levels of analysis, requiring multilevel, articulated analyses. "Complexity" is now the key word. Ferguson and Mansbach (2002: 163) argue that the rejection of the black-box model of state behavior has, ultimately, left scholars with "an acute case of theoretical overload" and "even more profoundly confused." That is certainly the case. Bringing into the field of international relations analytical problems such as Internet control, the impact of computer networks, or the security of NII can only increase the complexity and perplexity of which Ferguson and Mansbach speak. But can anyone really do otherwise?

Notes

1 Peter Steiner, "On the Internet Nobody Knows You're a Dog," *The New Yorker*, July 5, 1993, ID222230.

2 In the 1990s, when I wrote my doctoral dissertation, I felt it necessary to include a whole chapter on the "history of the Internet." Nowadays, even the casual user knows so much more about that story that a short paragraph will suffice. More compelling books and articles on the history of the Internet have also appeared. For example, Hafner and Lyon (1996) provide an excellent account of that story, Leiner *et al.* (1998) is the story told by some of the actual protagonists, and Rosenzweig (1998) examines how the different "histories" of the Internet can be compared.

3 The packet-switching technology converts data (including voice, sounds, videos, etc.) into bytes which are then "grouped" together in packets. In other words, the digitalized message is broken into "smaller messages" that can travel on telephone lines independently. Packets generated by different messages can line up and travel together, allowing a more efficient use of the same telephone line. Distributed networks were an idea developed by Paul Baran at Rand in the 1960s to guarantee a better survivability of communication networks. Robert Kahn and Vint Cerf are responsible for developing (starting as early as 1973) the TCP/IP protocol, the very flexible (albeit insecure) lingua franca thanks to which all computers connected to the Internet, regardless of their operating systems or brand, can communicate. In 1972, Robert Tomlinson wrote basic message send-and-read software and chose the symbol "@" to go between the address and the name of the sender/receiver. Bob Metcalfe invented Ethernet (the packet-based protocol that makes Local Area Networks, LAN, possible) in 1973. Jon Postel conceived the Domain Name System (DNS) in the 1980s and Tim Berners-Lee put together the World Wide Web in the 1990s. But many more helped and improved those ideas to make the Internet what it is today. All these ideas were simple, cheap, and flexible, which guaranteed their success.

4 In this work, for ease of comprehension, the terms "government" and "state" are used interchangeably.

5 Mowlana (1997: 34) categorizes four types of "control": (a) internal (i.e. within the members of the communication system) and actual (i.e. with concrete measures); (b) external and actual; (c) internal and perceived; and finally (d) external and perceived. In the case of the Internet, government control is definitively actual; it is external, because it is imposed by governments. But it is also internal, because governments are active members of the Internet community and, in several instances, willing providers of abundant official information. Mulgan (1991) has also classified control as exogenous (external) or endogenous (internal).

6 See also Pool (1990: esp. 66, 113, and 210).

7 The situation became further complicated when utility managements around the world began to use the Internet to perform SCADA (Supervisory Control and Data Acquisition) operations. Moreover, digital switches (called distributed control systems, or DCS) have almost completely replaced hardware parts in panels for process control that operate complex information or service distribution infrastructures. This change has several advantages: software is more easily upgraded, more scalable (i.e. more units can be added to the system), and cheaper than hardware counterparts. Maintenance personnel can remotely supervise (and even modify in real time) the software programs that control the functioning infrastructures such as power plants, oil and gas refining, telecommunications, transportation, and water and waste control. More and more SCADA systems rely on Internet packets (IP) that are highly vulnerable to denial-of-service attacks. For more details on SCADA, see Whatis.com at <http://whatis.techtarget.com/definition/0,,sid9_gci555434,00.html> [April 7, 2004].

8 Communication means can be divided into three categories, according to their communication modes. Whereas (a) the telephone is a *one-to-one* (from one source to one receiver) and (b) the television a one-to-many (from one source to many receivers) means of communication, (c) the Internet is a *many-to-many* (from many sources to many receivers)

means of communication. The Internet is an interactive medium. Unlike radios and televisions, the applications used over the network to communicate (that is, e-mail, mailing lists, newsgroups, Internet Relay Chat, and the World Wide Web itself) have been created to facilitate the exchange of information between senders and receivers and vice versa on a large scale. The awareness of being part of the transmission of news or creation of ideas is highly motivational for users, who act more as protagonists than mere passive spectators. The interactivity of the network allows it to function simultaneously as a medium for publishing and communication, unlike other traditional media.

9 Today the private sector produces not only weapons and hardware, but also services. Modern mercenaries have indeed become "corporate warriors" (Singer, 2003).

10 The term "cryptowars" (or "crypto wars") refers to the legal and technical battle that, in the 1990s, a civil liberties NGOs and ICT firms alliance engaged in with national security communities (in the United States and in several other democracies) to allow individuals to access and use encryption software to protect their on-line identities and personal communications. The cryptowars ended in 2000, when the United States renounced the prohibition on exporting encryption software and several other democratic governments resolved to adopt a liberal stance about individual use of encryption software.

11 See also the Human Rights Watch "Global Issues: Free Expression on the Internet," available from <www.hrw.org/advocacy/internet/index.htm> [April 9, 2004].

12 The cases of China and Cuba demonstrated that modern ICT may even help autocratic governments to control Internet users (Chase and Mulvenon, 2002; Kalathil and Boas, 2003; Kurlantzick, 2004).

13 Rarely, there are legal provisions that formally bar access on the basis of ethnicity or religious affiliation. More likely, limits are based on census (that is, resources to buy hardware or pay for phone calls), more subtle, implicit affiliation (in Saudi Arabia, for instance, only members of the royal family can afford, and are permitted, Internet access), or obedience to the orthodox political ideology (such as in Cuba or North Korea).

14 Bill Gates, "Software Breakthroughs: Solving the Toughest Problems in Computer Science," public lecture, Kennedy Hall, Cornell University, February 25, 2004.

15 I owe this concept to Fernando Mendez, personal conversation, European University Institute, Fiesole (Italy), September 20, 2000.

16 All the countries examined in this work have highly developed national information infrastructures and an active ICT/media sector. This means that there are plenty of ICT companies operating in these countries and that, either individually or collectively, they would try to influence governments' policies. However, when they act collectively through their associations there is some overlapping with the NGO groups of stakeholders.

17 For convenience, in this short summary I have used the term "liberalism" to stand for both institutionalism and the liberal/domestic politics approach.

18 The number of books covering these two theories is impressive. In fact, these theories still provide a substantial contribution to the field of international relations. For comprehensive (pre- and post-Cold War) overviews of these competing views see, for example, Keohane (1986), Baldwin (1993), and Risse-Kappen (1995a).

19 For instance, "states + nations + firms + confederations interacting across the political, economic and societal sector" (cf. Buzan *et al.*, 1998: 16).

20 See, for example, the defense of the Internet Corporation for Assigned Names and Numbers' independence that the US Department of Commerce has continuously exercised. ICANN is an NGO that oversees the management of domain names on the Internet and several other countries have pressured for its competencies to be transferred to international organizations like the International Telecommunication Union.

21 Social engineering is a technique that allows the person(s) performing it to acquire, exploiting the common willingness of most people to be helpful, critical information by posing as a legitimate recipient of that information. Such pieces of information may be used by malicious hackers to penetrate computer systems.

22 The exchange of information on European travelers to the United States requested by the US federal government is one such example. The EU objected first, because American standards on personal privacy were lower than European ones. Later, however, probably to avoid accusations of obstructing the United States in the fight against international terrorism, the EU gave in. Non-US travelers now have no say on the information that the federal government collects on them, nor on what it does with that information, nor on how long that information will be stored in the federal government's databases.

23 The World Trade Organization (WTO), the International Telecommunication Union (ITU), the World Intellectual Property Organization (WIPO), the Internet Society (ISOC), the World Wide Web Consortium (W3C), and many others would have participated.

24 Interview with Robin Urry, visiting scientist, EU Joint Research Center at Ispra (Italy), November 24, 2000.

25 Several economic issue areas remain nonetheless highly controversial. The EU, for example, supports strong protection of intellectual property rights as does the United States.

26 It is a fact that, for the 2000 elections of the quasi "Internet government," namely the board of directors of the domain name organization ICANN, Germany mustered more registered voters than the United States (where the organization is based) or any other European country, and all the top four candidates. One of them did become ICANN regional director for Europe (see Chapter 5).

27 National governments are usually rather unadventurous and conservative when dealing with unforeseen and unplanned occurrences such as the Internet explosion, and sending out security personnel on "scouting" missions is a not atypical response.

2 Sometimes security just does not prevail

The case of the "cryptowars"

Between 1990 and 2000, all Internet stakeholders were engaged in an international campaign to reduce or abolish all state control on the individual use of encryption software products. In democratic countries around the world, civil liberties NGOs and ICT firms forged an "accidental" alliance and fought long legal and technical battles, the so-called cryptowars, with national security and law enforcement agencies to allow Internet users to encrypt personal communications and protect their on-line identities. National security communities strove to securitize cryptography by maintaining a monopoly on its research and use. By 2000, democratic policy-makers accepted the economic and social arguments for private use of encryption. Cryptography was thus liberalized in the majority of democratic countries and has remained strictly controlled only in autocratic states. This chapter examines the events of the cryptowars and their consequences.

There is no date for when the struggle about cryptography began but June 5, 1991, the day when Phil Zimmermann released Pretty Good Privacy (PGP), the first popular encryption software based on public key crypto-graphy, could be considered a starting point.[1] By 1999, *The Economist* (1999a: 23) warned that, given the easy availability of increasingly complex codes, "governments may just to have to accept defeat, which would provide more privacy not just for innocent web users but for criminals as well."[2] The cryptowars ended in 2000 (Levy, 2001), after the United States, France (Segell, 2000), and other democracies relaxed their limitations on the export and individual use of encryption software (and in the midst of the dot.com crash). Against the background of the growing diffusion of the Internet and the increased international dependability on information infrastructures, the 1990s battle to guarantee the free use of encryption truly epitomized one of the epochal moments in Internet control.

Cryptography comes from two ancient Greek words that together mean "secret writing."[3] For most of its history, the science and technology of cryptography have been the exclusive domains of national governments that wanted to protect their communications and intercept those of their adversaries and competitors.[4] When the British and the Americans broke the Japanese and German codes during World War II, they secured an enormous strategic advantage. In the last two decades, the ICT and software revolutions, the diffusion of the Internet, and the meshing of the Internet and of public key information infrastructures (PKI) have popularized cryptography but also made it a controversial issue.[5] All communications exchanged on the Internet (personal data, system maintenance data, individuals' preferences, locations visited) are open; anyone with minimal training and technology could see or read anything. Security is guaranteed only through encryption. Several authors (Barth and Smith, 1997; Singh, 1999; Schneier, 2000; Levy, 2001) have identified this problem, and have emphasized the extreme importance of encryption software for Internet communications.

Presently, the private sector would stop functioning without strong encryption software; electronic business and financial transactions would be impossible, as would the business of government agencies and offices. Strong encryption means strong secrecy and secrecy is also at the foundation of privacy. But secrecy can be "a two-edged sword for a democratic nation" (Dam, 1996: xiii). If the privacy of law-abiding citizens is protected, then the identities and communications of criminals and terrorists are also protected. The double-edged sword is reflected, for example, in the words of Barth and Smith (1997: 283), who note how, since its advent, government encryption regulation has been driven by "two distinct interests": a foreign intelligence interest in gathering information implicated in national security and a law enforcement interest in collecting evidence of criminal activity. Szafran (1998: 45) wrote that governments face a real dilemma as two contradictory political objectives are at play.

In a networked environment, sophisticated cryptography is a necessity for protecting the privacy of personal information and the secrecy of confidential business or classified national security information. At the same time, the use of cryptography may impair the ability of law enforcement agencies to combat crime and protect national security. Since cryptographic freedom would allow everyone, including criminals, drug dealers, and terrorists, to be confident in their Internet communications, governments have had to face the fundamental question of whether or not they should legislate against cryptography (Singh, 1999). Denning also warned that the widespread availability of unbreakable encryption software, coupled with anonymous re-mailing services, could well lead to "a situation where practically all communications are immune from lawful interception (wire-taps) and documents from law search and seizure" (1997: 176).

How much information can a democratic nation collect in order to ensure public order and defend national security, without violating its citizens' "right to be left alone"? Tellingly, throughout the whole of the 1990s, the US government position on the question was torn between two conflicting interests. On the one hand, law enforcement (the FBI) and the national intelligence community (mostly the NSA) wanted to maintain the status quo, that is, cryptography under strict federal control. On the other side, civil liberties advocacy groups like the Global Internet Liberties Campaign (GILC), the Electronic Privacy Information Center (EPIC), the Electronic Frontier Foundation (EFF), the Center for Democracy and Technology (CDT), and several others argued that, since privacy is a fundamental human right (Mock, 2000; Steeves, 2000),[6] and cryptography is essential to communicate safely in a networked environment, there should be no restrictions on its availability and use.

Cryptography and encryption software are interrelated with privacy (Levy, 2001) and computer networks security,[7] but they are also essential to protect freedom of speech. Denning (1997: 176) notes that "encryption can protect communications and stored information from unauthorized access and disclosure." Barth and Smith (1997: 291) have also observed that "governmental controls on encryption technology often interfere with legitimate private sector needs for strong encryption." Finally, governmental regulation of cryptographic security technology endangers personal privacy, according to the Electronic Privacy Information Center (EPIC, 1999b). In a networked environment, encryption ensures the confidentiality of those personal records, such as medical information, personal financial data, and electronic mail, which are increasingly at risk of being stolen or misused. In sum, cryptography touches all aspects of today's global computer networks.

This chapter wants to stress the tools that both sides used to fight the cryptowars. Ironically, both sides employed powerful discourses derived from fundamental problems (assurance of NII, censorship and privacy, expectations of economic growth) that were all meshed together on the Internet and for which cryptography was vital. Realizing the implication of cryptography for computer networks, national governments (or more precisely their national security agencies) tried and often succeeded to securitize the issue of encryption.[8] On the other hand, civil liberties NGOs used the discourses on privacy and on freedom of speech (which were still rather forceful in the United States). In addition, the ICT private sector created a whole new myth (Gadrey, 2003) to show that the benefits of the new economy could not and should not be put at risk because of "cryptocontrols." In an unexpected synergy, ICT companies also used the privacy argument to counter government efforts to control encryption (BBC News, 2000c).

What is encryption useful for?

Encryption software has numerous applications in modern communication networks. Not only does it make secure computer-to-computer communications, but it can also protect wireless communication on cellular phones. Furthermore, the entertainment industry makes extensive use of encryption software to protect copies of movies or music. In the era of Internet downloading and extensive software piracy, encryption is vital for the survival of that industry. The availability of encryption software is crucial to protect both infrastructure and on-line content. Indeed, toward the end of the 1990s, more and more utilities providers installed remote-control systems based on the Internet protocol (TCP/IP). All these systems together with other communication networks constitute a modern country's national information infrastructure (NII). Since the basic Internet protocol is still in the "clear," all these systems are fairly vulnerable to denial-of-service (DoS) attacks. These attacks can disrupt the regular functioning of the NII. Hence, controlling encryption software could amount to controlling the Internet.

With regard to the Internet, telecommunications, and information infrastructures, cryptography is germane in at least three issue areas, namely freedom of speech, privacy, and the electronic economy. This section examines many of events that took place between 1994 and 2000 that were intermingled with, relevant for, and a consequence of the specific battle on encryption between the private sector and NGOs alliance versus national governments. Civil liberties NGOs were in the forefront of the free speech and privacy argument, although the ICT sector did intervene in the latter to some extent. In the case of commercial encryption, the ICT was clearly in the forefront, with scant contribution from NGOs.

Freedom of expression and censorship

Article 19 of the 1948 Universal Declaration of Human Rights clearly states that everyone has the right to freedom of opinion and expression. In addition, in all "real" democracies, this right is either explicitly asserted in their constitutions or, if not so, it is corroborated *ex post* by the prevalent jurisprudence as if, albeit implicitly, it were actually included in the constitution. Consequently, most individuals in democratic countries take this right for granted. Lessig (1999: 164) comments that freedom of speech (or of expression) in the United States is constitutionally protected in a "complex, and at times convoluted, way," and that this protection is intended to counterbalance government control. Writing on the American experience, Haiman (1978: xi) noted that of all the rights Americans take for granted, "the freedom to speak one's mind seems the most secure" or, he added, "so goes the mythology of our democracy."

In 1997, with specific reference to the Communication Decency Act (CDA) of 1996, the US Supreme Court (*ACLU v. Reno*) ruled that the Internet was a "unique medium entitled to the highest protection under the free speech protections of the First Amendment to the US Constitution."[9] This interpretation impacted other democracies, which have gradually included it in their national jurisprudence. Defining what free expression really is, however, is a demanding task, since "freedom of speech" is culture-dependent. Mayer-Schönberger and Foster (1997: 246) noted that regulating the content of speech on the network was "still thought of as a national issue." Traditionally, the United States has defined free speech more broadly than has Europe. In the United States, hatred and racist speech or neo-Nazi publications (which are considered a criminal offense in Germany or France) are protected under the First Amendment. American civil liberties NGOs fully support this viewpoint. To further complicate this matter, hatemongers have been among the first to realize "the tremendous power of the Internet to spread their hateful messages and recruit members to their hateful causes" (Mock, 2000: 141).[10] Paradoxically, this circumstance caused a battle between "free speech advocates and human rights advocates" (Mock, 2000: 147).[11]

Freedom of expression and the need for encryption software to protect it were also cited by civil liberties NGOs with reference to defending human rights activists around the world. Many human rights groups used encryption "to protect their files and communications from seizure and interception by the governments they monitor for abuses" (EPIC, 1999a: 3). NGOs have argued that if the United States and other countries with advanced software industries made it difficult for human rights groups to acquire strong encryption software by regulating the export and availability of that software, they would also have to consider that this action favors undemocratic governments. Autocracies are particularly attentive to the behavior of democracies because they might eagerly use that behavior against the democracies themselves, in a tactical manner, whenever it suits their goals (Delacourt, 1997).

Curbing freedom of expression and imposing censorship are state instruments to control information exchange. These are among the most unequivocal examples of resistance by governments to the Internet's role in enabling individuals' communications. Governments "know that unfettered speech can shape and transform individuals' expectations, giving them a renewed sense of the possible" (Shapiro, 1999: 65). By the same token, states aiming to control the exchange of information are fully aware that such an outcome is effectively attainable only by seriously infringing upon individual rights, such as the right to privacy and freedom of expression, the true hallmarks of democracies (Steeves, 2000: 188).

One of the frequent justifications used to restrain freedom of expression and privacy, or secrecy of communications, is that they threaten national interests, including national security interests (Cox, 1981). Democratic and non-democratic countries alike may use this explanation; however, the former have a much lower record of citing "national security" or "national interest" to curtail basic freedoms than the latter.[12] Even in democracies, however, the definition of certain issues as "national security matters" poses considerable obstacles to Internet users, civil liberties activists, and human rights activists alike. Since it is national governments that decide what is to be included in the classification of "national security," individuals who may want to challenge the state's exclusion of certain topics from public discussion are de facto deprived of a considerable portion of legal ground for actions against their governments. This process of securitization has been applied by national governments (and the US federal government in particular). But American civil liberties NGOs balanced the securitization move by resorting to the First Amendment and the need to protect freedom of speech. The most skilled countermove by the NGO stakeholder, which could count on the support of extremely knowledgeable users, such as early Internet developers and scientists, was to equate the compiling of codes for encryption software to the act of writing a poem, a novel, or an essay or simply publishing the results of one's own research. All these activities are undeniable manifestations of expression and thus were fully shielded by the First Amendment.[13]

Privacy and data protection

Privacy is defined as "the right to be left alone" (Warren and Brandeis, 1890). Privacy is a fundamental (but not absolute) right recognized in Article 12 of the 1948 Universal Declaration of Human Rights,[14] and it is constitutionally guaranteed in many countries (EPIC, 1999b).[15] But authors have now "given up trying to define privacy and there is no generally accepted definition" (Bennett, 1992: 26). The perception of what constitutes privacy has changed over time and across nations. Given the enormous amount of personal information that is now available in databases and the electronic messages that people[16] continuously leave behind, privacy has (or should) become an everyday concern. Rosenberg (1998) wrote that there was a "battle being fought in the US and elsewhere, with respect to the protection of privacy on the Internet." Indeed, two of the stakeholders of Internet control, namely national governments and the ICT sector, have conflicting attitudes toward privacy (Dam, 1996). Democracies try to protect their citizens' privacy but they can also dispose of privacy very quickly. The exponential increase in the ability of "electronic governments" to gather, store, and mine data about people should raise well-founded worries about privacy and civil liberties. Businesses who sometimes emphasize their respect for privacy as a marketing quality for their products and services would at the same time rely on consumers' information for their marketing strategies.

All the most important international organizations, including the United Nations, the OECD, and the EU, have stressed the significance of protecting privacy and personal data.[17] Privacy, however, is also frequently violated by governments. It often stands in the way of law enforcement, national security (Diffie and Landau, 1998), and companies' business practices. Furthermore, not all states offer the same degree of protection to their citizens. For instance, the treatment of personal data in Europe is more strictly regulated and enforced than in the United States,[18] which prefers to rely on "self-governance" for businesses. Europeans argue that self-governance alone cannot protect consumers sufficiently. EU directive 95/46EC, which entered into effect in October 1998, initiated a hot debate between the EU and the United States on the export of data of European citizens outside the EU, to the point that transatlantic trade relations could have been seriously hampered. In the aftermath of September 11 and the war on terror, however, the EU has given up considerable ground to US demands for more information, for example, on European travelers to the United States.

Computers, the digitalization of electronic signals, and the Internet itself have accentuated the problem of protecting individuals' privacy.[19] A survey by the Pew Internet and American Life Project in August 2000 showed that as Americans go on-line, they have "great concerns about breaches of privacy" (Fox *et al.*, 2000: 2). Bennett (1992: 17) observed that instantaneous access to vast quantities of information from multiple and remote locations had changed "the character of the modern organization and of the society in which it is embedded." Many of the early Internet users thought the original anonymity of the network would indefinitely remain as such. Anonymity was (and is) the most cherished feature of the network.[20] Companies as well as governments quickly realized that faceless users could lead to the failure of marketing strategies and an encouragement to unaccountable behavior on-line.[21] In addition, surfing and other activities on computer networks leave clear and easily followed tracks. At the same time, over cheaper computing power has allowed even small companies or governments in less developed countries to run large relational databases that permit efficient cross-referencing of users, a capability that only large corporations or rich states could afford in the past. All these actors have developed both techniques and software to track those paths, and possibly to ascertain the identity of previously anonymous users.

Violation of privacy can occur at different levels, personal communication being just one of these. More precisely, in telecommunications, the gathering of information about individuals can be done in any of the three layers that normally constitute the telecom system.[22] Layer one is the basic infrastructure, carrying undifferentiated digital data, which is reserved only for network providers (that is, telecom companies). In this layer it is not possible to screen what information the sender and receiver are exchanging. For this reason, privacy laws do not apply here. This level, however, is where traffic analysis takes place: for example, it can provide useful information on the locations of the sender and receiver, how long they communicate, and who else they contact. All this is extremely valuable information that law enforcement officials may obtain from a telecom carrier by a simple request without a judge's warrant.

Layer two is where service providers operate, for instance offering Internet access to businesses and individuals (that is, the ISPs) or storage space.[23] In this layer, data are roughly divided into general information about the identity of the senders and receivers and the contents of their messages. Data protection acts usually apply at this level, since here it is possible to pinpoint who is communicating with whom. A judge's warrant is usually required by the service providers to disclose this information to legally authorized personnel. Finally, layer three is the platform on which content providers (such as hosts of web pages) operate. At this level it is possible for the provider to gather plenty of information about the preferences and tastes of users and hence "profile" them.[24] Data protection laws clearly apply to this layer as well. Hence, ISPs should explicitly state their privacy policy.

Encryption may be applied to any or all these layers, thus making it impossible or very expensive to retrieve information and data. The "double-edged sword" of cryptography (Dam, 1996) is clearly evident: what helps to protect one's own NII and communications would hamper the effort to gather information about future adversaries or incoming threats. Governments have worried about this "double-edged" nature of cryptography for another crucial motive that has also long-term implications for individual privacy: encryption is a key factor for electronic government. At the same time, since digital signatures rely on encryption, electronic documents would be impossible without public key cryptography.[25] With the advent of the Internet, reasons of image (that is, to appear more "advanced") as well as the aim of reducing costs have increasingly encouraged political leaders in several industrialized countries to enthusiastically embrace e-government.

The more governments and companies become "electronic," the more efficient and less expensive their services should be (Symonds, 2000). Although the number of citizens familiar with the Internet will increase, thus reducing the "fear" of it so common in certain sectors of the population, it is also likely that the same Internet-savvy citizens will be more aware of the risks to their privacy. These individuals are likely to loudly demand more protection for the details of their personal lives. George Orwell's *1984* may only remain the visionary work of a literary genius, but it is undeniable that "vastly more efficient governments will also know vastly more about each and every one of their citizens" (Symonds, 2000: 26). The consumer-user might try to fend off threats to their privacy by sending a clear signal to the whole on-line industry, namely, "no privacy, no business." This request for privacy would impact many of the current on-line retailers, who have made the trade of personal information their main business. Nevertheless, as more traditional (that is, less dependent on information-gathering for profit) stores go on-line, providing such guarantees should not be a problem, and it can also become a mark of quality of service. Governments, however, cannot be subjected to that kind of pressure and hence it has become increasingly problematic to comply with the warning that "the price of happy e-citizenship will be eternal vigilance" (Symonds, 2000: 26).

To counter the requests by intelligence and law enforcement agencies to restrict access to encryption, both civil liberties NGOs and ICT firms quoted the need to defend privacy. Both stakeholders applied that discursive strategy to pursue different interest aggregations, but their efforts turned out to be fortuitously synergic. For users and NGOs, encryption would simply guarantee their right "to be left alone" while on-line. For ICT companies that did not use encryption, the rampant lack of privacy would put off customers afraid of exposing their spending preferences and their credit card numbers. Of course, this latter argument overlapped with the problem of establishing a reliable secure environment for electronic commerce.

Electronic commerce and the new economy

Banks and financial firms have a long tradition of applying cryptography to their communications. When money started to be transferable, the document on which the amount was indicated became as valuable as the actual currency. When those documents began to be transferred by wires, assuring their confidentiality and integrity became paramount. The credibility and the survival of financial institutions were at stake, and cryptography soon became indispensable to guarantee that survival. Finances and cryptography have thus long accompanied each other. What was brand-new with the Internet was that also *commerce*, to some extent, could be dematerialized as money had been.

The ICT portal Whatis.com defines electronic commerce as "the buying and selling of goods and services on the Internet, especially the World Wide Web."[26] Electronic commerce was born in the mid-1990s, when a handful of companies that had no physical infrastructures, such as Amazon.com, discovered that it was possible to sell some products (books or music CDs) on the Internet. Three changes have made this state of affairs possible: the Internet, cheap computing power, and public key cryptography (Levy, 2001). The Internet brought about electronic mail (the most popular communication medium since the telephone) and, as a virtual "window store," the World Wide Web. Cheap computing power has made the management of increasingly complex mathematical operations (indispensable for strong cryptography) available on the desk of the average PC user.

Public key cryptography has corrected the most serious flaw in the Internet protocol design, namely the lack of secure communications. This new form of commerce took everyone, including national governments, by surprise. Many governments accepted, at least in principle, that e-commerce should be market-led and free from burdensome structural and bureaucratic barriers. Such liberal precepts, however, could jostle awkwardly with the defensive anxieties that national governments, even democratic ones, tend sometimes to display. In 1998, even the *Financial Times* warned that, once the full power of the Internet was unleashed on the world, it would "challenge national laws and may eventually elude government control altogether" (Jonquieres and Kehoe, 1998: 14).

Electronic commerce then became electronic business in 1997, when IBM coined the term, adding servicing customers and collaborating with business partners to the buying and selling (thus including banking and financial services on the network). When business analysts included revenues and jobs from the ICT sector to the then anticipated returns from electronic business, they coined the definition of "new economy," characterized by speed and innovation (Barua *et al.*, 1999). This situation inevitably had a considerable impact on Internet growth. Secure communications were critical to boost the new economy and encryption software was indispensable for secure communications. Not only telecommunication and software companies saw cryptography as a vital element in their economic survival. Encryption was also essential to the entertainment industry. Since digital copies are the exact replica of the "original," piracy of movies, music, and software exploded in the 1990s. Thus, entertainment media conglomerates joined the battle on the side of those who wanted to liberalize cryptography.

As Barth and Smith (1997: 297) observed, "market realities based on continued rapid advances in technology make it likely that strong encryption will be an essential component of the international structure of electronic commerce." In fact, two of the most telling examples of these changes in government attitudes were the United States and France (Segell, 2000). In the cryptography survey of 1998 (GILC/EPIC, 1998),[27] both countries were reported as having restrictions on the use and export of encryption software. In 1999 and 2000, both eased their limits on that software because of industry pressure (GILC/EPIC, 1999). The expectation of benefits from the new economy was simply too persuasive for many governments to resist. These conditions made it harder for them to implement overly restrictive and obtrusive measures of Internet control, at least as long as those expectations are not shown to be unfounded. To date, more than half (57 percent) of the world's secure server computers, which rely on strong encryption algorithms, belong to dot.com firms.[28] A small minority of secure servers is owned by non-profit organizations (dot.org) (7.22 percent) and an even smaller minority by the US armed forces (dot.mil) (0.63 percent) or the US government (dot.gov) (0.51 percent) (E-soft, 2004).[29] The overwhelming preponderance of commercial and financial firms on the Internet is evident. For the world's ICT sector, ensuring that there were no limits to the exploitation of encryption necessitated engaging national security agencies on the issue of securitizing cryptography.

The "securitization" of cryptography

Paraphrasing Mueller (2002: 369), one may say that the term "national security" is problematic because it is applied in so many different instances as to have become almost useless.[30] Often, however, this practice is functional for a government to achieve precise political goals. By saying "security," Buzan *et al.* (1998: 21) note, "a state representative declares an emergency condition, thus claiming the right to use whatever means necessary to block a threatening development." Furthermore, once a government controls the definition of "national security," on the whole "there is no limit to what information it may decide to fall into that category" (Supperstone, 1981: 270).

All governments have indeed made use of the notion of national security to justify varying degrees of control on the Internet. Democracies want to protect their NII and, at times, to incriminate and prosecute those who preach hatred or terrorism on the Internet. Autocracies want to prevent dissent and silence human right activists and (less so) secure their NII. The case of the cryptowars shows how democratic and autocratic governments alike have securitized the issue of free encryption on the basis that it may endanger national security. That said, democracies have multiple stakeholders, and access points to the executive and legislative branches are plenty, thus allowing those stakeholders to influence the policy-making process (e.g. Risse-Kappen, 1995a, 1995b). Depending on the domestic political structure, those access points can be legally formal and institutionalized (as in the United States or Canada), institutionalized but less formal (as in Sweden), or formal (and personal, as in Japan) but not institutionalized. Furthermore, even after government policies are established, it is possible to prevent government agencies and bureaus from implementing them on legal or technical grounds. Depending on whether the different interests of the different stakeholders converge or diverge and allow or bar synergic approaches, attempts to change policies or prevent implementation may be more or less effective.

An important distinction to make is whether the focus of government control has been on infrastructures or on-line content. Whereas autocratic governments would make no distinctions, democracies have tended to concentrate on the control of infrastructure more than on content. Furthermore, within democratic states, diverse interest representations and interest coalitions have played a primary role in shaping national Internet policies.[31] Cryptography was essential for numerous applications in both types of control. If national governments could succeed in retaining their traditional monopolies on cryptography, they would have been exceptionally well placed with respect to the other players to mold the development of the Internet according to their specific preferences. Last but not least, cryptography was already an integral tool of national security policy in every country.

Nye and Keohane (Nye, 2004; Keohane and Nye, 1998) have developed the intriguing concept of "soft power," which in the globalized, interconnected world has joined economic and military power as a tool of foreign policy.[32] Soft power could be used by a state, but it could also be applied against that state in the form of propaganda and disinformation. The US Department of Defense invented the concept of information operations (after the 1990 Gulf War) to place those actions in the broader picture of modern warfare (Campen, 1992). Digitalization and the Internet as media have acquired a central position in that picture. Governments in general, and national security authorities in particular, have grown even more concerned because widespread access to Internet communications means not only that sovereign states can use their soft power and launch information operations, but also that non-state actors (e.g. NGOs) could do the same.

Indeed, non-state actors have shown a remarkable ability to do so in the most assorted forums and under the most diverse circumstances (Keck and Sikkink, 1998; Kidd, 2003; Vegh, 2003; Cogburn, 2004). The appearance of these new actors (which also include terrorist groups) with their Internet access made the need to control cryptography even more compelling for national security authorities.[33] Unrestricted access to strong encryption products, national security authorities argued, would have hampered all efforts to monitor those NGOs and groups and permitted them to plan and launch disinformation campaigns undisturbed (e.g. Harmon, 2004). Hence, the securitization of cryptography was justified by threats emerging not only from traditional state competitors but also from these new challengers, about which the Clinton Administration was particularly concerned (Bendrath, 2003).

The national security authorities' argument was consistent with what Buzan *et al.* (1998) call the traditional realist security studies approach. Such a viewpoint of the cryptowars emphasized the necessity to retain any relative advantage in encryption. A country with the capability of producing strong encryption algorithms (now embedded in software) would have to protect that advantage. Likewise, to preserve its own capacity to "snoop" into other countries' confidential communications, that same country would have tried to discourage a worldwide, unrestricted diffusion of strong encryption products. It would also have to take action, including lobbying hesitant friends or allies, to prevent unfriendly foreign governments from obtaining the necessary know-how to develop or foster their own domestic cryptography industry. This is precisely the course of action that the United States national security community took in the 1990s, taking the lead in an international campaign to oppose liberalization of encryption (Campbell, 1999).

The first multilateral response to the growing problem of liberalizing encryption for individual users came, in March 1997, from the Paris-based Organization for Economic Cooperation and Development (OECD), which issued its Guidelines on Cryptography Policy. OECD recommendations were non-binding, but its 29 members (all the EU members, the United States, Canada, Japan, and other advanced democracies) were expected to adjust their cryptography policies. The OECD guidelines encouraged the use of cryptography for the benefit of data protection and commercial applications. In the negotiations leading to the guidelines, the United States, backed by France and the United Kingdom, was inclined toward more restrictive rules. However, many of the other representatives, including the economics and trade representatives from Japan, Canada, and Germany, did not favor these efforts. The outcome was a compromise, but with a more "liberal" interpretation, closer to the desire of the latter group of countries. It should also be noted that the private sector in the United States was also in favor of a more liberal interpretation for the guidelines. In addition to the OECD arena, the governments of advanced countries used other international forums, like the G8 and the Council of Europe, to discuss and refine their positions on the issue of cryptography. European governments also tried to coordinate their policies within the EU framework.

The United States and many other countries like France, the United Kingdom, China, and Russia took some or all of the OECD steps. A group of 33 countries, which included Western-style democracies as well as democracies in transition (such as Russia and Turkey), joined forces, in 1995, to sign the Wassenaar Agreement (WA). The WA is not an international treaty but a pact among members and it indicates to whom and under what conditions encryption software, among other dual-use technologies, could be sold to third parties. Other countries not part of the Wassenaar Agreement, like China and Singapore, have retained full control on export of encryption products. China and Singapore restricted domestic access to those products to only a few well-known and licensed users, such as banks and companies providing financial services or government agencies. As the data in the next section demonstrate, despite the limits imposed by the WA, the large majority of advanced democracies had very liberal policies with regard to cryptography. The countries that most watchfully controlled cryptography were non-WA autocracies like Saudi Arabia or China. How may that difference be interpreted? Another key question is the following: in 1998, advanced democracies like the United States and France (Segell, 2000) *still* had rather restrictive rules on who was legally authorized to employ encryption software outside the national security and law enforcement communities. By 2000, even they had relaxed their restrictions. What can best explain that change?

Liberal democratic theory may provide a partial answer. States are not all alike and domestic political structures count. Unlike autocratic states, democratic societies do not normally need to monitor the private communications of their members. If citizens want to hide the content of their communications and enhance their privacy by encrypting their messages, within legally established limits, they are allowed to do so. Governments in democracies soon realized that, under these circumstances, their main function was to protect the NII and that a widespread use of encryption software products, especially to protect large, privately owned databases, would have eased their job. Liberal theory is also helpful in recognizing that different stakeholders rationally pursued their own interests and formed alliances when those interests somehow coincided. But liberal theory, which is notoriously weak when it comes to security issues, cannot say anything about the process of securitization. This outcome of securitization can best be explained by constructivism. In order to retain a certain degree of control on the Internet, national governments found it all too convenient to securitize encryption. Democracies, however, because of their multiple access points and their diverse interests' configurations (as liberal theorists argue), faced remarkably strong coalitions of interests that eventually obliged them to de-securitize cryptography.

Two of the world's oldest and most important democracies, the United States and France, took longer to move along the path of de-securitization. The change in these two countries is best understood by considering the allocation of interests of domestic players. Both France (Segell, 2000) and the United States started with very restrictive rules about what their citizens could do with encryption software. Repeatedly, the advocates of national security interests (law enforcement and intelligence agencies, the military) in both countries had warned against allowing individuals to use or freely distribute encryption software. In pursuing the implementation of restrictive policies for cryptography with policy-makers and government leaders, however, champions of national security met an unexpected and influential alliance of private business, consumer protection, and civil liberties organizations.

Advanced democracies have embedded in their constitutions and legal and social systems plenty of channels to voice discontent as well as access points to lobby policy-makers on new policies. Furthermore, curbing individual use of cryptography could represent, technically and legally, a severe hindrance for the companies in those countries that wanted to embrace e-business. In the United States, individual users and civil liberties NGOs joined forces with the private sector. Together (and with their remarkable technical understanding) they battled the advocates of the national security community and, in the end, convinced the federal government to drastically change its previous cryptography policy (Levy, 2001). The same pattern happened in France (Segell, 2000), although there the role of NGOs was less prominent. This was more than offset by the more liberal stance taken by France's top commercial partners, in particular Germany.

Both the European Union and the United States were actively involved in the debate on cryptography since they were the big developers of encryption software. But it was in the United States that the confrontation between the accidental alliance of civil liberties NGOs and the ICT private sector and government agencies was most evident. In the United States, civil libertarians were joined by representatives of right-wing movements (suspicious of government intervention), in addition to the ICT private sector. Between 1993 and 1998, the United States conducted sustained diplomatic activity seeking to persuade EU nations and the OECD to adopt their "key recovery" system and insisted that the purpose of the initiative was to assist law enforcement agencies. It was the National Security Agency that led the international campaign to prevent liberalization of cryptography, sometimes to the complete exclusion of police or judicial officials (Campbell, 1999).[34] Nevertheless, it was again the United States where civil rights NGOs successfully challenged federal laws on encryption on the basis of infringement of the First Amendment. During the cryptowars, the position of the United States was so central that, as Singh (1999: 304) concluded, "whatever policy" was adopted in there, it would ultimately affect policies "around the globe."

The American battleground for cryptography

As mentioned before, prior to the Internet, the use of cryptography to protect personal communications outside military and intelligence circles was essentially unknown. When the Internet became an indispensable tool for telecommunications, electronic commerce, entertainment and, most notably, the NII, the small and highly specialized field of cryptography achieved celebrity status almost overnight. National law enforcement and intelligence organizations also witnessed an unanticipated but steady increase in Internet users hiding their communications, which were previously transmitted "in clear." To continue the monitoring of this startling number of encrypted messages, those government organizations saw their interception and deciphering resources stretched to the limits.[35] Law enforcement and military intelligence had to disperse their energies and skills not only on controlling their enemies' encrypted communications, but had also to deal with encrypted communications of companies and individual users. The solution envisaged by governments, first and foremost by the United States, was to hinder the acquisition of encryption software by regulation. Throughout the 1990s, the United States government, under pressure from its intelligence and national security agencies, led an international effort to securitize encryption software.

Even before September 11, 2001, US authorities appeared extremely concerned that terrorists could take advantage of the Internet. US intelligence agencies stepped up their efforts to control the flow of information over the Internet. The FBI was among the most active players in the cryptowars, investing time and resources to stop the process of liberalization of encryption software and promoting controversial solutions like the "Carnivore."[36] But the NSA was by far the federal agency that embodied the image of "the enemy" for the accidental alliance of civil liberties NGOs and ICT firms. Consistent with the overall structure of American politics of multiple power centers, the "intelligence community" is in reality a euphemism identifying a large array of intelligence services whose activities often overlap or contradict each other. In addition to the CIA, the NSA, and other major agencies, each military service branch has its own intelligence, as does the State Department.[37] The task of making and breaking, communicating and intercepting secret messages has always been the principal business of the NSA, "a huge governmental intelligence apparatus, larger and more expensive than the CIA" (Ransom, 1970: 127). Anything pertinent to what is defined as SIGINT (Signal Intelligence) or COMINT (Communication Intelligence), such as Internet communications, comes under the scrutiny of the NSA.

Founded in 1947 and based at Fort Meade (whence comes the agency's nickname "the Fort"), located north of Washington, DC, the NSA was for long virtually unknown to the American public.[38] Secrecy surrounding the agency was so complete that even its name was not "listed on the organizational chart of the United States government" (Ransom, 1970: 128). For most of its existence, the NSA provided funds for cryptography research and hired the best mathematicians and cryptographers, and did not have to worry that its smartest employees might quit to find jobs in the private sector. Until the 1970s in the United States, "cryptography policy and information about cryptography were largely the province of the National Security Agency" (Dam, 1996: 414).

As the demand for encryption from the banking and financial sectors began to emerge in the 1970s, IBM researchers produced the Data Encryption Standard (DES) algorithm following the specifics of the US National Bureau of Standards (now the National Institute of Standards and Technology). The NSA, after a long tug-of-war with some ICT firms (principally Lotus) managed to have the original 128 bits of the key reduced to 56 bits, which were far more than the NSA would have liked (Levy, 2001). The export version would include 40-bit keys. The State Department could never grant licenses to export to those countries that were on the Pentagon's International Traffic in Arms Regulations (ITAR) list. In fact, until 1996, encryption software produced in the United States was classified as "ammunitions" on the ITAR.

The rationale behind that decision was that the NSA should be capable through a "brute force" attack to break any encrypted message.[39] The DES was approved and commercialized in 1977 and well into the 1990s it remained the standard encryption algorithm. However, with the plunge in the price of computing power the DES became inadequate for secure communications and financial transactions. Already by 1993 a custom computer costing US$ 1 million could theoretically be built to crack DES by brute force in seven hours. The software company RSA (owner of the RSA public key algorithm) launched 13 secret key challenges to test different encryption algorithms (four were solved by 2000).[40] The 56-bit key was found in October 1997 after 250 days of exhaustive key search on 10,000 idle computers.[41]

Civil liberties NGOs and savvy users long argued that the key lengths that the NSA was willing to support were too easy to break. The Electronic Frontier Foundation (EFF) repeatedly showed how to crack the 40-bit encryption technology that was the longest key permitted for export. In July 1998, the EFF DES Cracker easily won RSA Laboratory's "DES

Challenge II" contest and the US$ 10,000 prize.[42] In less than three days the machine completed the task, shattering the previous record of 39 days set by a massive network of tens of thousands of computers. In January 1999 Distributed.Net, a world-wide coalition of computer enthusiasts, worked with EFF DES Cracker and a world-wide network of nearly 100,000 networked computers, to win the RSA DES Challenge III. It succeeded in 22 hours and 15 minutes. Since then the DES is no longer officially considered "secure" by the US federal government, which, since 1997, has worked on developing the Advanced Encryption Standard (AES).[43] Nevertheless, despite the many criticisms, the DES had fulfilled its expectations well. As Levy (2001: 65) remarked, ultimately, the DES "*was* a problem for The Fort." It was a lesson for the agency that its mission in the age of computer networks would be much harder.

If the DES was the first lesson for the NSA, the second came from the steady, irreversible diffusion of public key cryptography (Levy, 2001). Invented in 1977 by Whit Diffie and Martin Hellman (with Ralph Merkle),[44] public key cryptography was first incorporated into an algorithm (the RSA algorithm) by Ron Rivest, Adi Shamir, and Len Adleman in the same year. The NSA knew that the spread of public key cryptography, with decreasing costs of computing power and the marrying of computers and telecommunications, would mean a complete overhaul of the agency mission. Hence, the agency undertook legal actions, pressured the MIT and Stanford (where the scientists worked) with threats to cut federal research funds, and lobbied Congress. Most importantly, all these initiatives were covered with the aura of "national security." The NSA repeated over and over again that what Diffie, Hellman, and the others did was not a scientific endeavor but an actual threat to the United States national security. That was a statement that, in the past, had completely nullified any opposition or resistance.

Overall, with its calculation resources, the NSA knew it could (and can) probably break any encrypted single message on the Internet via brute force attacks. However, two structural problems might considerably complicate the applications of those attacks, namely a surge in the number of encrypted messages and the increased length of encryption keys. If a large proportion of ordinary Internet traffic became encrypted with long encryption keys (128-bit, 256-bit, or higher), and the time and resources for breaking a message through brute force increased correspondingly, such an outcome would have put a tremendous strain on the analytic capability of the NSA. If one considers the billions of messages that are exchanged every day on the Internet in addition to the billions of faxes and phone calls (also monitored by the NSA partially through the Echelon system), it is not surprising that the intelligence community would be "stretched thin," as one knowledgeable observer put it.[45]

The NSA engaged in the battle against the free use of cryptography as if it was fighting for its own survival. Preserving this quasi-monopoly, however, turned out to be increasingly problematic for the NSA. In the case of the cryptowars, the NSA was up against opponents who could display impressive intellectual capabilities and strong technical understanding of the problem. Unlike the DES, which relatively few people and institutions used, a growing numbers of companies' and organizations' computer users needed strong encryption software, like the RSA. Furthermore, the private sector agued that if American ICT firms were not allowed to produce and export strong key encryption software, European software companies less burdened by their national security communities were all likely to outsell American firms in the global market. Thanks to the Internet, after 1995, "the market for cryptography has exploded" (Diffie and Landau, 1998: 47). Internet commercial potential boosted the demand for strong cryptography.

In June 1991, Phil Zimmermann, a long-time civil liberties activist, posted Pretty Good Privacy (PGP) ver.1.0 on a bulletin board on the Usenet, one of the networks of the Internet.[46] Zimmermann had been developing PGP for years with a combination of DES-like private key and RSA public key encryption algorithms, adding a user-friendly interface. As downloads of PGP grew, in February 1993 Zimmermann found himself under federal investigation for illegal export of "ammunitions" (the ITAR item). The investigation lasted for three years and ignited a debate about the positive and negative effects of encryption in the Information Age. This episode, Singh observed (1999: 303), "galvanized cryptographers, politicians, civil libertarians, and law enforcers into thinking about the implications of widespread encryption." The MIT Press ("with its thumbs firmly in its nose"; Diffie and Landau, 1998: 206) published the code of PGP as a 600-page hardbound book and sold it through its usual world-wide distribution channels. The book was an expression of free speech and academic freedom of research. At that point, the government could not solely prosecute Zimmermann and not MIT without inviting scorn, since "the MIT is three times as old as the NSA, just as well funded, and even more influential in the military-industrial complex" (Diffie and Landau, 1998: 206). Thus, in 1996, the US Attorney General's office dropped the charges. The main direct consequences of this investigation were that Zimmermann became incredibly popular and was supported by an international legal fund and, most of all, PGP became one of the most frequently downloaded software programs from the Internet ("if the *feds* are scared, it must be really good!"). The US government's action had indeed alerted a vast audience about the benefits of encryption and the risks of government control of on-line communications.

Another important case, albeit less well known, was *Bernstein v. The Justice Department*.[47] Daniel Bernstein, a computer science professor at the University of Illinois, challenged Department of Commerce regulations restricting the export of encryption products in 1995. Bernstein argued that computer source code is a form of speech and therefore not subject to censorship, while the US government maintained that the code was more functional than an expression of ideas. In May 1999, the US Ninth Circuit Court of Appeals ruled that United States controls on the export of encryption software violated the First Amendment. EPIC (1999d) defined the outcome as "a long-awaited landmark decision." While the Zimmermann case was unfolding, the government, aware of the growing and diverse opposition to curbing the use of encryption software, proposed basically two solutions: the "Clipper Chip" and the "Key Management/Key Recovery." The Clipper was a microcircuit to be attached to ordinary phones to protect private communications. At the same time it permitted law enforcement officials to circumvent encryption devices that, they claimed, hampered their ability to detect criminal activity (Abelson *et al.*, 1998) The Clipper used a key escrow system, in which two keys would be stored separately with two government agencies chosen by the Attorney General. Civil liberties NGOs criticized the solution because it failed to protect privacy rights of individuals and created an uncertain key escrow system.[48]

In an effort to ease the US export control policy and engage international competitors, in September 1995 the National Institute of Standards and Technology (NIST) presented the Commercial Key Escrow initiative, dubbed "Clipper II" for its similarity to its policy predecessor. Clipper II relaxed export controls on key lengths up to 64 bits, provided that an encryption key was escrowed with a US government certified agent. A "Clipper III" appeared in May 1996. In both the Clipper II and III, a spare set of keys would be given to a "trusted third party" who had been approved by the government and who would turn over keys in investigations.[49] This software could then be freely exported to most countries. Further liberalizing, the federal government freed the export of 56-bit DES equivalent products and higher to selected industries like banks and financial services in September 1998.[50] Civil liberties NGOs did not fail to criticize both Clipper II and III on the ground of the *quis custodiet ipsos custodies* argument. Who would oversee the trusted third party and ensure that it did not abuse its position? To avoid temptations, the NGOs argued, it would be better not to entrust anybody with that responsibility.

In September 1999, the Clinton Administration set forth the guidelines for its export policy of encryption software, which included promoting electronic commerce, supporting law enforcement and national security, and protecting privacy. In January 2000 the Administration announced the new encryption export regulations. The new rules confirmed that any encryption commodity or software of any key length could be exported under license. A technical review was necessary for non-government users, but, with the exception of states supporting terrorism, any country could purchase encryption software products from the United States. The federal government had, at least partially, accepted the claim of the civil liberties NGOs and ICT firms alliance that restrictions on encryption only damaged the private sector and the users' privacy. The national security coalition did not entirely capitulate and continued pressuring Congress to enact more restrictive legislation on the use and sale of cryptography software. After all, export controls had been relaxed, but not completely removed: the Department of Commerce would grant licenses, maintaining copies of the source codes exported. Many individuals and small businesses found the requirements daunting and civil liberties NGOs continued to pressure Congress to further liberalize, although it was "far from clear what direction Congress would take" (Diffie and Landau, 1998: 223). Thus far (2004) no further liberalization has occurred, nor have restrictions returned.

The cryptography debate in the United States brought to light the rival coalitions in the struggle over Internet control. On one side were the law enforcement and intelligence agencies that opposed the widespread use and export of strong encryption software. These actors considered those events as major impediments to their procedures, as well as preludes to more serious consequences such as deterioration of national security. The FBI and the NSA used their most powerful argument ("a threat to national security") and their privileged access to and knowledge of technical details. On the other side there was the accidental alliance of pro-liberties NGOs, consumers' organizations, users' groups, and the ICT industry. Not only were all the NGO and ICT private sector stakeholders in favor of unrestricted use, availability, and sale of strong encryption software, but together they could match the FBI and NSA in legal and technical expertise. These capabilities, coupled with the responsiveness of the American legal system to freedom of speech and privacy as well as the unique expectations that the new economy would generate (though less so), proved to be enough to overcome even the securitization proponents.

The situation in 2000, although not ideal, undoubtedly favored the accidental alliance. A criticism to the above conclusion is that it all that happened in the absence of a concrete danger. September 11, however, demonstrated that international terrorism could be a concrete danger. The then NSA director General Mike Hayden warned in February 2001 that "bin Laden had access to more sophisticated technology than did the agency" (CNN.com, 2001a). Nevertheless, the situation with reference to cryptography has changed remarkably little. Indeed, one would have expected a full reversal of the 2000 outcome, especially with the introduction of the Patriot Act (examined in Chapter 4). Not only was no evidence found that the terrorists had relied on encryption for their communications but also, well aware of the United States' superb interception capabilities, they deliberately used low-technology communications. Moreover, the ICT industry argued that *more* cryptography was needed, not less, if computer security was to increase. In the end, the genie of cryptography has remained "out of the bottle" for good.

Descriptive statistics and the data (1998–2000)

In April 2000 the last of the three surveys that EPIC/GILC produced since 1998 was released. The three surveys together provide a remarkable opportunity to evaluate the process of progressive liberalization and reductions in the use of cryptography that occurred in many countries during that period. As mentioned earlier, cheap computing power has made the management of complex mathematical operations (indispensable for strong cryptography) available to the average Internet user. This change has, in turn, allowed users to adopt public key encryption software that operates with two keys (both necessary to encrypt and decrypt messages). One of the keys can be given away on the Internet (that is, made "public") without endangering the security of the other since access to only one makes it computationally infeasible to discover the other. Once user-friendly software programs like PGP became available, it was the last straw that broke the effort to control cryptography.

In September 1993, the US National Institute of Standards and Technology launched a preliminary survey to collect information about the cryptographic policies of foreign countries. These countries were members of the Coordinating Committee on Multilateral Export Controls (COCOM), a grouping of Western nations that was abolished in 1994 and replaced by the Wassenaar Arrangement. Following this example, in 1998, the Washington-based Electronic Privacy Information Center (EPIC), on behalf of the Global Internet Liberties Campaign (GILC), embarked on the first international survey of cryptography policies (GILC/EPIC, 1998). EPIC researchers developed a cryptography index. The index took into account the numbers and typologies of laws related to the conditions of use of encryption software in the countries considered.[51] The survey was repeated in 1999 and 2000. After 2000, EPIC discontinued the survey, because, as Levy (2001) put it, the "crypto libertarians" had won the battle over encryption. For the moment, the accidental alliance of the ICT private sector and civil liberties NGOs had also won the fight over Internet control.

Using the GILC/EPIC cryptography index, it is possible to notice that more democratic countries decreased their control than increased it. The results of the three surveys are summarized in Table 2.1. In 1998, the relative majority (37.1 percent) of countries surveyed exercised no control on encryption software for individual use. If the figure for countries applying only low control (27.4 percent) is added, then in 1998, 64.5 percent of the countries in the sample did not consider if necessary to restrict individual/private use of encryption products. There were only a few countries where a strong domestic control on the use of cryptography was in place. These countries included Belarus, China, Israel, Pakistan, Russia, and Singapore; with the exception of Israel, all of them were autocratic governments. India, South Korea, and the United States were among those countries considering the adoption of new, stricter controls (GILC/EPIC,

Table 2.1 Results of 1998, 1999, and 2000 cryptography surveys

Level of control on cryptography	Cryptography score 1998	Cryptography score 1999	Cryptography score 2000
Full control	9.7	11.7	10.4
High	4.8	3.9	1.3
Medium	21	7.8	7.8
Low	27.4	37.7	31.2
No control	37.1	39	49.4
No. of cases	62	77	77

Source: Personal elaboration on the basis of GILC/EPIC (1998, 1999) and EPIC (2000).

1998). The policy of the United States was the most surprising given the fact that virtually all of the other established democracies had few if any controls on the use of cryptography. The dominant role that national intelligence and federal law enforcement agencies held in the development of encryption policy explains the US position. The influence of those players, however, was balanced by the alliance between the ICT private sector and civil liberties NGOs.

The stakeholders in the alliance backed different interests but they had the same goal, namely, the complete liberalization of use and export of encryption software. The ICT private sector had an economic rationale. They were afraid that the government opposition would hamper electronic commerce (for which encryption was indispensable) and that they would lose market shares to European software companies in the cryptography business. Civil liberties NGOs and users' group had socio-legal motivations, since law enforcement and national security agencies could prohibit individuals from legally using encryption products, hampering individual privacy. Autocratic governments could also seize on the US example to further curb their citizens' freedom of speech. Last but not least, NGOs would argue that function creep could allow national security agencies even in democracies to pry much more than was necessary. The state of affairs that emerged in the United States after September 11 justified those fears.

In 1999, the "controlling" states (Belarus, China, Kazakhstan, Pakistan, Russia, Singapore, Tunisia, Vietnam, and Venezuela) were all among the world's most undemocratic regimes (GILC/EPIC, 1999). In many of these countries controls on encryption products did not appear to be enforced. One democracy, Israel, had lowered control on encryption products from full to high. The United States dropped from high to medium level of control, but it continued to exert economic and diplomatic pressure on other countries in an attempt to force them into adopting restrictive policies. Among EU members, the United Kingdom and Spain had the most restrictive (medium) policies on encryption. Among the countries that had increased their controls were all the Scandinavian democracies

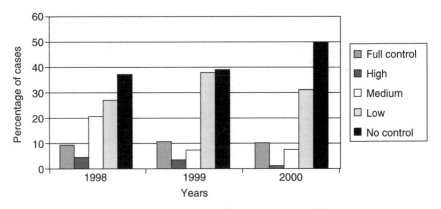

Figure 2.1 Crypotography score, 1998–2000. Source: Personal elaboration on the basis of GILC/EPIC (1998, 1999) and EPIC (2000).

(except Iceland). These, however, raised the level of control from no control to low (thus following the OECD specifications). EU members constituted the low control group. Ironically, an unmistakable autocracy like Kyrgyzstan appeared to have no control in place, since its government had probably not yet understood the problem.

In 2000, only a few countries still imposed restrictions on individual use of encryption software, and EPIC (2000) could conclude that the international relaxation of regulations concerning encryption had largely succeeded (cf. Campbell, 1999; Levy, 2001). The themes championed by the accidental alliance (namely, expectations for electronic commerce, privacy protection, and freedom of speech) overcame the resistance by the national security communities in the United States and other democracies. Figure 2.1 shows how the number of countries with no control on cryptography steadily increased from 1998 to 2000. The countries with low control increased in 1999 and decreased in 2000 while those with medium control moved either up or down. The number of countries with high control decreased steadily, demonstrating that those governments realized that it was unreasonable to maintain that level. The figure for full control countries (most of which are well-known autocracies) remained stable and actually increased a bit in 2000.

The United States continued its efforts for widespread encryption control until January 2000. As EPIC researchers concluded, by 2000 no countries in North or South America or Western Europe restricted domestic use of encryption products, and exports were only moderately regulated (EPIC, 2000). Indeed, by that time, most countries in the world had no controls on cryptography and encryption products could be freely used, manufactured, and sold without restriction. A most striking exception remained the United Kingdom, which alone among all democracies never ceased to advocate cryptography control. On the other hand, the group of controllers still included countries such as Russia and China, who routinely monitored the Internet and other communication media.[52] National governments and the ICT sector slowly began to address the many problems of the Internet before consumers started embracing it as a viable and secure channel to conduct their business. ICT firms made sure that consumers were informed that business transactions would be guaranteed by powerful encryption software and that they saw better protection for customers' personal data as a value-added service (for some companies it was marketing tactics, however). If national security authorities had prevailed in the contest over encryption, it would have dealt a deadly blow to electronic business. The accidental alliance, however, prevailed and electronic commerce ultimately took off (*The Economist*, 2004b).

Conclusions

Securitization, according to Buzan *et al.* (1998: 23), is a "more extreme form of politicization." The tragedy of September 2001 provided the US government with an enormous incentive to securitize a number of issue areas, including Internet control. Cryptography, however, despite its strong, almost "natural" bond to defense and national security, has largely remained untouched. The intelligence fiasco of September 2001 has been ascribed to lack of human intelligence and good analysis and disinterest in international terrorism on the part of the Bush Administration rather than to the failure of breaking al-Qaeda encrypted communications (Johnston and Purdum, 2004).[53] The cryptowars were over by the year 2000 (Campbell, 1999; Levy, 2001). By that time, expectations for electronic business and the unreasonable stock exchange frenzy for any product with an "e" before it made the Internet almost a sacred icon of the new millennium. Ultimately, it was a matter of marrying a suitable problem (electronic commerce) with an appropriate solution (encryption software). As far as computer networks are concerned, in no other case has the accidental alliance been more solid or more effective than in the cryptowars.

The conditions of control on encryption software analyzed in the previous section, however, substantially worsened after September 11, 2001. Before that dreadful date, the evolution of control by different national governments depended on the coalition of interests of three actors, namely governments, businesses, and individuals (as users and consumers, and as civil liberties advocates). The latter stakeholders, however, must be put in a position where they can use their "voice options." This outcome was (and is) only possible in democracies. In autocracies, governments can bar individual users and cajole private business into supporting government-led plans to develop electronic business. For autocratic governments, preserving the social fabric and control over the whole society are more important than allowing business as well as users to take full advantage of an uncontrolled

Internet. Under different conditions, within most advanced democracies, the three-player structure yielded business–NGO accidental alliances that thwarted the governments' efforts to control encryption. This outcome provided incentives to civil liberties NGOs to tackle the more general problem of Internet control, of which control of encryption was an important element. What happened in September 2001, however, changed the situation.

The attacks against the World Trade Center and the Pentagon prompted a rush for initiatives to increase control on the Internet, primarily in the United States, but also in Europe and other industrialized countries. The securitization of Internet control moved into a high gear, with fears that terrorists would soon strike the NII and that they had communicated before September 11 via encrypted messages. Even several months after those terrible events, evidence of both "fears" was lacking (McCullagh, 2001; Provos and Honeyman, 2002). The formidable increase in Internet control, however, was far too large for civil liberties NGOs to tackle together, especially at a time when the accidental alliance of civil libertarians and the ICT private sector was eroding. The ICT sector wanted to show that it was "patriotic" and ready to cooperate with the US government in securing the NII.[54] Encryption remained untouched, but freedom of speech and, above all, individual privacy were affected. Ironically, before September 2001, the EU, with its directive on personal data, was setting more stringent standards on privacy that the United States was willing to follow (Heisenberg and Fandel, 2004). After 2001, not only did the relative position change, but the EU (violating its own directive) complied with US requests to release personal information about air travelers to US law enforcement authorities.

Computer security experts like Bruce Schneier are skeptical that that computer information will be useful in stopping terrorism. Schneier (2003) noted how ICT industry leaders announced that they would privilege security over adding new features, but once they looked into costs and who would have to bear them, that enthusiasm slowed down. The most notable anti-terrorist bill affecting the Internet has been the US Patriot Act, passed by Congress in October 2001. The Patriot Act was not specifically tailored for the Internet, but several of its provisions relate to on-line communications, which basically expands the monitoring powers of US law enforcement and intelligence agencies without proper "checks and balances."[55] Even if "9/11" had not happened, the coming of age would have, in any event, changed the nature of the Internet, as it has done with many of its innovators. Once an individual-led phenomenon (with governments hesitant about what to do), the Internet has become more and more business-led. In a hypothetical new alliance, the balance of interests would change. Even in democracies, ICT firms have never been so ideologically committed to an uncontrolled Internet as many of its early users or civil liberties advocates. Now governments (including, or perhaps especially, the democratic ones) demand that, to foster assurance of the NII, the private sector should undertake more responsibilities. This question is likely to remain open, until the dilemma of who would bear the extra costs (whether the market or the companies themselves) is solved.

In this context, advanced democracies will play a crucial role in setting standards for the future development of the Internet. Indeed, if countries such as the United States, Canada, Germany, or Japan, which are regarded by many, whether rightly or wrongly, as true democracies, enact restrictive legislation on Internet content or access, then what will happen in countries such as Iran or China (Delacourt, 1997)? Their political leaders might comfortably address their public opinions by noticing that even advanced democracies, which constantly lecture other governments about their human rights records and lack of personal liberties, cannot tolerate an "uncontrolled" Internet. Ultimately, September 11 made the securitization of Internet control easier. The accidental alliance that had won the cryptowars had already been eroding because the convergence of interests was less compelling. The terrorist attacks accelerated that split and fuelled the Manichean "war on terror" rhetoric of the Bush Administration. Much has changed since Hersh (1999) noted how deeply distrustful Americans were of the NSA. Nonetheless, the outcome of the cryptowars demonstrated that, given the multiple access points of democracy and a strong enough aggregation of diverse interests, sometimes the power of securitization can be overcome.

Notes

1 "Pretty Good Privacy (PGP) is a popular program used to encrypt and decrypt e-mail over the Internet. It can also be used to send an encrypted digital signature that lets the receiver verify the sender's identity and know that the message was not changed en route. Available both as freeware and in a low-cost commercial version, PGP is the most widely used privacy-ensuring program by individuals and is also used by many corporations. Developed by Philip R. Zimmermann in 1991, PGP has become a de facto standard for e-mail security. PGP can also be used to encrypt files being stored so that they are unreadable by other users or intruders." Whatis.com, available from <http://searchsecurity.techtarget.com/sDefinition/ 0,,sid14_gci214292,00.html> [June 15, 2004].

2 Along the same lines was also Ari Schwartz of the Center for Democracy and Technology, interview, July 12, 1999.

3 Cryptography is the art of creating and using cryptosystems. A cryptosystem or cipher system is a method of disguising messages so that only certain people can see through the disguise. Cryptanalysis is the art of breaking cryptosystems – seeing through the disguise even when you are not supposed to be able to. Cryptology is the study of both cryptography and cryptanalysis. These definitions are available from Federation of American scientists, "Cryptography FAQ," <www.faqs.org/faqs/cryptography-faq/part03/>. Encryption software simply enables computers to perform fast and efficiently the mathematical processes (algorithms) to encrypt messages. In this chapter I use the terms "cryptography" and "encryption" as synonyms. However, while cryptography is the *entire* scientific field of information security, encryption is only the *process* of turning "plaintext" (ordinary text)

into "ciphertext." The reverse process is known as decryption. For more definitions see, for example, the Committee on National Security Systems (2003).

4 Cryptography is a well-developed field of research with numerous highly specialized texts. A classic reference textbook is Schneier (1996). There are also many books on cryptography history and achievements like Singh (1999) or more popular material such as Mackenzie (2003).

5 Most of the global information infrastructure is of the PKI type because it relies on public key cryptography invented by Whitfield Diffie and Martin Hellman at Stanford University in 1977. Diffie and Hellman first publicly proposed asymmetric encryption in their paper, "New Directions in Cryptography." The concept had been independently and privately proposed by James Ellis several years before when he was working for the British Government Communications Headquarters (cf. Singh, 1999; Levy, 2001).

6 See Article 12 of the Universal Declaration.

7 In its guidelines to protect personal privacy, the Electronic Frontier Foundation recommends to "use encryption!" available from <www.eff.org/pub/Privacy/eff_privacy_top_12.html> [May 5, 2004].

8 It would be more correct to speak about "re-securitization" in the case of cryptography. In fact, the whole field was already an integral element of the military sphere. In the United States, for example, cryptography had been a public field until World War I, when the Army and the Navy realized its value to national security and began surrounding it with secrecy.

9 For more details on the CDA, see the Center for Democarcy and Technology at <www.cdt.org/speech/cda/> [May 5, 2004].

10 Two excellent "hate-watch" websites are the Hate Watch at <www.hatewatch.org/frames.html> and the Simon Wiesenthal Center at <www.wiesenthal.com/watch/index.html>.

11 Mock recommends education for Internet users as the key solution to this problem. This is precisely the goal of organizations such as Hate Watch or the Wiesenthal Center.

12 Cox (1981) identified only one major post-World War II case in the United States, of conflict between First Amendment freedoms and national security that resulted in the "Pentagon Papers."

13 In all fairness, it should be mentioned that threats to freedom of expression and imposition of censorship may also come from the private sector. As Shapiro (1999: 67) pointed out, sometimes "the driving concern of the state seems to be that someone needs to rein the Net – if not government, then private actors." In September 2000, the Global Internet Liberties Campaign (GILC) singled out at the Internet Content Rating Association, a global consortium of corporations, which includes, among others, AOL, Microsoft, IBM, British Telecom, and Bertelsmann, aiming for a world-wide policy of self-rating. Content rating, complained the GILC, could threaten the freedom of expression, diversity of views, and accessibility that the Internet currently offers.

14 "No one should be subjected to arbitrary interference with his privacy, family, home or correspondence, nor to attacks on his honor or reputation. Everyone has the right to the protection of law against such interference or attacks."

15 There is also an interpretation of individual "privacy" that is seen as detrimental for democracy. This point is well explained, for instance, in Ruiz (1997: 9–10).

16 It is not only Internet users who leave behind a wealth of information about their preferences and personalities. Using ATM machines, cellular phones, and credit cards in the real world or simply walking across a shopping mall or an airport leave behind data and images that, if cross-matched, can reveal substantial information about individuals' behavior.

17 See "Guidelines Concerning Computerized Personal Data Files," adopted by the UN General Assembly on December 14, 1990, "Guidelines on the Protection of Privacy and Trans-border Data Flows," published by the OECD (1990), and the EU Directive 95/46EC of October 24, 1995.

18 For an overview on these differences in telecommunications see Ruiz (1997). The fact that privacy is more regulated in Europe does not mean that Americans are not fond of it. On the contrary, the "right to be left alone" is more strongly felt in a country the size of the United States than in many crowded countries of Europe.

19 Computers, more than other technologies in the past, have elicited impulsive fears in the larger public since their appearance (Bennett, 1992). It is the very idea of the *deus ex machina*, that a machine could search for and collect information on people's lives. In this respect, this image has fostered the demand for more regulations on privacy protection, at least in industrialized democracies. The effects of digitalization of the Net can be also seen, for instance, in the widespread use of digital cameras for surveillance. In Britain alone there are an estimated 300,000 cameras covering shopping areas, housing estates, car parks, and public facilities in many towns and cities. As Lessig (1999: 152) noted, in this constantly taped world, the burden of proof is on "the monitored" to first establish their innocence.

20 It is also the main reason why on-line pornography is so popular.

21 On this problem, see, for example, Rosenberg (1998).

22 I am grateful to Professor Hansjürgen Garstka, Data Protection and Information Access Commissioner of the State of Berlin, for his thorough explanation of this point (Berlin, June 27, 2000).

23 A storage service provider (SSP) is a company that provides computer storage space and related management to other companies. There are also ISPs that make available the same service to individual users.

24 A content provider of a web page can, mostly thanks to "cookies" (small text files placed on the user's computer) but not exclusively, know not only the IP address of users accessing that web page, but also how many times the same user has accessed that page and what other pages he or she has visited before. Cookies can generally be read only by the server that has placed them. However, "third-party cookies" could be placed on the user's computer (without his or her knowledge if the browser does not alert him or her) by other web servers than the one the user has visited.

25 For more on this aspect, see for instance Dam (1996: esp. 52–7)

26 See the definition at <http://searchcio.techtarget.com/sDefinition/0,,sid19_gci212029, 00.html> [May 10, 2004].

27 The first version of the survey was done under the name of Global Internet Liberties Campaign (GILC) by investigators of the Electronic Privacy Information Center. In 1999 and 2000, Electronic Privacy Information Center took the report under its sole name.

28 Public key encryption software is considered "strong" when it relies on 128-bit permutations (2^{128}). Encryption software is deemed secure when it relies on 1024-bit permutations.

29 Those surveys are based on public source information and it is thus probable that many military secure servers when "interrogated" by the surveying software simply did not respond.

30 National security is an extensive, all-embracing, and, for that matter, undefined concept that states use at their pleasure to justify controlling or repressing an equally broad variety of social behaviors, from human rights to organized crime or terrorism. It is intended here in the most comprehensive sense.

31 The works of Bessette and Haufler (2001) and Herrera (2002) have also focused on the interactions of the three Internet actors (i.e. states, firms and individuals) and the creation of interest coalitions.

32 Soft power, however, in the different disguises of "persuasion" or "socio-psychological pressure," has long been with economic power the main instrument of domestic politics. Charisma could be seen as an innate ability to yield soft power.

33 Even before September 11, the FBI feared that al-Qaeda terrorists were some sort of "masters" in the use of encryption, to the point of "getting jittery" (McCullagh, 2001).

34 It should be noted that, technically, legally, and organizationally, law enforcement requirements for wire-tapping differ fundamentally from communications intelligence, which is the primary business of the NSA.

35 Large government organizations, particularly in industrialized countries, have the resources (i.e. computing power) to monitor, encipher, and decipher large quantities of messages. However, if it takes, for instance, one day to read ten encrypted messages, with the same computing power 1,000 messages will require ten days of work, and 100,000 messages 100 days. With 10 million encrypted messages, the same organizations with the same computing power will be saturated, since it takes proportionally much more computing power to decipher than to encrypt messages. The best solution is simply to limit the number of individuals that can use cryptography. This solution is clearly more easily implemented by autocratic regimes than democratic states.

36 Carnivore is an FBI-developed software program that copies and saves e-mail messages that contain certain keywords.

37 In the movie *Sneakers* (1992), Robert Redford greeted two alleged NSA officers with the remark: "Uh, so you are the guys that I hear breathing when I pick up the phone." One of the two officers replied: "No, that's the CIA. We are the good guys."

38 Another unofficial nickname was "No Such Agency." In the past, two of the best-known books on the NSA had given an equally upsetting assessment of the agency. Bamford (1983: 378) noted that "like an ever-widening sinkhole, NSA's surveillance technology will continue to expand, quietly pulling in more and more communications and gradually eliminating more and more privacy." The conclusion that Ransom reached was no different. The National Security Agency, he noted, was "a huge, secret apparatus that bears watching, for it could become 'Big Brother's' instrument for eavesdropping on the entire population if '1984' were ever to come" (1970: 133).

39 A "brute force" attack is only possible by using a computer that simply tries to guess all the possible permutations to find the key. The more powerful the computer, the faster it can find the key. It must be noted that the DES was a private key algorithm, and therefore the length of the key measured in bits did not need to be as long as a public key would. David Kahn, author of *The Codebreakers*, noted that the DES code should be weak enough for the NSA to solve it when used by foreign nations and companies (quoted in Bamford, 1983: 347).

40 "RSA is an Internet encryption and authentication system that uses an algorithm developed in 1977 by Ron Rivest, Adi Shamir, and Leonard Adleman. The RSA algorithm is the most commonly used encryption and authentication algorithm and is included as part of the Web browsers from Microsoft and Netscape. It's also part of Lotus Notes, Intuit's Quicken, and many other products. The encryption system is owned by RSA Security. The company licenses the algorithm technologies and also sells development kits. The technologies are part of existing or proposed Web, Internet, and computing standards." Whatis.com, available from <http://searchsecurity.techtarget.com/sDefinition/0,,sid14_gci214273, 00.html> [June 15, 2004].

41 All information about the "DESCracker" challenge are available from the EFF website, <www.eff.org/Privacy/Crypto_misc/DESCracker/> [May 12, 2004].

42 The EFF press release on the event is available from <www.eff.org/descracker/> [May 12, 2004].

43 The AES can support key sizes of 128, 192, and 256 bits.

44 An employee of the British intelligence service, James Ellis, however, had devised the public key scheme in the 1970s but he could not publish his discovery (Levy, 2001).

45 I attended the lecture of this observer at the 20th ISODARCO Summer School, Rovereto (Italy), August 7–17, 1999. On this point see also Hersh (1999).

46 Zimmermann actually asked a friend to post it (Levy, 2001: 197).

47 In addition to the DOJ, the DOC, DOD, and other US agencies were actually involved.

48 The escrow system is risky because there are no guarantees that it will not be abused by government employees or that hackers may not break into it and steal the keys (*quis custodiet ipsos custodies*).

49 For a more extensive account, see the EPIC websites at <www.epic.org/crypto/> [May 12, 2004].

50 The liberalization rules included "retail" encryption products (widely exportable to all but certain "terrorist" nations) subject to a government review and reporting requirements, non-retail products (also exportable and subject to similar requirements) to most non-government users, and encryption products with less than 64 bits (freely exportable).

51 The surveys ranked countries from *green* (free and uncontrolled cryptography) to *red* (restricted and controlled cryptography). The 1998 and 1999 surveys are available from <www.gilc.org/crypto/crypto-survey.html> and <www.gilc.org/crypto/crypto-survey-99.html> and the 2000 survey from <www2.epic.org/reports/crypto2000/countries.html> [May 14, 2004].

52 The countries were Belarus, Burma (Myanmar), China, Kazakhstan, Pakistan, Russia, Tunisia, and Vietnam (EPIC, 2000).

53 See Murray (1997), who was strongly skeptical about the usefulness of much U.S. intelligence well before September 2001.With reference to information infrastructures, the change of focus (and discourse) from state to non-state actors of the Bush Administration is well analyzed in Bendrath (2003). See also Murray (1997) about the uselessness of more information to prevent surprise attacks.

54 The "rally around the flag" attitude, however, was quickly worn away by the unwillingness of ICT firms to fully bear the costs of further securitization (Schneier, 2003).

55 For an in-depth analysis of the Patriot Act, see Chapter 4 below and the "Analysis of the Provisions of the USA PATRIOT Act," by the Electronic Frontier Foundation (EFF), available from <www.eff.org/Privacy/Surveillance/Terrorism_militias/20011031_eff_usa_patriot_analysis.html>.

3 What democracies do?

An overview

This chapter provides a quick overview of the ways in which ten democratic countries, with varying population size, socio-political structure, and pluralist institutions (Lijphart, 1999), attempt to control the Internet, protect their NII and, more generally, develop an information society.[1] All the ten countries (Australia, Austria, Canada, Finland, France, Israel, Japan, the Netherlands, Spain, and Switzerland) identified on-line threats that required some control on the Internet. Cybercrime, child pornography, and computer frauds were the worries causing greatest concern for most of them. However, each country characterized those threats in light of its own specific national culture. In his study of counterterrorism policies, Katzenstein (2003: 734) stressed the importance of "how threats are constructed politically." National processes of threat construction are crucial elements in the debate on Internet control and so are the general political economic orientation of the governments in office and the aggregation of domestic interests.

If the private sector has the habit of working together with the cabinet or being closely associated with it, if the structure of political economic interests is corporatist, or if the necessity of "total defense" prevents businesses from being confrontational with the executive and so on, Internet users and civil liberties NGOs have a difficult time in steering government policies away from greater Internet control. The high level of pluralism in a country is necessary to guarantee multiple views on policy-making and to use the multiple access points to cabinets and legislation, but alone it is not sufficient. Only when companies support or sympathize with users and their NGOs that represent their interests, will they then work together to curb government control of the network. Users are also a sample of the public. Hence, if the public traditionally loathes neo-Nazi or hatred speech, it is likely that users will consider it "natural" that freedom of speech in their country does not protect hate crimes, whether on- or off-line. All these ten countries examined and their publics rejected any justification that might be used to exempt child pornography from prosecution. Child pornographers have indeed exploited the constitutional guarantees that protect freedom of speech in democratic states to hide the content of their communications.

The case studies cases presented here are short and are intended to support the analysis of the next chapters. King *et al.*, (1994) always recommend, if possible, to increase the number of observations. These observations are based on availability and richness of data as outlined by Van Evera (1997). The second reason is that the Internet is shaped by numerous forces, including active users, R&D spending, etc. All these forces are still concentrated within the relatively small OECD group of countries. The countries analyzed in this chapter, together with the United States, Germany, and Italy, are in essence a sort of "governing council" (or a board of directors) of the Internet. They currently own most of the Internet and are, thus, by far the major producer of Internet content. As Braman (2004:8) notes, there are now "three classes of nation-states from the perspectives of their relative impact on the global information policy regimes." The United States and the EU members are the two most powerful players. The United States, the EU, and Japan are also among the world's biggest spenders in R&D in advanced technology, including the ICT sector. North American and European Internet users are also the most active when it comes to Internet civil liberties and privacy.[2] If one adds countries like Canada and Australia, it could hardly be denied that this group is de facto the governing council of the Internet and of the global information infrastructure.

All the countries surveyed tend to consider telecommunications, banking and financial services, energy and water distribution, transportation, and critical government services as part of the national information infra-structure (NII) (Dunn and Wigert, 2004a). This definition of NII is consistent with what the formulation of the United States, the first country that has outlined the core elements of a NII, did. All the countries in this chapter, as well as the United States, Germany and Italy, in the next chapters qualify high in several international rankings. They are all ranked within the criteria to be in the first 25 positions (out of 75) in the Harvard University's Network Readiness Index (Kirkman *et al.*, 2002a: xiv). According to the UNDP Technology Achievement Index (United Nations Development Program, 2001: 45), all but one are in the group of "leaders" (Spain is a "potential leader"). Finally, all but one of the countries are in the "high access" category of the International Telecommunication Union Digital Access Index (Spain is in the second best "upper access" group) (Mingers, 2003). These indexes are valuable because they show what is the level of technological sophistication and dependability of the country considered, as well as its potential vulnerability to computer networks failure.

Most importantly, these countries are all democracies, which have different domestic institutions (government agencies, businesses, NGOs) with a varied aggregation of interests that compete to shape policies. Democracies are more interesting when it comes to exploring why their governments want to control the Internet. Autocracies tend to control all means of communication by default (Reporters Sans Frontières, 2003; International Press Institute, 2003a). In autocratic states, the competition among Internet stakeholders and their interest is non-existent. To them the merging of communication and infrastructure on the Internet poses no dilemmas and is not of great relevance. In this respects, autocracies are a like a constant, that is, they hardly change over time. Moreover (with the exception of Singapore and, to a lesser extent, China) most autocracies contribute little to the development of the world's information infrastructures. Instead, all those countries that do contribute are mostly democracies with advanced economies. These continue to invest in infrastructures, and their experience with Y2K was akin to a "crash course" in information infrastructure assurance. They hold overlapping membership cards in the international "democracies' network club," which includes the Organization for Economic Cooperation and Development (OECD), the European Union, NATO, the Wassenaar Agreement (WA),[3] the Council of Europe, the G8, the World Intellectual Property Rights Organization (WIPO), and others (Dunn and Wigert, 2004b).

All these international organizations have been the source of guidelines and recommendations about problems related to NII and the Internet for their members. For instance, as OECD members these countries are expected to be consistent with the organization's guidelines on, for instance, the protection of personal data and the use of encryption software. OECD guidelines are not, however, binding international norms like those of a convention of the Council of Europe or of an international treaty like the Non-Proliferation Treaty. Last but not least, most of the countries surveyed had a national chapter of the Internet Society (ISOC) or of the Electronic Frontier Foundation (EFF) or both. While the latter has always been more "socially" oriented, the former tried, over the years, to preserve the more pragmatic, problem-solving attitude of the original founders like Jon Postel.[4] The two NGOs were founded in the United States and are now two of the best-known stakeholders in the development of the Internet. The presence of several national chapters is a sign of a high level of international coordination on issues such as freedom of speech and censorship, privacy, and the individual use of cryptography.

Generally speaking, in Europe, Japan and elsewhere, national governments have been more likely to intervene in the course of the information revolution than the US federal government. European governments, for instance, have tried to balance the market in a way "to span the digital divide, promote equity, protect privacy and assure inclusion and social participation" (Pearson and Bikson, 2000: 69). At the same time, European governments have emphasized social and cultural capital development and the quality of life within the information society. Not accidentally, when it comes to social capital, European countries top the list in the Network Readiness Index (Kirkman *et al.*, 2002b, table 6). European trade unions also exerted some influence, limiting the power of governments and the market in the service of the quality of life. Pearson and Bikson (2000) also argued that Europe might provide lifestyle models for the future, in contrast to the United States, where the market has mostly been allowed to determine the shape of the information society.

The five EU members (Austria, France, Finland, the Netherlands, and Spain) included in this survey show interesting telling similarities. For example, several EU countries have struggled to adapt their legislation to the EU directives on privacy and personal data protection. The rules laid down by the directive were stricter than similar rules in the United States (in this respect, Canada is closer to the European viewpoint than to America's).[5] The EU as a group of countries is also important for the action of transnational actors (TNA), as more and more European NGOs coordinate their efforts at the "EU level" (for instance, Evers, 2001). After the attacks of September 2001, all EU governments agreed that terrorism, with its consequences for European NII, was an issue-area in which cooperation was essential. They went as far as setting up the European Network and Information Agency (ENISA), which began operating in January 2004. Despite the impressive-sounding name, however, the "agency" was designed simply to be a centralized center for knowledge and research, where national cybercrime centers could pool resources and information, rather than a European counterpart to the NSA.

The principal tasks of Europol police are to facilitate the exchange of information between member-states, and to obtain and analyze information and intelligence. In October 2000, the French Presidency tabled a proposal for the extension of Europol's mandate to the fight against cybercrime to the council of the European Union (Rand Europe, 2002a). The official definition of computer crime in that context was "all forms of attack on automated data-processing systems." To fulfill that goal, Europol would operate a centralized database that would be accessible by all EU member-states. Nevertheless, because cybercrime per se was outside the convention that established Europol, Europol officers could investigate cybercrime only if it is interwoven with other kinds of organized crime (Rand Europe, 2002a). The bomb attacks in Madrid in March 2004 disclosed how little had been done in terms of cooperation among European partners since September 2001 (BBC News, 2004b). European governments intend to extensively improve and expand electronic intelligence. But data gathering through electronic intelligence was already quite broad before March 2004 and even if it had been more far-reaching it would have helped little, since, apparently, there was no digital communication or "electronic chatter" by the terrorists (Gardner, 2004). What was really lacking, just as in the United States before September 2001 (Schneier, 2003), was more exchange (and coordination) of information among different (national) intelligence services and more analysis of data already available.

Some EU governments wavered for domestic reasons in the face of adopting other necessary measures, like the Europe-wide search-and-arrest warrant, which would have been more effective in fighting terrorism than simply increasing electronic data-gathering. For example, the Berlusconi government dragged its feet for years (upsetting the other partners) because the Italian premier feared that other European judges could use the warrant against him. Nevertheless, at the end of March 2004, the 25 EU members agreed to adopt a Declaration on Combating Terrorism. The declaration outlined a plan to adopt a "solidarity clause" for mutual assistance in the event of a terrorist attack, improve intelligence services cooperation, make better use of Europol and Eurojust (police and judicial cooperation bodies), create a counter-terrorism tsar within the Office of the High Representative for Foreign and Security Policy, and strengthen border controls. The declaration also affected the Internet and telecommunications with proposals for a European database on terrorists and for further extending the storage of data by telephone operators and ISPs (BBC News, 2004c). Katzenstein (2003) explains Europe's tardiness as the result of a trade-off. Europeans have surrendered their capacity to systematically control their national borders in exchange for an increasingly proactive surveillance of certain sectors of their populations, primarily foreign residents and immigrants. Greater control on computer networks is an indispensable condition for that proactive surveillance.

The half-hearted reforms on fighting terrorism displayed by EU governments before March 2004 were not anomalous. Indeed that seems to be the rule when it comes to developing the "most competitive and dynamic, knowledge-based economy in the world" by 2010 that EU members promised at the 2000 Lisbon European Council. An outline for reforms in areas such as education, the labor market, and information infrastructures was prepared at that summit. A report of the London-based Center for European Reform (Murray, 2004) exposed the cynicism (bordering with derision) with which Europeans look at those promises. Not only would EU countries be unable to catch up with the United States, but, on the contrary, they are falling further behind. According to the report, Denmark, Sweden, and Finland are the world-class exceptions that outperform even the United States on many indicators of innovation, while a second group, namely Britain, Ireland, the Netherlands and Spain, perform well on many (but not all) of the Lisbon measures. France and Germany, which began a slow process of structural social reforms, are considered "laggards" and Italy is Europe's "villain" for failing to undertake even the modest reforms of the other two major countries.

NATO itself had a taste of offensive information operations (IO) during the air campaign in Kosovo in 1999, when Serbian hackers tried to block the organization's web servers (although no important information was compromised). A few of its members (notably the United States and the United Kingdom) did launch limited IO against Serbia. These actions reinforced the conviction of many members that protecting one's own information infrastructures was even more needed. NATO had begun to develop its own plans for IO in 1997, based on its experience in Bosnia (Rathmell, 2001). There appeared to be a "division of labour": the EU and the G8 would concentrate on cybercrime while NATO would cover the military side of the NII protection. NATO in fact provided distinctive definitions for cyberterrorism and cybercrime.[6] Within the realm of national defence, another remarkable parallel among many of the ten countries considered here and the three in-depth case studies is the enhanced role of national intelligence services. Because of the relevance of cryptography and electronic signals, not only do these stakeholders fulfil their functional mission of controlling Internet communications, but now they are also expected to be proactive in "information assurance," that is, to fight back against cyber-attacks on the NII.[7] The American National Security Agency (NSA), the British Government Communications Headquarters (GCHQ), the Canadian Communications Security Establishment (CSE), the Australian Defense Signal Directorate, and others have all been earmarked for those tasks by their national governments.

The issues of cybercrime and cyberterrorism, dependability and information assurance have steadily risen up the G8's agenda. At the 1995 Halifax summit in Canada, G8 governments set up a special working group of senior experts on organized crime, called the "Lyon Group." At the 2000 Paris summit, G8 leaders declared that the dialogue between public authorities and the private sector was indispensable in guaranteeing security on the Internet and the dependability of NII. The G8 had also agreed to further increase cooperation to fight cybercrime at the conclusion of the Paris meeting. In 2003, another G8 cybercrime meeting in Paris gathered not only top-level experts (the Lyon Group) but also major telecom and Internet carriers from the eight countries. G8 governments finally looked at the draft proposal for the Council of Europe Convention on Cybercrime as the most appropriate international locus to foster their cooperation to fight cybercrime, because non-European countries like the United States or Japan could also join in. Talks on the draft dragged on because of divergent views on privacy and freedom of speech, mostly between the Europeans and the Americans. The events of September 2001 hurried many participants in the Convention to sign it, but five countries had to ratify the Convention before it entered into force and again different opinions between Europeans and Americans on freedom of speech and privacy led to delays. In fact, it is only fair to say that the already diverse interpretation that Americans and Europeans had of the concept of privacy (Bennett, 1992) has grown even more diverse during the 1990s (Jonquieres and Kehoe, 1998). Ultimately, EU members agreed to sign an ad hoc memorandum attached to the Convention that would allow them to fight hatred speech and neo-Nazi material on the web more forcefully. The Convention finally entered into force on July 1 2004.

Democracies, Internet control and domestic interests

Australia

Australia's NII is seen as "the backbone of the information society" (Bruno, 2002: 17) and one of the world's most comprehensive legislative structures when it comes to e-business and e-commerce (Rand Europe, 2002b). There is a large degree of self-regulation and the main telecom operator is the former government-owned monopoly, Telstra. The Australian federal government has focused on several priorities to guarantee better education and skills and to provide world-class infrastructure so that Australians will benefit from the Internet and ICT in general. Consequently, I2000, the National Office for the Information Economy, was established to fulfill these aims.

In a country of the dimensions of Australia, distances and costs make redundancy (the key guarantee against the failure of the NII) something to be kept to a "strict minimum" (Wigert, 2004a: 40). In 1997, an early report by the Defense Signal Directorate outlined the main vulnerabilities of Australia's NII that prompted the creation of an interdepartmental committee for the protection of the NII as well as of a consultative forum with the private sector. Another NII report further stressed the need for cooperation between the public and private sector and was followed, in 2002, by the launching of the "E-Security National Agenda" and the National Office for the Information Economy (Bruno, 2002). Australia's regulatory framework includes several laws that govern telecommunications interception (1979), radio communications (1992), and electronic transactions (1999). The Australian government has numerous agencies earmarked with protecting the NII, including the Australian Security Intelligence Organization (ASIO), which has as its primary mission "to protect Australia from threats to national security." At the same time, as with European countries and Canada, Australia has a Federal Privacy Commissioner. The commissioner investigates complaints which fall within the Privacy Act. Therefore, the commissioner's office can conduct audits of government agencies, health organizations (hospitals), and private businesses that are subject to the act.

The main forum for public–private partnership is the Business–Government Task Force on Critical Infrastructure, which gathers together government and regional agencies as well as private companies and trade associations. Australia considers Internet threats mostly as threats to the its NII, and the Australian government has been one of the most sensitive to this issue. The government has appealed to "national security" in the debate on controlling the Internet, but cybercrime appears to be the major worry and a mix of law enforcement and intelligence is required to tackle it. More importantly, even after 9/11, it seems that in Australia security imperatives are less relevant than economic and commercial motivations in the development of a framework for infrastructure governance.[8]

The struggle over Internet control has had ups and downs for all the stakeholders, whose alliances are constantly shifting depending on the issue at stake and the interests aggregation of the stakeholders. For instance, the Australian Broadcasting Authority (ABA) was authorized under the Broadcasting Service Act of January 2000 to ask ISPs to take "reasonable steps" to remove certain material (including child pornography, bestiality, real sex acts, or information about crime and violence). Civil liberties groups opposed these restrictions while Australian ISPs tended to ignore them (Reporters Sans Frontières, 2003: 16). After ABA refused to censor websites calling for anti-WTO demonstrations in November 2002, the government stated that it would directly act, but it appears that no concrete steps have been taken. In another instance, in 2002, under the pressure of civil liberties NGOs, even the federal government joined with opposition parties in parliament in voting against a proposed government amendment to interception laws.

In the aftermath of September 11, the proposed plan would have allowed government agencies to intercept e-mail, text messages, and voicemail messages without an interception warrant. Civil liberties NGOs argued that it would have unnecessarily extended government surveillance powers. Ultimately the federal government dropped the plan. In 2003, on the other hand, it was the private sector that linked up with government agencies. The Internet Industry Association of Australia (IIA) issued for public consultation a draft of the Cybercrime Code of Practice for ISPs. The Code had been developed in secret for over two years by the IIA and law enforcement agencies. Electronic Frontiers Australia declared that the code would result in massive invasion of Internet users' privacy and that the IIA was behaving like "Big Brother" (Electronic Frontiers Australia, 2003).

The struggle about censorship and Internet control and the protection of the NII has continued unabated ever since. The pluralism level (Lijphart, 1999: 177) of Australia (moderately high) seems to justify why that support has continued. Moreover, the fact that the Australian government exercises more control over the spending of NGOs than other OECD countries (Smillie, 1999) means that it has additional leverage on some of the non-governmental players. But Australians are also eager to stress that they do not want to replicate the situation in the United States. For example, civil liberties NGOs criticized the intellectual property clauses of the free trade agreement announced between Australia and the United States. The organizations argued that those clauses would leave average Australians at the mercy of legal action from multinational media companies, and represented a "massive step backwards" for Australian intellectual property law (Electronic Frontiers Australia, 2004).

Austria

In the 1990s, Austria eagerly embraced the ICT service sector. The country reformed its educational system, turning out more graduates in engineering and science than did many other EU fellow members. The diffusion of the Internet and of mobile phones is a clear demonstration of this reformation. Austria ranks ninth on the Network Readiness Index and shows a clear indication of moving its economy from more traditional sectors (such as tourism) to the high-tech industry. The main player for government R&D programs is the federal Ministry for Transport, Innovation and Technology, and researchers in sectors such as cryptography and access control have amply benefited from those programs. Despite the 1998 liberalization, the fixed telephony market, however, is still dominated by Telekom Austria, the former monopoly. The main regulatory law is the Telecommunication Act (Telekommunikationgesetz) of 1997 and Austria has a telecom control commission that supervises the application of that law. Austria also has laws on electronic commerce, personal data protection (as do all EU countries), intellectual property rights, and digital signature, and the government has "ambitious projects" (Rand Europe, 2002j) in the area of e-government. As one of the smaller countries in Europe, since World War II Austria has adopted the concept of comprehensive security (or "total defense" in Swedish terminology). Austria, a neutral country during the Cold War, had a structure of network defense (like Switzerland), according to which different areas had different values in terms of defense priority. To implement this security policy, like Switzerland or Sweden, Austria had to rely "on the systematic co-operation among various policy areas" (Wigert, 2004b: 54). Hence, when the need to protect the NII emerged in the late 1990s, Austrians knew what their template would be.

As with other EU countries, cybersecurity for Austria is mainly focused on fighting cybercrime. The Kriminalpolizei especially targets computer-related fraud, credit card misuse, and child pornography. The Federal Chancellery has directly undertaken the mission of fostering public–private partnership in the area of computer network security. Initiatives like the Austrian Digital Initiative are the direct result of this Chancellery policy. A specialized unit, created in 1999 within the Ministry of Interior, fulfills the task of surveillance and control.[9] Wire-tapping and computer searches are regulated by the code of criminal procedure, which was updated in 1998 to bring it more in line with other EU member countries (GILC/EPIC, 1998). Since criticism had been widespread, the new rules were supposed to be in effect only until December 2001. After 9/11, however, those provisions were maintained.

"Informal relationships, the absence of clear criteria, the tendency to avoid conflict and to find an 'arrangement' for everything" (Küblböck, 1999: 61) have long been typical traits of Austrian political culture. These characteristics, coupled with Austria's low level of pluralism

(Lijphart, 1999: 177), have long contributed to reducing division and confrontation among Internet stakeholders. In the past few years, however, "the political climate has begun to change, resulting in more confrontation between the government and various interests groups" (Küblböck, 1999: 61). The few political parties, trade unions, and the private sector have produced a highly corporatist political system in Austria, where the liberalization of the telecom sector has been a major watershed. The telecom liberalization and the diffusion of the Internet have given birth to several users' and civil liberties NGOs. Civil liberties NGOs had really to struggle to influence government policies. Among the small corporatist states (Israel and Switzerland), however, the Austrian government does not appear to have applied securitization moves to increase Internet control.

Canada

Canada, the second largest country in the world, has a strong resemblance to Australia, with a small population dispersed over a continent-size territory. Canada also enjoys a level of social capital higher than many other English-speaking countries (Kirkman *et al.*, 2002a: 18) and a very high level of pluralism (Lijphart, 1999). The country combines the inclination toward voluntarism of all Anglo-Saxon countries with a distinctive "social" attitude close to Europe's. Telecommunications, the Internet, and infra-structures in general are perhaps even more essential in these countries than in other advanced economies. Moreover, the extensive links between the Canadian and American economies have further encouraged ICT penetration (Rand Europe, 2002c). While the Canadian federal government has the responsibility, among others, for national defense, foreign relations, international trade and commerce, the banking and monetary system, criminal law, and fisheries, federal courts have awarded Parliament regulatory powers in areas such as railways, telecommunications, and atomic energy (Harrop, 2002).

The provincial governments are also responsible for local infrastructures. Hence the protection of the NII and Internet control requires, at a mini-mum, the cooperation of different federal and local institutions with the ICT private sector which, as in all other advanced economies, owns a large share of Canada's NII. Remarkably, in October 1998 the federal government issued a comprehensive policy statement on the conduct of electronic commerce, addressing national security, law enforcement, and consumer protection. Unlike other advanced countries, however, the same statement also referred to the effects that the necessity to "police" the public Internet would inevitably have on civil liberties (Rand Europe, 2002c).

If Canadians are closer to the Americans in their frequent use of telephone touch-tone services for banking, bill payment, and information services, they are more like the Europeans when it comes to legislation. In fact, computer crime violations are all included within the Canadian Criminal Code, unlike the United States, which has numerous laws, each covering a certain aspect of computer crime. Privacy is another area where Canadians lean more towards the European interpretation than that of Canada's southern neighbor. Although there is no explicit right to privacy in Canada, unlawful interception of private communication is a criminal offense and police are obliged to obtain a warrant (GILC/EPIC, 1998). Canada's attitude toward personal privacy is closer to the European template than to that of the United States. Nevertheless, Canadian privacy law hardly affects the private sector, which relies on "voluntary privacy codes" (Rosenberg, 1998). The Telecommunication Act of 1993 has specific provisions to protect the privacy of individuals. Canadians are closer to Europeans because they expect more from their government than they do from the private sector in terms of privacy and security. Canadians believe that since the government holds so much sensitive personal information about them (on their health, educational attainment, job history, social benefits, and marital and financial status) that the executive should demonstrate unquestioned commitment to the protection of that information (Government On-line, 2002). Their perceptions about how seriously the government views its stewardship responsibilities for safeguarding their personal data and respecting their privacy will have a tremendous impact on the take-up of on-line services.

Canada has a long tradition of defense cooperation with the United States, and so the Canadian government has coordinated in this area with its southern neighbor. In fact, Canada's NII is tightly interconnected with that of the United States and is largely in the hands of the private sector (Wigert, 2004c). Hence, Canadians have not failed to notice that a well-functioning public–private partnership is of key importance to protecting their NII. An infrastructure protection coordination center was created in early 2001 with the goal of guarding ("around the clock") the country's NII. The center is embedded within the Department of National Defense (DND). The National Critical Infrastructure Assurance Program, which the government launched after September 11, has worked as a national focus for cooperation between the federal and local governments and the private sector. One of the most important goals of the program is the circulation of information among its many stakeholders. The Canadian parliament passed a new anti-terrorist law in December 2001 that extended the electronic surveillance powers of the police. Furthermore, the National Defense Act allows the defense minister to authorize the Communication Security Establishment to intercept private communications but not those of Canadians or people living in Canada. Since 2002, the federal government has pressured ISP to develop the necessary technical means to allow national security officials to access their data. Canada's Privacy Commissioner has "fiercely attacked" these actions (Reporters Sans Frontières, 2003: 27).

Despite the high pluralism (even higher than in the United States), Canada has not experienced the kind of antagonism about Internet control that the United States and even other countries had. Several factors contribute to explain this anomaly. Canadian pluralism is a consequence of the country's cultural and linguistic differences that presuppose that there are multiple players that defend those differences. The multiplicity of players implies a multiplicity of access points to the federal and local governments to influence their policies. Canada also has a notion of privacy that is very close to Europe's. This shared understanding between civil liberties NGOs and the Canadian government also lessens the conflict among stakeholders. No matter how many misgivings Canadians may have about their government, they are inclined to trust it more than most Americans or even Europeans. Finally, the federal government has not considered any securitization of Internet control. Even in the case of the cryptowars, the federal government has refused securitization, preferring a more liberal approach to the issue.

Finland

Rand Europe (2002d: 3) considers Finland "one of the most successful ICT countries in Europe," with innovative ICT products, high export rates, skilled programmers (for example, Finland is home to Linus Torvald, inventor and "spiritual" guide of Linux), a reliable economic environment for electronic commerce, and enthusiastic population users/consumers of ICT. All Finnish schools have Internet connections, and Finland was the first country in the world to launch third-generation mobile phones as early as in 1998, giving away licenses for free (unlike what most EU countries did). According to Murray (2004), Finland is one of the Nordic EU countries (the others being Denmark and Sweden) that have outdone even the United States in creating a true knowledge-based economy and society. The recipe for Finland's success has been strong investment in the NII and in ICT-oriented public education programs.

The main regulatory sources include the Personal Data Act (1999), the Electronic Services in the Administration Act, which includes electronic signature (2000), and the Communication Markets Act (1999) to harmonize digital telecom networks. E-government and electronic commerce, despite the burst of the dot.com bubble in 2001, still rank very high on the government's agenda, which, by 2004–2005, hopes to establish Finland as a fully knowledge-based interactive society. Given its dependability on computer networks, Finland is more vulnerable than even the United States. Hence, protecting the country's NII is one of the highest priorities for the Finnish government. A study of six European countries' response to terrorism found that, in the area of cybersecurity, only in Finland was the adoption of adequate measures considered "well under way," despite the fact that "the Finnish authorities do not believe the country is significantly threatened by terrorism in any way" (Linde *et al.*, 2002: 8, 34). The study also showed that other countries with a longer history of terrorism (France, Germany, Spain, and the UK) were behind Finland.

There are two main bodies concerned with the protection and development of information networks: FICORA, an agency under the Ministry of Transport and Communications, and VAHTI, the government's IT security board. The latter overviews all IT-related fields, but it has a predominantly consulting role, while the former supervises data protection and information security in the operations of telecom carriers. FICORA can undertake inspections of these operators and has established the CERT-FI to detect and prevent security incidents (Rand Europe, 2002d). The National Bureau of Investigation and the Security Police, internationally and domestically, have jurisdiction to fight cybercrime. The Finnish Information Society Development Center (a neutral and non-profit organization) is the meeting point for ICT private and public sectors. The Information Society Advisory Board also draws members from both the private and public sectors.

The picture emerging from this examination of the Finnish situation is that of a country that has no less than its own economic survival dependent on the functioning of its NII. At the same time, Finland maintains one of the world's highest standards for privacy protection and freedom of speech. Indeed, FICORA guarantees that operations by ICT operators intended to strengthen security of their infrastructures are fully compatible with the legislation on privacy protection. The Finnish case strongly confirms how it is possible to combine protection of the NII, respect for citizens' privacy and civil rights, and maintain Internet control within the reasonable limits for a democracy.

France

In France (Natalicchi, 2001: 129), "telecoms have for long been a national priority." Hence, cabinets of different political creeds have all intervened in the telecom sector. This tendency has "never ceased" (Natalicchi, 2001: 129 – 30) and is not limited to the telecom sector but, rather, it is a distinctive characteristic of French economic policies (Hulsink, 1998). Currently, France is "one of Europe's most advanced ICT countries" (Rand Europe, 2002e: 3) but it has been one of the slowest countries to adopt the Internet for three reasons. The first reason is that the French society and private sector are accustomed to follow the state's initiative (the French *dirigisme*). Unlike other countries, the public perceive the French government as cohesive and united. Turf wars are hidden and inter-agency disputes rarely reach the public, leaving the public with the impression that the "government decides." These conditions, coupled with the moderate level of pluralism of in the country (Lijphart, 1999: 177), imply that users' and civil liberties NGOs often have to struggle considerably to make their voice heard by the cabinet and legislature to change their policies.

Second, since almost all information on-line is in English, the French have been reluctant to accept yet another sign of Anglo-Saxon cultural pervasiveness (or of "America's soft power"). Cultural and linguistic considerations also led to the adoption of the "made in France" computer communication tool, the Minitel, in the 1980s. But the diffusion of that France Telecom proprietary communication system also made many French people hesitant about switching again to the Internet. After that slow start, however, the French have embraced the Internet with enthusiasm, albeit with a mildly more conservative attitude than in other countries (Hutchison and Minton, 2002). Furthermore, French investment in "knowledge" (R&D, software, and education) is always high (Rand Europe, 2002e). The Internet itself is considered an important exogenous factor that contributed to the change of telecommunication policy in France (Hulsink, 1998).

In some respects, the early French attempts at controlling the Internet resembled the situation in the United States in 1996. As the United States government (and Congress) failed to make a convincing case for the Communication Decency Act (CDA) before the Supreme Court in 1996, in the same year, France's Conseil Constitutionnel, the French highest court, struck down the Telco Act. According to the Association des Utilisateurs d'Internet (AUI), who filed the lawsuit, article 15 of the Act was both technically inapplicable and "dangerous for democracy and freedom of expression." For the then French Minister of Posts, Telecommunications and Space that article should have been the basis for increasing government control on the expanding network in France. Despite the failure of the Telco Act, which had been introduced to increase governmental control of the Internet, the French government could nonetheless rely on existing legislation to discipline certain aspects of the Internet. Like many other European countries, French laws forbid the use of any media for racist and anti-Semitic propaganda and sexual exploitation of children. The impact of these laws on the evolution of the Internet in France became evident with the Yahoo! case in 2000. Before that year, it appeared that France would emphasize more self-regulation in its effort to regulate the Internet.

The 1990 legislation forbade individual use of encrypted communications, which was reserved only for the military, intelligence, and diplomatic services. France's position changed drastically in 1999, when the socialist government of Lionel Jospin recognised that the Internet was having a tremendous impact on the growth of the French economy, but that the limitations on the use of encryption software could undermine that process. Not only did French firms complain that without encryption electronic commerce could never take off, but also that they could not sell their encryption products to foreign customers, who would buy encryption software from those countries that had no such limits.

As in other democracies, the tone of Internet control changed after September 2001. With the United Kingdom, France was one of the first European countries to toughen anti-terrorism legislation (CNN.com, 2001b). In November 2001, the Assemblée Nationale passed the Law on Everyday Security, proposed by the government. The law obliged ISPs to retain their customers' records for at least a year and allowed judges to use "secret methods" (for reasons of national defense) to decode e-mail messages or to obtain encryption keys from software companies (Reporters Sans Frontières, 2003: 56). Moreover, the Internal Security Policy and Planning Law (July 2002) allows law enforcement agencies, with previous court permission, to make remote on-line searches or have direct access to personal data necessary "to establish the truth in a criminal case." A bill that reintroduces the civil and criminal responsibility of ISPs (previously rejected by the constitutional court) was also considered by the parliament.

The main French body that deals with national and international security affairs, and hence with cyberterrorism and cyberwar, is the Secretary General for National Defense. The secretary is directly subordinated to the prime minister and was first called into action for the Y2K problem (Wigert, 2004d). France has been one of the most fervent supporters of the Council of Europe Cybercrime Convention and of cooperation with other EU partners in the area of legal and internal affairs to fight cybercrime and cyberterrorism. Nevertheless, as in almost all other advanced countries, the main cyber-threats are considered to be Internet frauds and scams, credit card theft, and child pornography. Like other many Europeans, Canadians, Americans, and Australians, French users are also concerned about their personal privacy when surfing the Internet. Initiatives to exchange information about the dependability of the NII between public, private, and individual actors are still extremely limited (Rand Europe, 2002e). Most of the public – private partnership is only in the R&D sector.

Because of its experience in World War II, France, like Germany and Italy, is very sensitive to the presence of neo-Nazi propaganda or memorabilia on the Internet. In 2000, French Jewish and anti-racist groups sued the California-based Yahoo! over items such as SS daggers, swastikas, propaganda films, and photos of death camp victims being sold on its auction pages in the United States (BBC News, 2000a).[10] Although, according to US laws, Yahoo! was not bound by the French ruling (a California judge heard the case nonetheless), the Internet company decided to comply autonomously and blocked access from France to those pages. American civil liberties NGOs considered this action to be a dangerous potential precedent undermining the unfettered freedom of speech of Americans. *The Economist* (2000i: 101) did not miss the opportunity to remark that the French initiative might set an "uncomfortable precedent" for the ways in which national governments might try to impose their laws in an on-line world.[11] Yahoo! was ultimately cleared in 2003 (Henley, 2003).

What is important to underline in this occurrence is that the French public supported the action by anti-racist groups, as in Germany the public supports the ban on neo-Nazi material. Hence, it could not be considered a case of censorship on French (or even European) free speech.

The French government had to bow to pressure from the private sector and civil liberties NGOs in the issue area of encryption software, which was an important exception. On the other hand, even the Socialist cabinet showed a penchant for securitization moves. If, as in the case of the cryptowars, two stakeholders (NGOs and the ICT sector) cooperate, they may overcome securitization. Otherwise a cohesive state with a long practice of securitization moves, the solid tradition of closeness between firms and the national government, and the fact that, for a long time, NGO interest groups have not been well organized (Natalicchi, 2001), suggests that antagonism among stakeholders on Internet control is still strongly unbalanced in favor of the executive. This state of affairs is unlikely to change in the near future.

Israel

Like many other countries, Israel privatized much of its telecommunications industry, and concurrently experienced privatization of telecoms and substantial technological innovation in the 1990s. The ICT boom of those years has, indeed, convinced many Israelis that the country had an opportunity to move from an agriculture-based to a high-tech-based economy. Some authors (Miyashita *et al.*, 2000) have grouped Israel with India and Ireland as emerging major international software players. One of the reasons for this success appears to be the mass influx of well-trained immigrants from the former USSR republics after 1991 (Ein-Don *et al.*, 1999). Indeed, in 1999, Israel achieved the remarkable result of having over 70 companies listed on the NASDAQ, second only to Canada among foreign non-US countries.

Despite this success and its great potential, Israel has been quite slow in the process of liberalization of telecommunications. The Israeli government, in the past, has tended to follow the example of continental Europe (with over 20 ministries) and has heavily regulated their market (the Ministry of Communication playing a leading role). Bezeq, the former telecom monopoly, still enjoys a powerful position within the telecom market and the ICT sector in general, mostly because the government has been unable to force full compliance on the company. Connectivity costs are thus still high, slowing the diffusion of the Internet in the country. Currently, three players interact to determine the development of the Internet in Israel, namely private ISPs, Bezeq, and the government itself. The Israeli chapter of the Internet Society, a private, non-profit organization, administers domain names. As is the case of ISOC chapters in other countries in this survey, ISOC Israel has tried to present itself to the public as a "technical" NGO rather than a civil liberties advocate. Israel, however, has a low level of pluralism (Lijphart, 1999: 177) and also a low number of users' NGOs.

Attempts at Internet control and the protection of the country's NII are unavoidably affected by the long-standing confrontation between Israelis and Palestinians. Defense and national security are obviously paramount concerns for the whole of Israel. The country has regular armed forces (the Israeli Defence Forces), but most of the population is subject to military reserve duties and is regularly called up for training and exercises as well as "real" wars. Israel's secret services have world fame. The 2001–2003 *Intifada* witnessed an information war ("Internet-faida") fought by skilled Israeli as well as Palestinian individuals. However, the whole conflict was limited to perception management and psychological operation[12] and resulted, mostly, in defaced websites or linking the adversary's websites to pornographic sites (Hershman, 2001). Since Israel is more dependable on computer networks and the Internet than all other Arab countries combined (Trendle, 2002), the protection of Israel's NII, given the growing reliance of the country on it, is a primary concern for the government. This long period of low-intensity conflict has also had consequences for freedom of the press. For instance, according to the International Press Institute (2003a), the Israeli government announced a new press law, apparently in order to control journalistic work and to discriminate against unwanted journalists. A combined protest by press freedom groups and others, however, prompted the government to delay implementation. The law would also have applied to Internet content.

The development of the NII and the diffusion of the Internet in Israel have benefited from a highly educated population, from military research, and from the ties with the United States, although, at times, Israel has been on the side of the "attackers" of the United States (MSNBC, 1999). One of the Israeli software industry's most successful products has been the peer-to-peer chat software ICQ, which is extensively used around the world for chats and file exchange. The widespread software piracy and the poor protection of intellectual property rights, however, have hampered the expansion of the promising software industry. Among the OECD democracies, Israel is comparable to the United States and the United Kingdom (and to a lesser extent France) in that they have identified cyber-threats as a clear national security contingency with a strong military relevance. Both Israeli and Arab hackers (including those from North America) have long engaged in extensive information operations (CNN.com, 2000), defacing each other's websites and redirecting users to other websites. Although it is unlikely that Arabs or Palestinians may launch cyber-attacks that could damage Israel's NII, the "low level cyberwar" waged by Palestinians has provided the justification for the Israeli cabinet to set up stricter limits for users and their NGOs. The business's long tradition of cooperation with the executive has also contributed to making that government's securitization move all the more successful.

Japan

Japan's passion for communication technologies is almost legendary. Few other countries in the world are so ready to embrace new forms of communications as Japan. It is therefore unsurprising that the country always scores very high when it comes to the Internet, information infrastructures, or telecommunications. The Japanese government has been explicit in wanting to preserve the image of Japan as a highly technological nation and foster a "knowledge-emergent society."[13] Nevertheless, Japan's NII is thought to lag three years behind the United States and concern about the protection of the NII has emerged only in 1999–2000 with the Y2K scare (Rand Europe, 2002f). Furthermore, the idea of public–private partnerships, essential for the protection of the NII, has only recently appeared in Japan. For a country that prides itself on being a technological giant, these are issues that cannot go unnoticed.

As Miyashita *et al.* (2000) noted, in the early 1990s, in only four to five years, most Japanese industries were very anxious to introduce the Internet and extranets[14] into their business structures, for functions such as supply chain management and marketing. Soon, the Internet became "a kind of infrastructure for Japanese industries and society" (ibid.: 45). In that phase of digitalization, the strong central government played a compelling leadership role, which, on the other hand, resulted in high degrees of "standardization and uniformity" (Miyashita *et al.*, 2000: 46). This factor, the low level of socio-political pluralism, conservative and passive consumers, and the lack of a challenging attitude to change society meant that, in Japan, the debate on the protection of the NII and on controlling the Internet was extremely restricted. That debate never remotely approached the antagonistic intensity that characterized the confrontation between the government and the private sector and civil liberties NGOs on those issues in the United States or even in Europe.

By 2000, the Japanese government had produced a series of guidelines to increase awareness of the private sector for protecting the NII. It was a demonstration that, in an era of high digitalization, even the paternalistic and angst-ridden national government had to rely on non-governmental stakeholders to fulfill a key mission for the security of the country. The basis of this public – private partnership would be the structure that had been put in place to tackle the Y2K problem. Japan revised its criminal law to include some computer crimes like on-line fraud in 1987, passed a specific law on unauthorized access in 1996, and moved on to establish a "cyber-police force" within the National Police Agency. The Defense Agency (the Japanese ministry of defense) was also required to maintain the security of its information system. The Japanese leadership considered it important to support international cooperation with other OECD members and within the G8 framework, especially in the fight against cybercrime (Interagency Director-Generals' Meeting, 2000). Despite its technological prowess, Japan pursued a low-tech, reactive counterterrorism policy (Katzenstein, 2003). This approach has been consistent with a presence of the police in the society that has been "pervasive, unofficial, and low key" (Katzenstein, 2003: 744). Even in the face of the chemical/bioterrorist attacks by the Aum sect in the 1990s, the reaction of the Japanese government was slow and tepid. September 11 offered Japan the opportunity to symbolically support the Americans so as to avoid possible criticisms. In reality, Japan's response was "mute" (Katzenstein, 2003: 754).

Spotless performance in international cooperation has long been a top political priority for the Japanese government, which is traditionally highly concerned with the perception of its international standing. This mind-set has generated some embarrassing situations. In June 2001, following the initiative of a group of NGOs before the parliament, the Japanese government had to admit that New Zealand and the United States had been spying on Japan through the Echelon system[15] and that the Japanese government had built its own monitoring system (Reporters Sans Frontières 2003: 70). According to Reporters Sans Frontières, in 2001, the parliament authorized Japanese security agencies to develop and install monitoring software for ISPs, whose technical details apparently were unknown to the parliament itself.

As one would expect, the government has made only minimal moves toward securitization with regards to Internet threats. It did not need to do more. The low level of pluralism (Lijphart, 1999: 177),[16] the cultural homogeneity of the country (which implies shunning excessive antagonism on public issues), and the long tradition of patronage politics between the private and public sectors meant that the debate over Internet control has been extremely limited in Japan. Although violations of citizens' privacy and personal liberties have been rare and young Internet users are sometimes rather vocal, the government still enjoys remarkable and mostly uncontroversial room for maneuver when it comes to policies on Internet control.

The Netherlands

The Netherlands is a decentralized unitary state. The country has a social market economy, characterized by a "large redistributional role for the government (i.e. welfare state), an active involvement of organized business and labor in the formulation and implementation of socio-economic policies" (Hulsink, 1998: 173). "Power sharing" and interdependence in public and private decision-making are traditional rules common in this country. Hence, the level of pluralism is quite low (Lijphart, 1999: 177). Nonetheless, during the 1990s, Dutch users were staunch libertarians providing users in other countries with free storage and mirror websites, and anonymous remailers.[17]

The availability of highly skilled labor, a population the vast majority of whom speak English as a second language, and a favorable tax environment are advantages that would have favored the diffusion of the Internet in any country, and the Netherlands has not missed the opportunity. Indeed, the Netherlands is an advanced ICT country with a strongly liberalized telecommunication infrastructure and the political leadership intends to maintain that position by strengthening trust in ICT among users (Rand Europe, 2002g). Fiscal incentives, promotion of ICT clusters, and emphasis on improved performance of government services and education have also contributed greatly to the superior position that the Netherlands enjoys.[18] The Dutch government took the first step to support ICT development already in 1994. While most of the regulation can be found in the 1998 Telecommunications Law, as in all other EU countries, current legislation at the national level is heavily influenced by the implementation of European directives (Schut and Essenberg, 2002). The "central" geographical position of the country has made the Netherlands home to the headquarters of the Network Coordination Center of RIPE (the Réseaux IP Européens). For the same reason, the European Police Force (Europol) is also based in the Netherlands.

The Dutch government made public its ICT policy program in 1999 with the report "the Digital Delta," which, among other factors, also includes the necessity to increase trust in the Internet and the ICT among the public. In the same document, however, terms like "safety" and "supervision on the Internet" were never mentioned, and for this the document was highly criticized (Rand Europe, 2002g). Another official paper, the "Dutch Defense White Paper 2000," highlighted the great degree of dependency on ICT and computer networks that the Dutch armed forces had reached (Wigert, 2004f). The White Paper concluded that attacks against military networks could not be ruled out for the future. Nevertheless, Dutch counterterrorism policy is that "conventional weapons, including explosives, are being considered much more likely to be used in terrorism than unconventional weapons of mass destruction," like nuclear, biological, radiological and also cyber-weapons (Linde *et al.*, 2002: 88).

The Netherlands was one of the first countries in Europe to encourage self-regulatory and industry-based initiatives on the Internet. The Dutch Foundation of Internet Providers, the Dutch Internet Users, the National Bureau against Racial Discrimination, the National Criminal Intelligence Service, and the Dutch police all undertook collaborative efforts to guarantee a smooth growth of the network. These circumstances, coupled with the belief that most potential Internet crimes can be covered by existing laws, has permitted the government to abstain from proposing major legislation about Internet content. Following two ad hoc reports (in 2000 and 2001), the Dutch government has increasingly seen protection of the NII as an issue for national security (Bruno, 2002; Wigert, 2004f). In October 2001, the cabinet tasked the Ministry of Interior with establishing coherent measures to defend the NII as part of the national anti-terrorist plan. Different ministries are in charge of protecting the information infrastructures that fall within their jurisdiction. Ironically, well after September 2001, Dutch legislation had no specific definition of terrorism, and terrorists are prosecuted as "violent criminals" (Linde *et al.*, 2002: 78).

In terms of public – private partnership, the Dutch government has favoured a role as "facilitator," bringing together the actors concerned (Wigert, 2004f), unlike other European governments that prefer to have a larger role in the same circumstances. The Dutch chapter of the Internet Society, founded by Internet users in 1997, is highly regarded for technical proficiency and is supported by banks, cable companies, and the Dutch Consumers Union. Dutch users have been among the most active in protecting anonymity and privacy during the 1990s.[19] Tradition of consensus, power-sharing, and the reluctance of the Dutch cabinet to "issue warnings that are too general" about the NII have helped moderate the clash between the government and users' NGOs. These factors also mean that the Dutch cabinet has been reluctant to securitize the issue of Internet control. Fighting cybercrime and the protection of the NII are priorities for the executive, but the level of Internet control has remained moderate and well within what it is expected by an advanced democracy.

Spain

The bombs that exploded on March 11, 2004, in Madrid were the worst terrorist attacks that not only Spain, but also the whole of Europe, had experienced since the end of World War II. EU members reacted fairly quickly and decided to speed up the adoption of several measures that had been planned but not put into practice since the aftermath of September 11. Spain had passed a law to fight terrorism and cybercrime in June 2002, almost a year after 9/11, and had a long experience with the independent Basque terrorism. A 2002 study found that Spain appeared "to have been more active than any of the other countries in urging the EU to take steps in many facets of counter-terrorism" (Linde *et al.*, 2002). Nevertheless, Spain and Europe were as unprepared for the attacks as the United States was unprepared for September 11. The attitude toward cybercrime has also been lax. Although criminal law did protect against on-line crimes, Spain did not have, as of 2004, a coherent system of data collection about these acts. Because of these conditions, Spanish users and companies tend to think that cybercrime and on-line scams are more common than they are and hence are more reluctant about adopting electronic commerce (Rand Europe, 2002h).

The Spanish university system had produced its the first Internet users in the mid-1980s. As in many other European countries, these were physicists working with the Geneva-based European Center for Nuclear Physics, CERN. As the Internet began to spread outside academia, users started to complain loudly about the exorbitant rates that the national telecom monopoly imposed for the Internet. The many campaigns against the monopolistic power of telephone companies created a sense of community among Internet users. The Spanish government had been slow to react to the recent rapid growth of Internet use. But after the liberalization of the telecom market, the executive enthusiastically embraced the Internet and its business potentiality, and so did the public at large.

The Spanish Press Law includes a controversial article that regards authors, editors, and publishers responsible for the content they publish. Civil rights advocates have challenged the article several times before the Constitutional Court, because it may have serious consequences for ISPs. As of 2004, however, there has been no instance of application of that article to ISPs for Internet content. As in other European countries, the law obliges ISPs to retain traffic logs of their customers for at least a year. At the same time, it is not clear who has the authority to shut down websites that might "undermine certain social values," which is also included in the same law (Reporters Sans Frontières, 2003: 108). Moreover, privacy NGOs and civil liberties lawyers have denounced the new law as contrary to article 20 of the constitution which protects freedom of speech. After the attacks of March 2004, EU governments are likely to request that ISPs keep records of traffic data for an even longer period of time (over five years).

Both the Policia Nacional and the Guardia Civil deal with cybercrime. Unsurprisingly, the most common instances of cybercrime in Spain are telecommunication frauds and child pornography (Rand Europe, 2002h). The main body of the public administration earmarked for the development of Spain's information society is the Consejo Superior de Informatica, while the main focus for public – private partnership is the Consejo Superior de Cámaras de Comercio. R&D in the Council for Scientific Research and some universities principally focuses on intrusion detection systems, public key infrastructure, cryptography, and so on. With a lively and diverse multicultural society, Spain has a high level of pluralism (Lijphart, 1999: 177). Users' NGOs, the national government, and the private sector have focused on different aspects of the development of the Internet and the level of control of the network has not been excessive, although the government often used "terrorism" to justify monitoring the network.

Switzerland

According to a report by Rand Europe (2002i: 3), "Switzerland is an advanced ICT country." In terms of ICT penetration, Switzerland is more advanced than most OECD countries. In the Network Readiness Index, Switzerland scores higher than larger modern economies such as Germany, France, Italy, and Spain, but lower than other small, advanced countries, like the Scandinavian countries, the Netherlands, Taiwan, or Singapore. Switzerland became aware of the growing opportunities offered by the ICT sector toward the end of the 1990s, but also that its economy and its society were increasingly dependent on the information infrastructure. Deregulation of the sector began in 1996, and in 1998 Switzerland launched its "Strategy for the Information Society Switzerland," based on open access to information, freedom of development of the information society, and acceptance of new technologies. The same year, a new federal law on telecommunications came into effect. Most of the cantons (15 out of 21) into which Switzerland is divided also adopted specific Internet strategies by 2001.

The first major event related to ICT security in 1997 (the Strategic Leadership Exercise) unveiled the new threats to its NII that Switzerland, like all advanced, industrialized countries, had to face in the new millennium. In 2001 another exercise assessed the information protection process that had started in 1997 and confirmed that the personnel in charge of ICT security needed more training. To guarantee the full penetration of ICT in the Swiss society and economy, the federal and local governments have undertaken a major revision of most legislation, including the Swiss penal law code, the telecommunication and broadcasting laws, the law on data privacy (Switzerland intends to follow the EU model in this respect), and several others (Rand Europe, 2002i). In addition to various federal ministries (Communications, Information Technologies, and Defense), Switzerland has an ad hoc bureau for cybercrime control that is part of the federal police and that citizens can access to report various Internet crimes, such as unlawful access, virus spreading, and data destruction. This bureau is also responsible for "in-depth analysis of cybercrime" (Wigert, 2004g: 179).

In November 2001, Switzerland signed the Cybercrime Convention of the Council of Europe. Adopting the Convention has obliged the country to undergo a further legislative revision that will take up to three years to be completed. The main on-line crimes in Switzerland are computer frauds, child pornography, unauthorized access, and infringement of copyright laws. The Swiss criminal code provides that, if the author cannot be found, the publisher or the host of illegal material could be prosecuted. This also applies to on-line material and thus to ISPs. A federal law of January 2002 requires ISPs to retain records of their customers for six months and, by court order, to hand them over to law enforcement personnel (Reporters Sans Frontières, 2003: 111). That period, however, is considerably less than what the EU is considering for data retention.

Switzerland has a long tradition of public–private partnership. Historically, this is due to the practice of "part-time participation in a strong 'militia' system" (Wigert, 2004g: 19). A successful career in politics implies a successful record in the military. Moreover, several Swiss public institutions rely exclusively on part-time staff, with many full-time private-sector professionals in a supporters role (Rand Europe, 2002i). The "InfoSurance" foundation and the Commission for Technology and Innovation are two such examples. In the R&D sector, Switzerland is particularly active in the fields of data-secure data transmission and cryptography. Most Swiss companies that trade internationally are world-class, but the domestic sector is much less competitive, and is heavily protected or subsidized. Moreover, the Swiss economy, which depends heavily on exports, suffered badly when the dot.com bubble burst in 2000–2001 (*The Economist*, 2004a).

If Switzerland is often praised for its efficiency and direct democracy system, it is also criticized by the Swiss themselves for being "stodgy and slow" and extremely reluctant to change (*The Economist*, 2004a). Switzerland is, with Austria, the most corporatist state in this sample of countries. Furthermore, Swiss policy-makers strongly support the "total defense" concept, which traces its origins to the tradition of Swiss neutrality and was further emphasized during the Cold War. The bedrock of this concept is exactly the intimate relationship between the federal government and the private sector. This state of affairs has made it extremely difficult (if not impossible) for civil liberties NGOs to effectively oppose any securitization move by the federal government.

Conclusion

The findings of this chapter, which has added ten more short case studies, confirm the model outlined in the previous chapters. Democratic governments want to guarantee assurance of their NII. But the Internet is at the same time an information infrastructure and a content carrier (bytes are indistinguishable and information is intertwined). If not properly performed, control to protect the NII might "spill over" to information content. Censorship increases and privacy decreases. In most of the countries in the sample, protecting the NII means fighting cybercrime, namely computer frauds, identity theft, child pornography, and illegal access. Israel may be seen as an exception, because of its ongoing information war with the Arabs. Nonetheless, even that is more of a nuisance than a real risk for the functioning of Israel's NII. Corporatist countries like Israel and Switzerland have securitized the issue of Internet control, and taken advantage of their domestic interest aggregation to basically ensure that NGOs stakeholders are not too influential. Some bigger countries, like Australia, France, and Spain, have also tried to limit the influence of NGOs, but have been less successful because they are more pluralistic than Israel or Switzerland. The historical association of private and public interests has helped France to curb the impact of NGO stakeholders, but considerably less than one would have expected. Japan has taken advantage of its domestic structure and the network relationship between government agencies and companies to quell excessive discussions about Internet control. The situation may change when younger generations of Japanese become more critical of the government and increasingly technologically savvy Countries like Canada, the Netherlands, and Finland have limited securitization of Internet control and maintain an active, open dialogue with other Internet stakeholders.

The countries considered above are all democracies and, thus, Internet stakeholders like the ICT sector and civil liberties and users' NGOs have multiple access points to cabinet and legislation. As seen in this chapter, the stakeholders might cooperate or oppose or form alliances depending on the specific domestic interest structure of the country. Civil liberties NGOs groups and the private sectors can pressure and change the position and policies of their governments. Therefore, the ultimate outcome of how much control is exercised by the government depends on their specific domestic structure, as well as on the different interest aggregations within their societies. If the lawful exceptions to freedom of speech and privacy in democratic countries remain few (for example, neo-Nazi propaganda or child pornography), then the level of Internet control should stay low. If that level rises above a reasonable average, that is because the most powerful stakeholder, the national government, buys out or otherwise overcomes, through various means like securitization, the opposition of the other two players and proceeds to implement its own political agenda. This is what happened in the United States in the aftermath of September 11. As we shall examine in the next chapter, the definite securitization move of the US federal government, however, only marginally increased the assurance of the United States national information infrastructure.

Notes

1 A high dependency on computer networks implies, usually, a high vulnerability. Time, lack of resources, and multiple private owners in fact conspire against making a country's NII truly secure. The universal policy seems to be "go ahead and worry about security later." The more dependent a country is on computers, the higher should be the investment in computer security, but even the United States does seem to not follow this recommendation thoroughly. Furthermore, it should be noted that, although issues such as data protection, critical information infrastructures, Internet control, cybercrime, etc., are all grouped together here, each of them is very different and sometimes treating them as part of a single set of problems might equal to comparing apples and oranges.

2 See, for example, the the numbers of anonymous remailers in these areas. The remailer software re-sends an e-mail message, erasing the information about the sender. As of 2003 there were 19 remailers in Europe and 22 in North America (Remailer Geographical Mapping Project, 2003). Users can access anonymous remailers to hide their real identities.

3 The Wassenaar Agreement is the "heir" of the Cold War Export Control Committee (COCOM), which coordinated the export of "dual-use" technologies to third-party countries. The organization, for instance, has worked extensively to standardize legislation and policies on cryptography (considered a "dual-use technology") of the members. More details on the Wassenaar Agreement are given in Chapter 2.

4 ISOC, however, has never avoided taking part in the all the controversial battles about the evolution of the Internet.

5 Had September 11 not happened, the pervasiveness of surveillance and the treatment of personal data would have become major flashpoints between the EU and the United States, introducing a novel and particularly fascinating theme in the realm of international politics.

6 The NATO report on "Technology and Terrorism" of October 2001 (Mates, 2001) defines the two activities as follows: "cyberterrorism is any act of terrorism ... that uses information systems or computer technology either as a *weapon* or a *target*" (emphasis in the original). The report stresses that cyberterrorism and cybercrime are similar in their use of information technology but different in their motives and goals (the confusion is particularly evident in the media). Cyberterrorism, the report argues, is politically, socially, or religiously motivated, aimed at generating fear and panic among civilians, or at disrupting military and civilian assets. Finally, two different components of cyberterrorism can be singled out: (1) terrorist use of computers as a facilitator of their activities; and (2) terrorism involving computer technology as a weapon or target.

7 Routinely, signal intelligence services are also called in to gather evidence and forensics when governments' websites are attacked.

8 A. Cobb, quoted in Bruno (2002: 22).

9 The *IT Security Handbook* for the public administration, published in October 1998, was substantially updated in September 2001.

10 There was no material on sale on Yahoo's French website, but users in France could easily reach web pages in the United States.

11 *The Economist* did not fail to remind its readers about the "chilling effect" that the pretension to apply every national regulation in every area of the world would have.

12 Perception management and psychological operations refer to the use of the Internet to spread false information or discredit different political, cultural, or religious views. Both were considered parts of the "propaganda machinery" in the past.

13 See, for instance, the "e–Japan Strategy" of January 2001, available from<www.kantei.go.jp/foreign/it/network/0122full_e.html. [March 25, 2004].

14 Extranets are private networks that rely on the Internet protocol (TCP/IP).

15 Echelon is a world-wide intelligence-gathering system operated by the governments of the United States, the United Kingdom, Australia, and New Zealand.

16 According to Pharr (2000: 184), however, in the last three decades, all types of interest groups have been "dramatically multiplying."

17 Users could post material that was illegal in their countries on the mirror websites and use anonymous remailers to communicate (Remailer Geographical Mapping Project, 2003). Human rights activists have used them extensively in many parts of the world (Metzl, 1996; Stevees, 2000; Wright, 2000).

18 The Netherlands is the only non-Scandinavian country that could fit in that top class of ICT countries along with Iceland, Norway, Sweden, Finland, and Denmark.

19 As of 2003 there were three anonymous remailers based in the Netherlands, including one of the "oldest" (1994), that is, XS4ALL. Only Germany (seven) and Italy (six) have more in Europe (Remailer Geographical Mapping Project, 2003).

4 The United States
The sole information superpower

Because so many key components of our society are operated by the private sector, we must create a genuine public/private partnership to protect America in the twenty first century.

(President William J. Clinton)

The United States is the country where the Internet was born and, in fact, for a while it was the only "information superpower." In the Network Readiness Index (NRI) the United States ranked first (Kirkman *et al.*, 2002a: xiv). But in the Technology Achievement Index (TAI) the United States is number two, with Finland in the top position (United Nations Development Program, 2001: 48). In the International Telecommunication Union Digital Access Index (DAI) the United States is only number 12 (International Telecommunication Union, 2003a). Other advanced countries in Europe, Japan, and elsewhere, however, have slowly but steadily started to close the gap. The United States was also the first country among the advanced democracies to experience the merging of the Internet and the national information infrastructure. That merging has progressed to the point where 90 percent of the national security command and control communications passes through the civilian network (Haimes and Longstaff, 2002: 443). Ultimately, the public Internet, run by universities and research centers, fused with several other privately owned infrastructures to give birth to the current national information infrastructure (NII) which is held together by the same (Internet) protocol.

This chapter examines the attitude of the US federal government toward Internet control and the protection of the NII before and after September 2001. Before that momentous time, the "information economy" (prominently represented in this work by the liberalization/privatization of the telecom sectors) and the exigencies of national security were on diverging paths. The plain fact was that the US national security complex had to acquiesce. The informal alliance of ICT businesses (which backed telecom liberalization) and civil liberties NGOs held the upper hand (Levy, 2001). The September 2001 attacks changed all of that. What has also changed in the past few years is the relative position that the United States enjoyed in the Internet world.

When, in 1998, a report published by the National Telecommunication and Information Administration (NTIA, 1998) at the request of Vice-President Gore found that Americans increasingly embraced the information age through electronic access in their homes, it seemed that the "information society" and "United States" would remain synonymous for a long time. Figures for computers, modems, and telephones kept growing. Whether measured by the location of Internet users, websites or direction of traffic flows, the Internet was accurately described by the International Tele-communication Union (ITU, 1999: 1) as "US-centric." Now, only a few years later, the United States increasingly resembles a *primus inter pares* among the many countries that are on-line. It cannot dictate Internet policy the way it used to. Some estimates predict that by 2015–2020 the Chinese, with their educated and assertive young population, will become the largest group of users on the network. Indeed, the most recent of the three indicators used in this work, namely the 2003 DAI, shows the United States somehow removed from the vertex.

Despite this progressive erosion of its once unmatchable superiority, it would be impossible to write a study of government control of the Internet without investigating the United States. Historically, structurally, and with respect to content, the overall position of the United States was so vital for the future of the Internet that analyzing the American political debate on this issue corresponds closely to examining *the* core debate on the Internet. The United States, de facto, still influences all major policy decisions. The strong position of ICANN governance on domain names, which is backed by the US Department of Commerce, or the signing of the Council of Europe Convention on Cybercrime, which the US government strongly backed, are indicators of the still crucial role of the United States. Several reasons – historical (the Internet was "made" in the US), technical (principal backbones are in the US), and cultural (English is the dominant language of the network)-contribute to explain this state of affairs.[1] On the other hand, the country has remained behind in several areas where it was already behind, before the erosion of its overall leadership began. For instance, disparities among the different racial groups and household incomes have remained considerable. Indeed, the digital divide between racial groups has increased since 1994.

As Risse-Kappen (1995b: 208) pointed out, the United States represents a "society-dominated structure," with a strong organization of interest groups, in which societal demands can be mobilized easily and quickly. Access to federal and state legislatures and bureaucracies is ample and structured. Interest groups are highly institutionalized and very efficient. Transparency, at all levels, is highly valued by US public opinion.[2] The availability of independent sources of information is remarkable, and the American public appreciates the diversity and autonomy of media. Similar to transnational alliances, domestic, intra-sector alliances can influence specific policies in the short run, since they can directly access decision-makers. In the American political system, the identification of lines of decisions is complicated and laborious. The US federal government and the whole political system is highly decentralized. Different political actors, including the President, compete for influence and are often obliged to compromise. But also, many of the fundamental solutions pertaining to the development of the Internet have been informally generated by individuals or groups who were preoccupied with the efficiency and functioning of those solutions. These people would not bother finding out who was officially designated or held the executive power to authorize the solutions to be implemented; technical and management problems were simply tackled by those confronted with them.

This political environment has offered the Internet an effective, pragmatic arena to deal with unavoidable technical bottlenecks. At the same time, however, it has made the attribution of executive responsibilities hard to ascertain. For instance, the origins of the crucial dispute on the domain names system (DNS) traces its origins in numerous documents that several scientists have written since the early 1980s. In one of those documents describing the system, Jon Postel (1994), the father of the DNS, simply wrote that a decision had been taken to register under the domain name "dot.gov" only agencies of the US federal government. He did not specify who made the decision or why, but thus went one of the most important choices in the history of the network.[3]

This chapter acknowledges that September 11, 2001, was such a cultural and political watershed for the United States that it was almost unthinkable that anything could remain untouched. It signaled that, from then on, security would prevail over any other concern or any other debate, including civil liberties and Internet control. Interestingly, however, it did not. Although civil liberties NGOs now face a harder, uphill fight, privacy, freedom of speech, and censorship have remained on America's agenda. The decisions made about individual access to encryption software, (a long-standing anathema for the intelligence community) have not been reversed. ICT companies now agree that product security is essential, and perhaps even profitable, and they are more inclined to work with federal agencies. But the core belief held by most business people that the government should stay clear of the private sector is too embedded in the American culture to be subdued for long. This chapter first examines the situation of the NII and the foremost debates on ICT in general and the Internet in particular before that date, and then considers how the situation and the debates changed.

In a modern democracy, the complexity of many public interests, ranging from health care to taxation, immigration or economic growth, has brought about the proliferation of interest groups as well as an expanded role of the government in these matters. Although formally parts of the same institution, the federal government, many of these actors often do not coordinate their actions and pursue conflicting interests and different agendas. The most noticeable of these conflicting interests is the attempt by the intelligence community (led by the NSA and FBI) to restrain the use of cryptography for individual use, while the Department of Commerce (DOC) is trying to ease the rules for exporting strong encryption software produced by American companies. After September 2001, the ICT sector has supported some of the requests of the national security community in terms of NII security, but this position is far from universal or permanent. Indeed, the "rally around the flag" was and will continued to be observed by ICT companies as long as its cost does not impact too heavily on future revenues (Schneier, 2003). The accidental alliance of pro-liberties NGOs and users' groups with private industry has given way to an even more fluid situation, where the main stakeholders – government agencies, ICT companies, civil liberties and consumer NGOs – shift alliances and cooperation depending on the issue areas, trying to influence the executive or Congress in one direction or another. This state of affairs is likely to persist for a long time.

The complexity of America's decision-making machinery

Karl Deutsch (1980: 231) once remarked that nobody really understands the United States, "neither foreigners, nor its own people." Dahl (1994: 13) shared Deutsch's conclusions, noting that "Americans must now cope with a political system that works in opaque and mysterious ways that probably no one adequately understands." The opaque and fragmented nature of the US political system is an important intervening variable. It helps explain why the federal government cannot afford to ignore any of the several actors involved in the struggle of setting the level of control on the Internet. Law enforcement and intelligence agencies, pro-family groups, ICT associations, ICT companies, and civil liberties organizations through multiple (and sometimes overlapping) channels promote their own agendas with policy-makers in the executive branch and in Congress. Compromised agreements and watered-down initiatives are inevitable while the executive has to include the interests of several political players so that consistent federal policies may be approved. This is the reason why the United States scores so high on the Lijphart (1999) ranking of pluralism. The complications of understanding the American political system originate from a multiplicity of factors: an inconsistent political system, resting on a societal mosaic and contained by an incongruous federal state. Such a degree of fragmentation and lack of integration is unmatched in other advanced democracies, especially those with a strong state tradition like Japan or most European countries (Deutsch, 1980; Bowles, 1993; Chamorel, 1994; Dahl, 1994).[4] If the American federal system has never been a neat system of distinct governmental activities and functions (Lees, 1970: 49), the Tenth Amendment to the Constitution[5] reflects an American antipathy to government in general, to a unitary state in particular" (Bowles, 1993: 259).

The main and most direct consequence of the constitutional principle of "separation of powers" is that pluralism, rivalry, and competition creep into the very center of government. It also elicits, according to Dahl (1994), the representation in the executive and legislative branches of differing and possibly divergent interests, while the President and Congress press for conflicting policies. Finally, Bowles (1993) notes that the separation of powers, combined with a federalist structure, renders the bureaucracy decentralized but also complicated and dispersed. Bureaucratic accountability to representative politicians is thus problematic. Not accidentally, the process of identifying the lines of authority in the country is perplexing and complex, since even presidents are constantly obliged to negotiate and compromise with other politicians who have their own agendas and constituencies (Bowles, 1993).

Another peculiar feature of the American political landscape that contributes to the complexities of analyzing the decision-making process in the federal republic is the "interest industry" (Bowles, 1993). Dahl (1994) observed that in last few decades the number and variety of interest groups with significant influence over US policy-making have greatly increased. The occurrence of such a large number of interest groups in American politics is a result of the First Amendment to the Constitution, which endorses the right of the people "to petition the government for a re-address of grievances." Unsurprisingly, the federal government is deeply penetrated by private groups and its policy-making process is "the product of particularistic patterns of interaction between groups and public officials" (Bowles, 1993: 211).

Nevertheless, ascribing the responsibility for this inefficient fragmentation solely to the constitutional system (hardly modified since its inception) would be misleading. Indeed, this state of affairs seems rather in accordance with the prevailing mood of the American public. Americans recognize that government is necessary, but they still think of it as "potentially dangerous" (King, 2000: 79). A clear confirmation of this cultural aversion toward any concentration of power comes from analyzing the organization of the law enforcement system in the United States. Proliferation of law enforcement agencies and of their level of competence (the federal, state, county, local, private) creates enormous problems of coordination and duplication, without increasing efficiency. The self-evident solution to such a problem would be to concentrate the investigative and repressive functions of law enforcement agencies into one or two police institutions. But this solution would imply a tremendous concentration of power, which could (and probably would) be abused.

September 11 was the event that partially altered that attitude. American citizens accepted the privacy intrusions allowed under the Patriot Act and witnessed the largest organizational revolution since the end of

World War II with the creation of the Department of Homeland Security (DHS). Americans have accepted showing proof of ID in many circumstances that would have been objected to previously. Americans have allowed this cultural transformation of trading some liberty for more security. What pragmatically made this possible is that Americans perceive the situation as temporary. The informal alliance between the ICT sector and civil liberties and users' NGOs dissolved in the aftermath of September 11. In fact, ICT companies understand their enhanced role in securing the NII and the NGO watchdogs have had some setbacks in their activities. Nevertheless, if the American public were to sense that the restrictions are permanent and ICT were to find the government requests too taxing, the pendulum might swing back in favor of the defenders of digital rights.

Public and private sectors in ICT before 2001

For a country like the United States, telecommunications have always had strategic importance. The size of the country coupled with government and business requirements have obliged Americans to pay particular attention to this domain. Indeed, it is common that Republicans and Democrats in Congress tend to have similar voting patterns when it comes to federal legislation involving telecommunications. The oldest piece of legislation on telecommunications is the 1934 Telecommunications Act, which serves as the basic law governing the regulation of communications by wire or radio within the United States and between the United States and overseas (ITU, 1998).[6] The 1934 act also established the Federal Communications Commission (FCC) as the government authority for radio and wireless communications. The modernization of the 1934 act came with the 1996 Telecommunication Act signed by President Clinton on February 8, 1996. The 1996 act laid the ground rules for competition and regulation in virtually all sectors of the communications industry, from local and long – distance telephone services to cable television, broadcasting, and equipment manufacturing.[7]

The performance and reliability of the telecom sectors have had the long-standing attention of American legislators and public officials. In this respect, US government awareness of computer security is not a new phenomenon that has arisen with the diffusion of the Internet. Computer security and the protection of the NII have simply deteriorated with the advent of the Internet. Until 1984, responsibility for computer security standards in the civilian realm was assigned to the National Bureau of Standards (NBS) within the Department of Commerce (DOC). The NBS became a pivotal player in the development of computer security standards. It developed the Data Encryption Standard (DES), which was then adopted to protect non-military government communications (EPIC, 1998).[8] Security of military communications and foreign eavesdropping (namely encrypting and code-breaking) were the exclusive domain of the National Security Agency (NSA).

In 1984, the NSA convinced President Reagan to sign the National Security Decision Directive 145 (NSDD-145) which authorized the agency to develop means to protect "unclassified sensitive" information and "to curb the use of public cryptography" (EPIC, 1998: 5). The NSA took over from the NBS responsibility for setting security standards for civilian communications and data. This condition also meant that the NSA had the power to question private companies about their security procedures or customer relations. Noting that NSDD-145 had "raised considerable concern within the private sector and the Congress" (EPIC, 1998: 11), Congress passed the Computer Security Act (CSA) in 1987 to limit that power. However, in 1989 a memorandum of understanding between the NBS (then renamed National Institute of Standards and Technology, or NIST) and the NSA returned many of the competences (especially in cryptography) restricted by the 1987 act to the NSA. The NSA association with computers and networks came with two incidents involving electronic intrusion between the late 1980s and the early 1990s that were noted by US and international media. In the first case, West German hackers offered their intruding "services" to the KGB (Stoll, 1989). In the second, Dutch hackers who had stolen military information from 34 US Department of Defense (DOD) sites offered it to the Iraqis, during operation Desert Storm (Hafner and Markoff, 1995).[9]

The majority of the historical decisions that have transformed a sophisticated research tool, the Internet, into an international communication network have been made by American scientists in the United States, who were also acting on the behalf of the federal government. The Internet was thus born as the quintessential example of governance, as before the 1990s the US federal government backed all the decisions that engineers and scientists made about the development of the network. The National Science Foundation (a federal agency) decided to cease its operational management of the Internet backbone (the NSFNET) in 1995. This choice ultimately made it easier for millions of non-American users to access the Internet under reasonable conditions and costs.[10] At the same time, alerted by the intelligence community, the executive branch became aware of the increasing risks to the NII that such a decision might entail. Through uncontrolled Internet access points, foreign nationals, either government-sponsored or terrorists, could reach and exploit the security vulnerabilities of critical infrastructures, compromising America's national security. Given the manifest reliance of the United States on computer-assisted operations to manage energy, financial, transportation, and communication networks, it is not surprising that the Clinton Administration took the alert seriously.

Immediately upon entering office in the early 1990s, the Clinton Administration tried to claim credit for establishing the "information superhighway," with Vice President Al Gore as the leading figure (Hundt, 2000). Indeed, Al Gore introduced the US vision for the Global Information Infrastructure (GII) at the ITU World Telecommunication Development Conference held in Buenos Aires in March 1994 (Hundt, 2000). Among the principles declared at the conference and later incorporated into the "Buenos Aires Declaration" was the encouragement of private sector investment and promotion of competition, as well as the provision of open access and universal service. At the same time that the governments and international organizations were discussing the top-down approach to the global information highway, the Internet, with its scientist-run governance, was growing to become the "accidental highway" (Anderson, 1995). Although the unexpected explosion of the Internet took the federal government by surprise, the strategic vision of the information society did not change. Thus, in 1997, President Clinton declared that world governments should adopt a "hands-off" policy for the Internet, eliminating taxes and unnecessary regulations that could hinder the development of the new medium. While the Internet was developing into a mass phenomenon in 1994–1995, however, some branches of the administration became increasingly disturbed by the inherent frailty and openness of software and computer networks. The United States had grown more and more dependent upon these software and networks, certainly more than any other industrialized country.[11] The Internet, with its open protocols and evident lack of hierarchical control by any authority, further amplified the known problem of the protection of America's NII. Chapman (1998) noted that in the 1990s national security officials came to view the Internet as a new field for international conflict. For them the new medium-cum-infrastructure required national security to take on new forms.

The Internet was used for greater shares of international commerce but also for delivering government services or conducting critical communications. Hence, US government officials and experts in the private sector argued that the expansion of the Internet combined with its "blending" into critical national infrastructures made the protection of computers on the Internet a matter of national security. Both government official and private experts have high stakes in the field of computers and national security. These individuals might sometimes exaggerate the vulnerabilities of the network to enhance the status and commercial value of the services that computer security firms offer or improve the negotiating position of government agencies that were seeking more funding or clout (Chapman, 1998).

Traditionally, intelligence and defense personnel enjoyed a quasi-monopoly of information about national security issues (most noticeably in nuclear warfare). The impact of the Internet and of ICT in general on US national security, however, triggered an unexpected situation. Since the beginning, Internet developers and engineers prized the maximum distribution and availability of technical information. Plenty of on- and off-line sources displayed and explained drawbacks, defects, "bugs," patches, and upgrades for the network. All this information was available to any moderately knowledgeable user. Pro-liberties NGOs, users' groups, and consumers' organizations have seized this mass of information and reinforced it with competent legal expertise. With the open support of the ICT industry, which, like all American businesses, was traditionally skeptical about government intrusion (King, 2000; Taft, 2000), NGOs and users' groups engaged the national security community on technical grounds to fight off state control of the Internet. As expected in a democracy, all the stakeholders in this struggle sought the public's support. The American public tended to favor the unusual alliance between the ICT sector and civil liberties NGOs that prevailed against the government stakeholder in the cryptowars examined in Chapter 2.[12]

Given the importance of telecommunications and ICT in general for a country of the size and status of the United States, one would expect that the federal government would play a key role, which indeed was the case. Americans use the term "government" to indicate both the elected officials (such as the President and Congress), as well as the bureaucracy that is designated to implement the decisions made by those officials. For all practical purposes, most of the time, the majority of citizens connect with "the government" through the bureaucracy, not the elected officials. Thus, they often identify civil servants with "the government" (King, 2000). In the United States, the bureaucracy is, nevertheless, more than just a mere appendix of the executive. Bowles (1993) called it the "fourth branch," thus attributing it with independent decision-making powers distinct from the other traditional branches, namely executive, legislative, and judiciary. The key organizational units are usually not departments but the semi-autonomous agencies or bureaus within them.

The Department of Commerce (DOC) is the branch of the federal government that oversees trade, both domestically and internationally. Given the growing share of the US workforce that is employed either by the ICT sector or by industries that are intensive users of ICT products and services, the DOC has steadily increased its involvement in the sector and in e-commerce in particular. The most important branch of the DOC with regard to ICT is the National Telecommunications and Information Administration (NTIA). NTIA is the principal executive branch voice on domestic and international telecommunications and information technology issues. In fact, it serves as the President's principal advisor on telecommunications and information policy matters. The DOC influence on Internet developments has been (and is) substantial. Before September 2001, it was even superior to that of the Department of Justice (DOJ) or any other federal departments. This influence was evident in two critical areas. The DOC had the prime responsibility for authorizing the export of over 40-bit encryption software (via the Bureau of Export

Administration).[13] Moreover, the DOC operated closely with the non-profit Internet Corporation for Assigned Names and Numbers (ICANN) for the management of the domain name system (DNS). Both these factors were indispensable for electronic commerce and the implementation of the Internet economy and the latter is still fundamental for the daily function of the network.

Another important actor in the bureaucracy is the Federal Communications Commission (FCC), which is an independent agency responsible for regulating interstate and international communications by radio, television, wire, satellite, and cable. The FCC reports directly to Congress. With the Internet economy booming, the FCC set its mission to create a regulatory environment in which the Internet could flourish. The FCC official position on Internet-based traffic was to resist government intervention, guaranteeing fair competition and open access to the network to users and companies alike. Furthermore, the growth and continued success of the Internet was solely to be attributed to the openness of both the Internet and the underlying telecommunications infrastructure (Oxman, 1999).

The FCC embraced governance for the Internet, but not indiscriminately. For instance, in 1999 the FCC adopted rules that require new TV sets to be equipped with the "V-chip," a technology that allows parents to block certain TV programs.[14] Civil liberty NGOs criticized the initiative because it could set an example for the Internet and help champion web-page rating initiatives (in fact a similar proposal appeared later). Perhaps more importantly, the FCC oversaw the implementation of the Communications Assistance for Law Enforcement Act (CALEA) of 1994. According to civil liberty NGOs, if activated, the act would endanger individuals' privacy in communications.[15] Despite strong opposition from industry and civil liberties organizations, Congress voted for CALEA in the last session of 1994, after the government offered to pay telephone companies $US 500 million to make the proposed changes. The main purpose of the act was to make the national telephone system more suited to wire-tapping by law enforcers (primarily the FBI). CALEA required the telecommunications industry to redesign its systems in compliance with FBI technical specifications. The FBI and industry representatives, however, were unable to agree upon those standards, resulting in a proceeding before the FCC (EPIC, 1999c).

Since then, the contest between civil liberties organizations and telecom companies and the FBI has been lingering, inasmuch as the private sector and the FBI have been unable to find common ground on the technical standards of CALEA. Telecom operators were afraid that granting the FBI and other law enforcers extensive wire-tapping capabilities could result in excessive surveillance, thus seriously upsetting the public and provoking severe financial losses, and Internet NGOs emphasized these particulars.[16] The FCC directed that "packet-mode communications" (that is, Internet communications) had to be made available to law enforcement agencies by no later than September 2001. The Electronic Privacy Information Center

(EPIC, 1999c) observed that such a ruling could ultimately result in a significant increase in government interception of digital communications.

Throughout the 1990s and until 2001, the American ICT industry was another powerful player in the battle for Internet control and frequently sided with civil liberties NGOs. The industry "battle cry" in the electronic marketplace was "thank you, and the government should just butt out" (Taft, 2000).[17] This attitude led to an accidental alliance with a collection of pro-liberties NGOs, users' groups, and consumers' organizations. Involuntarily, these actors joined forces because of their overlapping concern in limiting government interference in the network.[18] In so doing, they created a formidable obstacle for the national security community, which was insisting on greater government power for Internet control. In the continuing struggle between privatization and market regulation, the fact that the mood was in favor of privatization and government disengagement helped fend off determined efforts by the federal government to consider the Internet a strategic utility, like electricity. Had the Internet emerged as a communication and information medium in the 1960s or 1970s, the US government (and many other governments world-wide) would have regarded the Internet as another of those assets that only the state can efficiently own, manage or, at least, supervise. The whole debate about controlling the Internet would not even have happened.

In the last thirty years, the share of GNP devoted to services has become predominant in all advanced economies. Within this share, the ICT sector along with the entertainment industry, which also has increasing interests in the Internet, have predominated. A study by the University of Texas (Barua *et al.*, 1999) showed that the size of the Internet economy was over $US 301 billion in 1998, rivaling that of older and more established industries such as automobiles ($350 billion), telecommunications ($270 billion), and energy ($223 billion). If the value of the telecom sector was added to that of the Internet economy, the impressive sum of $US 571 billion would result, making these sectors the "crown jewels" of the American economy. Despite the considerable problems of definition and classification of the several companies operating in the Internet economy in a multilayered fashion, investigators identified four layers of the Internet economy. The first was the infrastructure layer, that is, companies concerned with the network infrastructure (that is, Cisco, MCI WorldCom, AOL, Network Associates). Second was the applications layer including companies with products that make on-line business possible (that is, Microsoft, Netscape, Oracle, IBM, Adobe). Third was the layer of Internet intermediaries such as Yahoo!, Geocities, ZDNet, E*trade, eBay, TravelWeb. Finally, the commerce layer that clustered vendors of services and products to users and businesses, such as Amazon, eToys, Cisco, Dell.

Given the magnitude of wealth considered, it is not surprising that the professional associations representing ICT companies enjoyed considerable benefit with the federal government and Congress during the dot.com bust.

Two of the most prominent industrial associations, for instance, are the Information Technology Industry Council and the Telecommunication Industry Association. Many companies like Microsoft, America On-line (AOL), Cisco Systems, Sony, Apple, 3Com, Panasonic, and IBM have memberships in both. The member companies of an organization like TIA manufacture or supply virtually all of the products used in global communication networks.

As meaningful illustrations of the involvement of the private sector in the policy-making process, it is worth addressing the reports and statements prepared by these trade associations on various Internet issue-areas. On the crucial case of cryptography, for example, the position of the TIA is that telecommunications equipment manufacturers should be proactively represented and included in any effort to deregulate encryption technology. These and other organizations stressed the importance of policy issues such as privacy protection (especially through encryption software), fighting cybercrime, and setting international standards. In all cases, the recommended solutions were industry self-regulation and governance, with little or no involvement by any level of government. There was thus some substantial overlapping among the main professional ICT associations and civil liberties and users' NGOs, grouped together as stakeholders.

It was not only the ICT sector that was enthusiastic about the Internet, but also more traditional industries such as car manufacture. In November 1999 two car industry giants, General Motors and Ford, announced that from that date on they preferred to deal with their business partners only through Internet-based communications. This change was not mandatory, but they strongly "encouraged" those businesses that wanted to continue operating with them to increasingly rely on that method of doing business. *The Economist* (1999a: 77) called that "the moment when e-business grew up," since the near 50,000 small and medium businesses working with the two giants were soon obliged to switch to this new mode of communication and procurement. Under such circumstances, it would have been unlikely that any government, parliament, or policy-maker in any country would have felt comfortable ignoring electronic commerce.

The Internet economy (also known as the new economy) was the big hype voiced by many business people, government officials, and laymen when referring to the future of the Internet. But this new economy was not a precisely defined issue such as, for instance, "freedom of speech." Rather, it was a macro-issue made up of other sub-issues that involved the domain name system, cryptography, privacy, information infrastructure, open access, in addition to the demands and high expectations that business and the general public had for the new economy. The policy of the federal government on electronic commerce and the new economy in general was minimal government intervention and the recognition of the leading role of the private sector. The White House also urged other governments to accept that, given the decentralized nature of the Internet and its bottom-up governance, regulatory frameworks established over the past sixty years for telecommunications, radio, and television could not fit the new medium. International cooperation would be necessary in areas such as taxation, intellectual property rights, privacy, and ICT infrastructures to preserve the Internet as a non-regulatory medium.

Gadrey (2003) asserts that it was this type of normative discourse, originating from political and media circles, which fed the "myth" of the new economy. Leading political figures (including President Clinton), journalists, and larger numbers of investors and consumers selected certain characteristics of the American economy and idealized ICT. The combined effects stimulated the image of strong economic growth without inflation. After the dot.com bubble burst in 2000, the skepticism and doubts of Gadrey and others have become commonplace. However, it was not only the idea of a "new" economy that was shattered in 2000–2001. It was also the notion of Internet governance and self-regulation championed by the private sector and embraced by governments and, to some extent, civil liberties NGOs, which was profoundly discredited. The events associated with the domain name system and the creation of ICANN are illuminating examples that will be described below.

No one within the small, cohesive Internet community that originally developed the domain name system (to facilitate memorizing Internet addresses by users) could ever have envisaged that the DNS would become a major bone of contention within private industry, regulating authorities, and users. Mueller (1999: 509) observed that the DNS, as a centralized point of interconnection, gave whoever controlled it the leverage to impose almost any terms they wished upon domain name registrants, registration services, and registries. Similarly, the Web's inventor, Tim Berners-Lee (1999: 126), defined the DNS as the one centralized Achilles' heel by which the Web (and hence most of the Internet) could all be brought down or controlled. In July 1997, following a presidential directive on electronic commerce, the Department of Commerce was designated to be the lead agency on domain names and instructed to privatize the management of the DNS.[19] This action was expected to increase competition and facilitate international participation in its management. All the most valuable name domains (that is, dot.org, dot.net and dot.com) were to be affected by this decision. Following an extensive public consultation process, in June 1998 the DOC issued a statement of policy known as the "White Paper" (Department of Commerce, 1998). The document called upon the private sector to create a new, not-for-profit corporation to assume responsibility, over time, for the management of certain aspects of the domain name system. The paper also articulated the fundamental policies that would guide US participation in the transfer of DNS management responsibility to the private sector.

In November 1998, the DOC officially recognized the Internet Corporation for Assigned Names and Numbers (ICANN, founded a month earlier) as the global, non-profit consensus organization that was to undertake administrative and management functions for the Internet names and addresses. One of the tasks assigned to ICANN was to specifically introduce competition in the process of name assignment. Network Solutions, under contract with the DOC, was the only registry and registrar for those domains and enjoyed a true monopoly. The Internet Society, which had lobbied for the establishment of ICANN, was thoroughly disappointed when ICANN could not break that monopoly and the DOC would not help either.

The White Paper also called on the World Intellectual Property Organization (WIPO) to investigate domain name trademark conflicts and make recommendations about how to resolve disputes (Mueller, 1999: 504). This move by the federal government was inevitable, since, in 1998 a dubious practice, "cyber-squatting," was starting to seriously disquiet the private sector. In 1994–1995, before the Internet frenzy, some individuals began to register well-known brand names (such as Disney or McDonalds) as Internet domains with Network Solutions for an annual fee of $US 35. Around that time, presence and visibility on the Internet quickly became a vital commercial necessity for companies worldwide. When a world-brand company turned to Network Solutions to register its domain, it might discover that what it considered "its" domain name (e.g. cocacola.com or nike.com) was already owned by someone else. These individuals would then charge the company large sums of money to turn the rights on the domain over to the company itself. Sometimes, another company with the same name or ordinary individuals in "good faith" had no intention of yielding their rights on the domain, thus initiating lengthy legal battles. So important was the copyright protection of brand names that Congress had to pass an anti-cyber-squatting law. Moreover, at the end of 1999 Congress approved a proposal to prevent average citizens from using well-known names as domain names. Civil liberties and users' NGOs voiced strong objections to such legislation because it might curtail free speech.

Overall, private business and civil liberties NGOs viewed the handover by the DOC of its policy authority over domain names and the creation of ICANN as successes for the supporters of Internet self-regulation and self-governance. They also knew that the domain name was the issue area in which disagreements and quarrels among "partners" of the coalition were most likely to occur. The private sector had huge stakes in the DNS and the impact on e-business of domain names was massive. Then again, civil liberties NGOs and users' groups maintained that, as a matter of principle, anybody should be able to access the DNS and register names. The greatest hopes of this unusual coalition were on ICANN, which was to be the model of self-regulation and self-governance. In its first years of activity, ICANN failed that test and pressure mounted to give national governments a greater say in its management and operations.

America's NII before 2001

The United States was the country most critically dependent on information infrastructures.[20] As Diffie and Landau (1998: 102) pointed out, it was "catastrophically vulnerable to corruption of that information." After 1988, when the Morris Worm struck the Internet and crashed about 6,000 machines,[21] American policy-makers became concerned with the possibility that domestic or foreign enemies could exploit vulnerabilities in the NII "to bring the country to its knees." The expression "information warfare" began to circulate on the media more and more frequently, and although the meaning of the term was far from settled, anyone would presume it meant attacking the enemy with information alone. Attacks could consist of unleashing malicious viruses or worms against a country's NII, but it could also mean spreading on the Internet negative and unfriendly information about a country's government, political system, or domestic situation. Furthermore, the Department of Defense had to assume that any enemy it engaged would then counterattack the department computers to disrupt its military operations (Libicki, 1997).

In the 1990s, the US critical information infrastructures included eight sectors: (a) information and communications, (b) electrical power systems, (c) gas and oil transportation and storage, (d) banking and finance, (e) transportation, (f) water supply systems, (g) emergency services, and (h) government services. The NII thus comprised the Internet as well as the public switched network, cable, wireless, and satellite communications, both private and public. Protection of the NII meant assuring the integrity, reliability, availability, and confidentiality (the four factors essential to attain computer security) of the information present on the infrastructure. Protecting the NII posed substantial technical and legal challenges to policy-makers in a democratic country. In fact, it concerned assets that were not only decentralized and privately owned, but also used by individual for their personal communications (O'Neil and Dempsey, 1999–2000). Overall, in the spring of 2001, the FBI via its National Infrastructure Protection Center had identified more than 5,000 public and private sector sites as critical and vulnerable (Vise, 2001).

During the early 1990s, the Internet developed in the United States simultaneously along two lines. As more and more users logged in, the computer network turned into a public medium for communications. At the same time, utility service providers also found it more and more convenient to use the network for communications and remote diagnostics. Users and providers were overwhelmingly American, thus making the protection of NII and monitoring communications a domestic affair. Law enforcement agencies, in particular the FBI, had to bear the burden. In addition to its traditional law enforcement mission, the FBI has also responsibility for foreign counterintelligence, as set out in a strategy document known as the national security threat list. The list combined national security threats (regardless of the country of origin) and a classified list of foreign nations that pose a strategic intelligence threat to US security interests. On the list, key threats to the NII were terrorism and espionage and, quite interestingly, perception management, which is a new definition for the old propaganda or counterinformation. Accordingly, the FBI might also tackle the spread in the media of information that could be damaging to the status, prestige, or policies of the United States.

The national security community was primarily involved through the NSA, which is part of the Department of Defense (DOD). The DOD considered security threats to the NII likely to come from foreign countries. But the NSA was drawn into the domestic battle about the export of encryption software. If American companies could export strong encryption software (or if a user developed a program and then sent it abroad via the Internet, as happened with PGP), encrypted communications could become more common in foreign countries and the job of the NSA would be harder. The FBI and the NSA thus personified the "bad guys" or "Big Brother" for civil liberties NGOs and users' groups throughout the whole 1990s.[22] However, while the NSA was exposed in the media and the public mostly for the cryptography wars, the FBI supported controversial initiatives such as CALEA, the Communication Decency Act (CDA), and Carnivore.[23] The FBI was thus more in the media limelight, fostering the conviction of the larger public that the federal government was already too intrusive. Traditionally the law enforcement and national security communities are supposed to operate separately, one inside and the other outside the borders of the United States. But the technical nature of the Internet (and of ICT in general) made it problematic to distinguish between "domestic" and "foreign" flows of information. It was logical to expect an overlapping of competencies and greater cooperation between the two communities. Indeed, the Intelligence Authorization Act of 1997, while it did not permit spying on US citizens directly, opened up the way for unprecedented collaboration between the intelligence and law enforcement communities so that the distinction was blurred (Diffie and Landau, 1998).

In 1996, both the DOD and the DOJ, along with the NSA and the FBI, were represented in the first crucial body earmarked for the protection of the NII, namely the Presidentials Commission on Critical Infrastructure Protection (PCCIP).[24] Other members of the PCCIP were the Departments of the Treasury, Transportation, Energy, the DOC, the CIA, and the Federal Emergency Management Agency. The PCCIP was to identify "physical and cyber threats" to the NII. The Presidential Decision Directive 63 (PDD-63) in 1998 further specified the Clinton Administration's policy on the protection of critical infrastructure. Critical infrastructures were those physical and cyber-based systems essential to the minimum operations of the economy and government and whose incapacity or destruction would have a debilitating impact on the defense or economic security of the United States. The directive specified that every department and agency of the federal government was responsible for protecting its own critical infrastructure, especially its cyber-based systems. The PDD-63 also established the Critical Infrastructure Assurance Office (CIAO) to oversee implementation.[25]

Before PDD-63 was issued, the FBI had already constituted the National Infrastructure Protection Center (NIPC). Located in the FBI building in Washington, DC, the mission of the NIPC was both a national security and law enforcement effort to respond to and investigate computer intrusions and unlawful acts that threatened or targeted the NII. The mission of NIPC was not only to investigate and respond to attacks after they occured, but also to learn about preventing them. The center was also an early model of a public – private partnership to protect the country's critical infrastructures, because in addition to FBI agents, and other federal government and state officials, representative of the ICT sector would contribute their expertise. The NIPC ranked disruptions of NII according to their gravity and premeditation. There could be natural or inadvertent interruptions, like natural events, accidents, blunders, or errors. Intentional interruptions by insiders, recreational hackers, or criminal activity would be more serious. Finally, intentional disruption by terrorists or governments, industrial espionage, and information warfare would be the gravest.

Such an extensive list, however, remained speculative. Documented cases of attacks remained relatively low throughout the 1990s. Given the growing numbers of millions of new Internet users (and billions of computer operations), there was little to support the claim that serious damage to the NII was likely to occur. That key policy-makers talked about an "electronic Pearl Harbor" did not contribute to a sober assessment of the existing threat.[26] Statements such as these were not accidental. They were often employed at the highest levels of the Administration. Former national security advisor Anthony Lake (2000) evinced the same belief, putting cyberterror and cybercrime on the list of the six most dangerous nightmares that the United States had to face. In January 1999, in an address delivered at the National Academy of Sciences, President Clinton equated the risk of attacks to the critical infrastructures, computer systems, and networks with the emerging threats posed by biological and chemical weapons. A year later, the President launched the National Plan for Information Systems (White House, 2000). The plan included specific new initiatives to defend the nation's computer systems from cyber-attacks, such as training and recruiting IT experts, and the creation of Fidnet, a cyber "burglar alarm" to alert the government to in-progress cyber-attacks.

A month later (perhaps incidentally) a much reported "cyber-attack" was launched against some of the most famous websites, including Yahoo, CNN, ZDNet, eBay, and Amazon (Dugan, 2000; Hamilton, 2000). It was a distributed denial-of-service (DoS)[27] attack that considerably slowed down access to those websites, in effect preventing them from continuing their business operations. The media coverage was extensive, with a tendency toward overstatement. When it seemed that some of the malicious hackers were operating from Germany, the FBI went on full alert and the White House convened meetings with ICT security experts and high-tech industry leaders. The disruption of commercial activity, however, turned out to be more feared than real (Hamilton, 2000), and hackers' sites denounced the new "witch hunt" by federal authorities. The media frenzy coupled with the inability of public opinion to grasp technical details and minutiae contributed toward reinforcing the negative attitude of the federal government toward Internet control.

Despite the emphasis that the federal government placed on the need to protect the NII and the conferences, meetings, or war games devoted to the subject, Diffie and Landau (1998) noted that there had not been a single case of an attack against another nation's computer networks using only digital tools. This statement also held true for terrorist groups. Alberts (1996) agreed that, although infrastructure attacks could be quite serious if they were well planned and coordinated, the vast majority of attacks on infrastructures had been by hackers whose motives ran from financial motives to "having some fun." It did not help sober assessments of risks for the NII or ongoing debates on how to balance civil liberties and security that badly informed media reports tended to transform any news related to hackers' interference or computer networks problems as a "prelude to cyberwars." This was the case, for example, of the DOD-sponsored exercise "Eligible Receiver." In 1997, a group of NSA specialists simulated cyber-attacks on the US power grid and telephone system. The main goal was to make DOD personnel aware of the issue; details of the simulation remained classified. Yet, the story began to circulate in the press and slowly acquired a life of its own. In two years, Eligible Receiver became the "undisputed" proof that the electronic Pearl Harbor was indeed feasible and likely.[28]

Some independent experts do not agree with the military's evaluation of the risk. John Pike, then with the Federation of American Scientists, identified a weaker and a stronger type of information operations attack.[29] In the former, system managers are concerned with protecting their systems against the annoyances of "script-kiddies."[30] The latter version was the electronic Waterloo (or alternatively Pearl Harbor), which signified to "switch off" the whole country. In this case, a determined adversary could be extraordinarily annoying for the country, provoking considerable financial losses and the loss of some human lives, but it could not bring the country to its knees. Chapman (1998) also shared this view. The problem with the stronger type of attack was that often policy-makers, generally in their fifties and sixties, were not very knowledgeable about computers and truly believed that an electronic Waterloo was possible. This fear was confirmed, for instance, by the fact that the DOD slowly withdrew most of its unclassified information previously available on-line (sensitive un-classified), although that information was still publicly available in hard copy upon individual request. After September 11, 2001, data and figures on the US military have become even scarcer.[31]

As illustrated in Chapter 2, for a long time (until 2000) a battle between federal government agencies and civil liberties NGOs centered on access to and export of encryption software. So much were these actors focused on that fight, that the former saw it as the emblem of its determination to protect the NII, while the latter considered it the ultimate example of Internet control. The NSA and the FBI won some ground in the Clinton Administration, with proposals such as the Communication Decency Act, the CALEA, the Cyberspace Electronic Security Act (CESA), and many others. Most of these proposals, however, either did not pass Congress or the Supreme Court ruled them unconstitutional. The backing that civil liberties organizations received from the ICT sector was crucial. For instance, at the same time that the federal government was circulating the draft for CESA, a presidential subcommittee on encryption (an advisory body) recommended that the Administration should substantially revise its restrictive stance on the export of encryption products. (Interestingly, the chairman of that subcommittee was a former deputy director of the NSA and other members had ties to the intelligence and security communities.) Nonetheless, the subcommittee stated that it was necessary that the US government recognize market realities and reverse its course on encryption policy (EPIC, 1999b). Although the NGOs – business coalition prevailed in the battle on encryption, other problems like the trade-off between individual privacy and security on computer networks would not go away so easily. These problems remained fused within the NII and became aggravated with September 11.

Historically in the United States, intelligence, counterintelligence agencies, and military organizations are extremely reluctant to discuss defense issues (including the protection of NII) outside the "inner circle" of the national security community. Moreover those issues prevailed over any other concerns, including economic affairs. Information operations or cyberter-rorism were the areas in which the national security community possessed the largest amount of classified information and the greatest expertise. For a long time, the main linkage between national security and the Internet had been young pranksters (the script-kiddies) trying to imitate Matthew Broderick's character in the 1983 fiction movie *War Games*, who gained access to classified computers. This state of affairs changed drastically with the growth and internationalization of the Internet.

Unexpectedly for the national security community, by the late 1990s, the debate on Internet control and the risks for the NII epitomized a new and different situation from the past. New stakeholders and elites with competing interests were involved and there was a new, unusual alliance of public and private actors. Civil liberties NGOs, users' groups, and private businesses were not willing to uncritically accept the viewpoints of the national security community because they had considerable technical expertise to refute those viewpoints. According to them, Internet threats should be properly debated and assessed, taking into consideration contradictory views. The stalemate that ensued was a testimony to the technical and legal proficiency of the accidental alliance, and of its ability to mobilize support. For once, not even the powerful national security coalition could win the day on such a flimsy argument as the Internet as a national security risk.

What stood in the way?

In February 1996, John Perry Barlow, co-founder of the Eletronic Frontier Foundation, published "a declaration of independence of cyberspace," asking the governments of the industrial age to leave cyberspace alone, because they had not been invited and did not have sovereignty therein (Barlow, 1996). The government of the United States was one of those cited in the declaration as trying to restrict civil liberties in cyberspace. The declaration came at a moment when it seemed that civil liberties NGOs could actually convince many democratic governments to relinquish their sovereignty in cyberspace. Given the Internet's nature and its historical development, it was not surprising that a considerable number of non-government organizations flourished, tackling important civil liberty issues related to the diffusion and use of the network. Questions such as privacy, cryptography, security, and hackers' ethics have been the topics on which most of these organizations normally work. Many NGOs in fields such as privacy, consumers' protection, and civil rights often overlap, cooperate, and sometimes disagree.

Speaking of the peculiar political alliances that were active in the debates about privacy and freedom of speech, Wayne Madsen, senior researcher at Electronic Privacy Information Center (EPIC), referred to them as the "red-brown" coalition (brown from the Nazi party shirts).[32] This accidental partnership of extreme left and right sympathizers was born to oppose the federal government's intrusions into individuals' privacy. Normally these activists hold opposing political views, but their common perception of the government as Big Brother threatening to curtail the privacy of US citizens coerced them into becoming temporary, albeit awkward, bedfellows. The existence of a red-brown coalition gives an accurate indication of how many segments throughout the whole political spectrum of American society could feel passionately about issues of privacy, freedom of speech, government censorship, and control.

The oldest (1920) civil liberties organization (and the country's foremost advocate of individual rights) in the United States is the American Civil Liberties Union (ACLU). ACLU's main mission is to defend the Bill of Rights which includes, among others, freedom of speech and the right to privacy.

In this respect, ACLU has been active on these issues along with other Internet NGOs. ACLU's activities are not limited to the Internet, but extend to other non-Internet-related topics such as prisons, racial equality, and workers' rights.[33] The first (1990) organization specializing in Internet civil liberties was the EFF, the Electronic Frontier Foundation.[34] The EFF is a non-profit, non-partisan organization active in the arena of computers and the Internet to protect fundamental civil liberties, including privacy and freedom of expression. The EFF wants to represent the interests of "netizens" in general. Chronologically, after EFF, the Internet Society (ISOC) was founded in 1991 and it has enjoyed a special place in the history of the Internet. In fact, it was the result of the joint efforts of the Internet Engineering Task Force (IETF) and the Internet Architecture Board (IAB), the two groups primarily responsible for the Internet infrastructure. IEFT and IAB included the late Jon Postel and most of the scientists who had actually built the Internet such as Vint Cerf. ISOC now gathers more than 150 organizational and several thousand individual members in over a hundred countries. The society sees its primary mission as providing leadership in addressing issues that confront the future of the Internet. In addition to public policy issues, the society continues to have a strong emphasis on technical topics like standards and protocols and remains the editor of crucial "request for comments."[35]

The Electronic Privacy Information Center (EPIC) was established in 1994 as a public interest research center, through the transformation of the Washington-based office of the Computer Professionals for Social Responsibility.[36] EPIC has focused public attention on emerging privacy issues such as the Clipper Chip (a monitoring device for telephones), the digital telephony proposal, national ID cards, medical record privacy, and the collection and sale of personal information and free speech. EPIC international reports on cryptography and privacy policies have been particularly useful for scholars working in those areas.[37] EPIC relies entirely on private donations and has no corporate members.[38] Concrete actions by EPIC have included publication of newsletters, Freedom of Information Act litigation, and policy research. Also based in Washington, DC, is the Center for Democracy and Technology (CDT). In addition to its public policy work on free speech, data privacy, cryptography, and wire-tapping, CDT also has a more "political" agenda. In fact, the center seeks to promote democratic values by building consensus among stakeholders in ICT and new media. Financial support to CDT is provided by private as well as corporate donors (including AOL, ATT, Bell, Disney, IBM, Lotus, MCI, Microsoft, Netscape, Time Warner, and others).[39]

One of the principal organizations for consumers' protection is the National Consumers League (NCL), the oldest non-profit consumer organization in the United States. In 1992, the league set up the National Fraud Information Center, and in 1996 the Internet Fraud Watch. The Consumers League's mission is to provide advice for consumers. The Internet

Fraud Watch was created to offer advice about promotions in cyberspace and route reports of suspected on-line and Internet fraud.[40] Other examples of consumers and users' groups are the Domain Name Right Coalition (to counter ICANN abuses), the Digital Future Coalition, which focuses on the balance in law and public policy between protecting intellectual property and affording public access, or the "cypherpunks" (hosted by UC Berkeley).[41] There are also international non-governmental organizations, the most popular of which is the Open Source Initiative (OSI), which is devoted to promoting the diffusion of open source software such as the operating system Linux.[42] The number and variety of these volunteer associations is once again proof of how right Tocqueville was about the American passion for involvement. The American attitude toward voluntary organizations and individuals' initiative explains the high level of pluralism (Lijphart, 1999).

The main goals of these organizations and groups have been to gather and disseminate technical/legal information, and build support in public opinion for their activities. The overlapping interests of civil liberties and consumers' organizations, and users' groups and the ICT industry, for a government-free Internet triggered cooperation and joint action. Furthermore, several of these groups have international links. For instance, the "internationaliza-tion" of privacy and the growing number of non-American users prompted EFF, ISOC, EPIC, and CDT with other non–US organizations to create the Global Internet Liberty Campaign (GILC), a transnational coalition to better coordinate their efforts.[43] All these NGOs were aware that the outcomes of debates and litigation on issues such as intellectual property rights, consumers' protection, domain names, and censorship would affect the Internet economy, the NII, and government presence on the Internet. As illustrated in Chapter 2, the NGOs – ICT sector alliance could muster a considerable success in the struggle on cryptography. But encryption software was just a tool to preserve two more important notions, namely free speech and personal privacy. In these two crucial issue areas the alliance was not that cohesive and the outcomes have been more indeterminate.

Freedom of speech in the United States is directly protected by the First Amendment. The American appreciation for freedom of speech is very distinctive. Liptak (2004: 3) wrote that "American tolerance for even the sort of dissent that calls for violent overthrow of the government and for racial hate is unique." The international war crimes tribunal investigating the role of radio stations and newspaper in the Rwandan genocide declined to use the near-absolute American standard for freedom of speech. European countries, Japan, and other democracies also put some limit to free speech. The different appreciation of the Americans for that freedom prompted the Europeans to sign a separated protocol, attached to the 2003 Council of Europe Convention on Cybercrime, because the United States, which had pressured for the convention, did not want hate and racial speech included in the convention itself.

For a long time, threats to freedom of speech on the Internet were not even considered a problem. The community of engineers and scientists that contributed to building the Internet, in fact, regarded the freedom to express divergent views and criticisms as one of its most valuable assets. Many of them saw the Internet as an experiment in free thinking, and attempts to raise profits from any product (as the University of Minnesota did in 1993 with its gopher) were considered almost an act of treason in the academic and the Internet communities (Berners-Lee, 1999). Freedom of speech per se is not indispensable for commercial activity, as demonstrated by the flourishing of commercial transactions under authoritarian regimes. After the privatization of the Internet in 1995,[44] the growing presence of the private sector on the Internet worried users and scientists that business would become a priority, pushing on-line free speech to the margin. Recognizing the sensitivity of many Internet users (and potential future customers) to this issue, the American ICT companies sided with civil liberties organizations in that early period, putting freedom of speech and privacy high on their agenda and demanding less government interference on the Internet.

In the same period, the American public begun to perceive the judiciary, and more specifically the Supreme Court, as an important actor in the struggle over freedom of speech on the Internet, after the Court rejected the Communication Decency Act (CDA). The CDA had been ratified by Congress in February 1996. In the same year, Congress had voted for the Telecommunications Act, which contained the legal prerequisite for the CDA. Under the CDA, individuals apprehended while disseminating "indecent" or "patently offensive" material could be fined up to $250,000 and face two years in prison. The law was the result by a long campaign by pro-family advocate groups (such as the Family Research Council), concerned with the pornographic material widely available on the network. These organizations worried, in particular, that the Internet was growing popular with children and teenagers who might more easily become victims of pedophiles and pornographers.

The American Civil Liberties Union immediately targeted the act. Along with ACLU, many NGOs like EPIC, EFF, and CDT were particularly active in emphasizing how the CDA constituted a dangerous precedent that could easily lead to more control on contents exchanged over the computer network. Internet technology, they argued, was "neither good nor bad." It would ultimately be about individual choice and educating children about actual risks. Finally, given the ample availability and effectiveness of filtering software (e.g. Surf Watch),[45] there was no room to justify infringements of the First Amendment. A three-judge court in Philadelphia, which challenged the CDA compatibility with the First Amendment, had already blocked the application of the controversial law in 1996. After that, litigators appealed to the Supreme Court for a constitutional decision. In June 1997, in *Reno v. ACLU*, the Court expressed its opinion on the CDA. Voting seven to two, the judges argued that some provisions of the act amounted to illegal government censorship. In the explanatory opinion of the judgment, Justice John Paul Stevens wrote that the CDA applied to a medium that, unlike radio, receives full First Amendment protection. Furthermore, the act raised special First Amendment concerns because of its obvious "chilling effect on free speech".[46]

The Supreme Court ruling on the First Amendment and free speech principles to the Internet had far-reaching effects, blocking further similar initiatives in Congress, at least for a while. The strategy of pro-family advocates changed. They moved from the federal to the state level of legislation. Currently, several states fashioned their own laws to regulate Internet speech. These activist groups also tried to render future drafts for federal legislation in Congress more "court-proof." Next, the pro-family groups targeted public libraries and other public interest places with numerous initiatives leading, for example, in March 1998 to the US Senate Commerce Committee approving the Internet School Filtering Act. This act required schools and libraries receiving federal Internet subsidies to certify that they were using filtering software.

The legal battle over Internet free speech resumed in February 1999 in Philadelphia, where a judge declared that the Children On-line Protection Act (COPA), voted by Congress in 1998, imposed technological and economic burdens on free speech. COPA established criminal penalties for any commercial distribution of material harmful to minors. The legal dispute furthermore became known as CDA II or *ACLU v. Reno II*, thus linking the two acts together as major threats to on-line freedom of speech. The Justice Department filed the appeals against the court proceeding and appealed, in 2001, to the Supreme Court to reverse the decision. In 2002, the Supreme Court rejected the appeal and ordered a lower court to decide the case on a wider range of First Amendment issues. In 2003, the lower court once again ruled that the act was unconstitutional.

Because in the correct opinion of the lower court, COPA had been likely to be found unconstitutional if challenged before the Supreme Court, the act was not enforced during the appeal process. As the battle on CDA – COPA continued, several bills were introduced in Congress to require the use of filtering software in schools and libraries receiving federal funding (e.g. the Children's Internet Protection Act), which were also immediately challenged before federal courts. Cases like COPA, CALEA, Carnivore (the FBI-designed computer program to intercept Internet communications), and others revealed an recurrent pattern: federal and local law enforcement agencies backed by a bipartisan combination of Congress members faced civil liberties NGOs, the American Libraries Association and local libraries, but also corporate and conservative organizations.

As Internet stakeholders, civil liberties NGOs showed how the subject of free speech can still attract support from segments of American society, even after September 11. Although national security and law enforcement are still high on the Congressional agenda, to pass more restrictive federal legislation to control the use of the Internet is not as easy as it was in the immediate post-September 11 period. The majority of members of Congress are fully aware of the importance of the Internet and of telecommunications in general to generate a full "information economy," as well as of the political prowess exhibited by Internet users.[47] Moral issues such as whether or not schools and libraries should install filtering programs in their computers to protect children will persist in sparking intense debates in Congress. If controversial bills are passed, it is likely that the Supreme Court will receive appeals.

The awkward spin-off of this situation is that racist and hatred websites cannot be banned or stopped on legal grounds in the United States. Hence, Europe and other countries will continue to find it excessive that Americans may impose their notion of freedom of speech. In opposition, American NGOs will probably defend that right even more staunchly, because amid the shrinking of all other liberties in the war on terror, freedom of speech might become a sort of a "moral Alamo." If Americans do have a peculiar interpretation of what free speech is, the approach to privacy could not be more different in the EU compared with the United States. In the former, information gathered by companies on individuals belongs to those individuals, while in the latter it becomes the property of the company. Furthermore, while in the EU the goal is to defend the public from information misuse in the private sector, in the United States the focus is on safeguarding individuals from the government's misuse of information.

The privacy issue has had serious implication for both Internet control and the protection of NII. Stronger privacy protection implies greater obstacles for law enforcement and counterintelligence agencies. The main technical reason why there was (and is) such a grave lack of privacy on the Internet was that information was transmitted "in clear," that is, it is not encrypted. A solution to that problem would be for users to regularly encrypt all of their communications. The digitalization of communications has made encryption almost a synonym for privacy and a necessity for which, as analyzed in Chapter 2, there was the long struggle about the individual use of strong-key cryptography. Nonetheless, although the NGOs-business alliance prevailed in this issue area, Internet users never truly embraced encryption for their daily communications, thus nullifying the most efficient tool to protect privacy on-line. In the United States, there is no explicit right to privacy in the Constitution and no comprehensive privacy protection law for the private sector. However, a patchwork of federal laws covers some specific categories of personal information (EPIC, 1999b). Although, as Cavazos and Morin (1995) noted, privacy plays a unique role in American law and is considered a core value by most citizens, "laws that protect consumers from having their information resold or given away are very weak" (Berners-Lee, 1999: 146). This contradictory situation was confirmed by a report that found that Americans had great concerns about breaches of privacy (Pew Internet & American Life Project, 2000).

As in other advanced democracies, surveillance of individuals for criminal investigation in the United States is strictly governed by federal laws. The United States was actually one of the first countries to pass a law governing privacy in electronic communications (the Electronic Communication Privacy Act of 1986). The information-gathering capability of the intelligence community is well known and impressive, and abuse and malpractice happen even within democracies. Furthermore, intelligence agencies cannot operate domestically and prefer to focus their efforts on foreign nationals. Nevertheless, in the 1990s, the American public seemed more and more concerned about the progressive loss of its privacy and growing intrusion by the federal government. Several polls conducted between the late 1990s and 2001 repeatedly showed that the loss of personal privacy was the first concern of American citizens, even surpassing topics such as terrorist acts or racial tensions.[48] Despite this concern (and the array of bills before Congress), there was no provision for a major privacy protection law or for a data protection agency like Europeans have.[49] With the notable exception of medical information, only children's privacy might enjoy some specific protection through the Children's On-line Privacy Protection Act, which was approved by Congress in the same bill that contained COPA in October 1998.[50] The White House and the private sector believed that, for all other individuals, "self-regulation was sufficient" (Berners-Lee, 1999: 146). In fact, before September 11, although in the United States there were already over 500 commercial databases, the data collected by the US government "dwarfs that by private enterprise" (Diffie and Landau, 1998: 137).[51]

When, at the end of the 1990s, EU countries began to implement the EU directive on personal data protection (95/46/CE of October 24, 1995), the private sector in the United States feared that the new EU privacy standards could hinder its traditional business practices. Under the new rules, US businesses would have to treat information about Europeans the same way that information would be managed in Europe. Companies lobbied Congress and the White House to convince the Europeans to ease their positions about how American companies should treat information about European customers. Some went as far as claming that the Europeans could not impose their concept of privacy onto Americans (Heisenberg and Fandel, 2004). After two years of negotiations, in order to meet the requests made by the Europeans that American companies comply with the EU directive on data protection, the DOC launched in 2000 the "safe harbor" proposal. Under this proposal American companies could voluntarily adhere to the EU guidelines. Several businesses, although wary about the "safe harbor" idea, enrolled in the program, because they recognized that offering greater privacy guarantees could become a quality service that might attract consumers and help secure their loyalty (Heisenberg and Fandel, 2004).[52] With the Internet and the blurring of communications and infrastructure, privacy has been "internationalized." The general public now needs to worry not only about its own national government and businesses but also foreign governments and companies. The war on terror simply aggravated these conditions. Several of the American civil liberties NGOs and users' organizations now have international ties with European and Asian counterparts. But the fact that individual privacy has become an international issue (in the same way as the environment) still fails to stir heated debates and keen attention in the way pollution, for example, does.

As Singh (1999) pointed out, digital technology had aided communications, but it also raised the possibility of those communications being monitored, even before September 2001. Large databases and data-mining techniques allow companies and governments to have detailed profiles of most individuals in advanced societies. Individuals had little control or influence on information legally stored in those databases held by private companies or law enforcement agencies, or to whom a bank could transmit borrowers' credit ratings or personal data. The convergence of cellular phones and computers has further worsened this state of affairs, because the former were so easy to wire-tap that *The Economist* called them the "enemies of personal privacy" (Wooldridge, 1999: 36). This impressive amount of information was already largely available to law enforcement and intelligence agencies in the United States and yet it did not have the slightest effect on preventing the September 2001 attacks. In 1997, the military historian Williamson Murray (1997: 63) wrote that the United States "did not need more information at Pearl Harbor, and it is doubtful that that we will need more information in the future." The response of the federal government in the aftermath of the 2001 attacks was simply to acquire more information about individuals.

After 9/11

The most striking feature of what happened on September 11, 2001, was that it was unexpected for everyone: the US and other governments, intelligence services, democratic societies, and the general public. Virtually within hours of the attacks, all major ISPs received FBI warrants and in the days immediately following 9/11,[53] law enforcement agencies investigated all possible sources of digital information. Months of searches confirmed that the use of ICT by the terrorists was rather ordinary. Even the speculation that al-Qaeda operatives had utilized steganography to hide their communications remained only a rumor (Provos and Honeyman, 2002). But the Internet, ICT, and the NII became even more sources of concerns.

Less than a week after the attacks, the Bush Administration presented Congress with the draft of the USA Patriot Act (Uniting and Strengthening America by Providing Appropriate Tools Required to Intercept and Obstruct Terrorism). Congress voted almost unanimously in favor of the act, which made substantial amendments to several existing laws, further enhancing the surveillance and investigative powers of law enforcement agencies in the United States. The act, however, was introduced with great haste and passed with little debate (Attorney General John Ashcroft gave Congress a week to pass the bill). Therefore, this important piece of legislation lacked the traditional checks and balances that normally safeguard civil liberties.[54] Some of the surveillance provisions would end after four years, unless Congress expressly renewed them at the end of 2004.

The second most noteworthy innovation (and the largest bureaucratic reorganization since 1947) that the September attacks caused was the establishment of the Department of Homeland Security (DHS), in November 2002. The department evolved from the Office of Homeland Security that was created within the White House just weeks after the 9/11 attacks.[55] The main purpose of the new department was to merge together 22 agencies (and nearly 170,000 federal employees) that were responsible for domestic defense, intelligence, and law enforcement but were accountable to different departments, such as Justice, Agriculture, Treasury, and Energy. A unified leadership would increase the efficiency of all these organizations. The amalgamation process was long and characterized by several turf battles as, for example, the FBI struggled to remain outside. The Secret Service, the Coast Guard, the Immigration and Naturalization Service, and the Federal Emergency Management Agency were among the several agencies that became part of the new cabinet department. Two of the most important players for the protection of the NII, namely the FBI's NIPC and the DOC Critical Infrastructure Assurance Office, were also fused into the DHS. Of the five division of the DHS, the National Cyber Security Division was explicitly earmarked to protect the NII.

All civil liberties NGOs quickly reacted to what they saw as the greatest threat to privacy and civil rights. The NGOs did not explicitly argue against new measures, but, rather, that more discussion was needed and that guarantees should be introduced in the act. More multifaceted was the position of the private sector. Private businesses own up to 85 percent of the country's NII; all ISPs are private. Hence, the cooperation of the private sector was indispensable in the post-attacks investigation as well as to enhance the overall level of security of the NII. ICT companies offered their full cooperation to the federal government, although, only a month after the September attacks, some ICT sector representatives already voiced their doubts about the usefulness of projects like Carnivore to help hunt for terrorists (Lee, 2001). The fear of being considered unpatriotic stemmed most criticisms in the private sector. At the same time, ICT companies that wanted to share with the DHS details about vulnerabilities of their networks claimed that exposing their vulnerability through the Freedom of Information Act (FOIA) might harm their business and help the competition. They negotiated exemption from the FOIA, thereby making it hard for civil liberties and users' NGOs to acquire information about faults and vulnerability of the NII from the DHS under the FOIA. The Bush Administration, which had shown a tendency for excessive secrecy (*The Economist*, 2003a), was ready to grant that exemption. But this position backfired against the executive since businesses wanted to protect their intellectual property rights from the federal government too (Bruno, 2002). Furthermore, they did not want to risk being liable for federal offences if some flaws that they had not disclosed surfaced later.

Finally, in the months after the 9/11 attacks, all major ICT companies, especially Microsoft, talked about how to improve the reliability of their products, which, in turn, would improve the dependability of computer networks. In the end that was not more than lip service. Since 2001, the federal government has tried to persuade the corporations that owned nuclear power plants, oil refineries, and software companies to improve the security of their infrastructures and products, mostly by appealing to their sense of patriotism. "That this had little effect should surprise none," Schneier observed (2003: 41), since security for private businesses is an extra cost that they have to bear, not an added feature that they can pass on to customers.

Despite the Patriot Act and the impressive intelligence apparatus, the increased control of the Internet and the ICT in general yielded only marginal evidence for the war on terror, as al-Qaeda leadership and operatives switched to non-electronic communications. This result did not cause any rethinking of information gathering and intelligence policies in the administration. On the contrary, the executive, forgetting the lessons of pre-September 11 when not lack of information but bad analysis was the problem, pressed on with its plan that more information was the key to more security for the country. The Bush Administration revealed plans for more surveillance on the Internet (Markoff and Schwartz, 2002) and launched the Total Information Awareness (TIA) project. The goal of TIA was to track individuals through collecting as much information as possible. A centralized database would collect transaction data (like financial records, medical records, communication records, and travel records) contained in numerous other databases. Intelligence information would also be included and then, using computer algorithms and human analysis, TIA, it was hoped, would allow federal agents to detect potential terrorists and criminals involved in "low-intensity/low-density" forms of warfare and crime. Retired Admiral John Poindexter (the same of the Iran – Contra affair) was appointed as director of the project, which was hosted by the DARPA, the DOD agency that financed the first computer network.

TIA did not make any distinctions between US citizens and foreign nationals and was so controversial that at first the DOD changed the name from Total to Terrorist Information Awareness, hoping to win some support from the public, and then put the whole project on hold. Poindexter's directorship had become so divisive, as he advanced more radical ideas (such as starting a stock exchange that would trade futures about terrorist acts), that he stepped down in the fall of 2003. The Bush Administration nonetheless continues to implement other initiatives to collect more information. The new approach of the federal government was to subdivide the items that were incorporated in TIA. It presented a Patriot II draft, quarreled with the EU Commission to obtain details on all passengers traveling to the United States,[56] and ended up with fingerprint scanning for all foreign travelers with US visas. The new approach worked. For example, based on an appropriation bill passed in December 2003, the FBI can now obtain personal financial information from banks, insurance companies, travel agencies, real estate agents, stockbrokers, the US Postal Service, and car dealerships without a warrant.

The federal government justified many of these highly controversial decisions with the new phobia, namely cyberterrorists. These new foes with digital tools (like viruses and Trojan horses) could exploit vulnerabilities of the Internet and of software in remotely controlled critical applications (like the air traffic or the gates of a dam) to wreck havoc. The claimed human and economic costs would be enormous. Some press reports seemed to substantiate alarm (Anderson, 2002; Arena and Ensor, 2002). But several authors (Denning 2001; Green, 2002; Hutter, 2002; Lewis, 2002; Schneier, 2003; Giacomello, 2004) demonstrated that for the time being cyberterrorism is not a realistic threat, and that resources should go elsewhere. The administration has not altered its line. The National Strategy to Secure Cyberspace of 2003 indicated as its primary concern "the threat of organized cyber attacks capable of causing debilitating disruption" (p. 6). The same document, however, points out that the "required technical sophistication to carry out such an attack is high" (p. viii) and that "the likelihood of suffering a severe cyber attack is difficult to estimate" (p. 9). In another federal document, the National Strategy for Homeland Security, the administration warned against the possibility that terrorists could become more proficient in destructive cyber-attacks (some time in the future). The same document indicated that terrorists were already exploiting ICT and the Internet "to plan attacks, raise funds, spread propaganda, collect information, and communicate securely" (White House, 2002: 7). These actions all belong to the class of perception management activities, which are the least dangerous form of cyberterrorism. Ironically, under certain circumstances, some of those actions could even qualify for protection under the First Amendment.

There is a serious (almost tragic) flaw in the logic of the Patriot Act and similar post-September 11 laws. In a democracy, the public is willing to accept that its government reduces civil liberties in time of war, as the United Kingdom and the United States did during World War II. The safeguard is that the restraint on civil liberties is only for the duration. Moreover, most traditional wars of the last two centuries have rarely lasted for more than a few years. Civil or unconventional wars usually last longer, but no war of that type has occurred in an advanced democracy in the last sixty years.

The war on terror, however, may have an exact starting date (September 11), but its termination is many years (decades probably) away. Or it may even never end (like other endless wars on poverty, famine, drugs, and so on). In his State of the Union address of 2002, President Bush introduced a permanent "war on terror," and the National Strategy for Homeland Security expressly stated that "the United States will confront the threat of terrorism for the foreseeable future" (White House, 2002: 7). There is absolutely no previous example of a democracy permanently suspending civil liberties for "the foreseeable future."

Conclusions

A few years ago, in reference to the cryptography debate, Singh (1999: 313) concluded that the ultimate fate of encryption in the United States would be determined by "whom the public fears the most, criminals [including terrorists] or the government." In 2004, another cryptography and computer security expert, Bruce Schenier (2004), answered that question, "the United States is looking more and more like a police state." After September 11, the American public fears terrorists more than the federal government. The Bush administration exploited the apprehension and alarm to secure a level of Internet control that would have been unthinkable without September 11, with only marginal increments in the protection of the NII, because funds and resources were wrongly allocated. With 9/11 the US federal government launched the second wave of securitization of Internet control, after the cryptowars. The Pentagon found the enemy that it had been searching for since the end of the Cold War (Kaldor, 2001; Bendrath, 2003; Barnett, 2004).

In the late 1990s, debates on cryptography and privacy alerted users and NGOs about the dangers arising from the federal government's monitoring activities. The "victory" in the cryptowars restored some privacy in communications, but privacy in the broader sense, as the *Economist* noted (2000b), continued to be eroded. September 11 gave a tremendous boost to that erosion. A formidable obstacle to the public discussion on Internet control was that American decision-makers could not really grasp the technical nature of the network. This mixed state of mind of admiration and fear for computers and computer networks, however, is also common among the general public, and does not contribute to a sober evaluation of the strengths and weaknesses of the Internet, and, above all, of what should be deemed legal or illegal. As early as the mid-1990s, Eli Noam (quoted in Mitchell, 1997) recalled how the public had long looked with apprehension at Big Brother, centralized government databases, mysterious computers, and 14-year-old hackers starting nuclear wars on their own. From the beginning, the public vision of computer networks and the Internet (let alone the NII) was never sober and informed. 9/11 and the emphasis that the executive branch has put on terrorism, cyber-attacks, and NII vulnerabilities could only make the picture gloomier.

The occurrence of the accidental alliance of principles-oriented (pro-liberties NGOs, consumers' organizations, and users' groups) and profit-oriented (private businesses) actors successfully opposed the national security community on Internet control until September 11. Because both actors mastered technical and legal information and were very capable of voicing their interests in the appropriate settings, even the federal government shared the alliance's hands-off policy of private self-regulation. Instinctively, given the traditional distrusts of Americans for the executive, the sympathy of the public tended slightly toward the accidental alliance. Undoubtedly, the legal, moral, and technical intricacies of the Internet made the opinion of citizens and administrators swing back and forth between demanding more control to protect children and fears of undermining the First Amendment. The different stakeholders demanded attention and action on the multiple facets of the Internet all at the same time, generating a Babel of mixed and contradictory opinions. Nonetheless, this was Lijphart's multi-interested nation at its best, where "constitutional arguing" with one's government was the perfectly acceptable procedure. After September 2001, the Bush Administration seized patriotism's high ground, thus making disagreement about its policies at home and abroad an act of anti-Americanism, but the pluralist society did not turn mute.

There are also international, far-reaching consequences for this state of affairs. The evolution of Internet control and the NII security debate in the United States and in other democracies will also be critical for the example that it will set for "less" democratic states. Delacourt (1997: 208) correctly noted that although the United States was regarded among those nations placing the fewest restrictions on expression, it was also among "the first to approve legislation governing the content of on-line communications" like the CDA. The CDA was eventually abandoned, but then came CALEA, COPA, the Patriot Act, and TIA and the list will likely continue. If a country like the United States, which prides itself with being "the first democracy," might put in place severe restrictions about Internet content, then what could happen in countries such as Iran or China? Political leaders in less than democratic states may now comfortably address their publics, pointing out that even the advanced democracies, which constantly lecture other governments about their human rights records and lack of personal liberties, cannot endure an unrestricted Internet. Autocratic states may point out that the United States decided to step up Internet control to protect the NII and Europe overcame all resistance and signed the Convention on Cybercrime, which was contested by civil liberties NGOs. These actions will also facilitate the discourse of more "control-prone" governments. Already in the late 1990s, Delacourt (1997) called this behavior of Western democracies "irresponsible."

Civil liberties NGOs and users' groups were aware that the ICT private sector could be a very influential ally against government's intrusion on the Internet, and that an ally was indispensable when facing the national security community. But because most of the Internet and of the NII as well as of databases are privately owned and the US government needs them for the war on terror, the private sector could be a "double-edged sword." The judiciary was early drafted in the struggle: if civil liberties NGOs could not change draft bills in Congress, they could try in court. The executive has now rebutted that line of attack as well, pointing out that it cannot fight terrorism in courts. The overall outcome of this state of affairs has been an excessive increase in the level of Internet control with a minimal protection of the NII, but with considerable opportunity costs, wrong allocation of resources, and enormous loss of personal privacy and civil liberties. Civil liberties NGOs will need to renew their strategies and efforts. The point is that, within the federal government, multiple agencies have multiple (and often conflicting) agendas. NGOs should work to exploit those competing agendas. For instance, the same administration that pushed friends and allies to sign the COE Convention on Cybercrime, supported ICANN when, at the UN World Summit on the Information Society in 2003, the NGOs resisted attempts by other governments to have greater influence in the management of domain names. NGOs will have to somehow revamp their odd alliance with the ICT sector, pointing out that too much leverage has been handed on to the federal government in the last few years.

Security is a trade-off, as any security expert would say: Benjamin Franklin reportedly noted that those who would give up essential liberty for temporary safety deserved neither liberty nor safety. Squandering an enormous amount of liberty for not even temporary safety in return, just as Americans have done lately, might be the most perverse of all trade-offs.

Notes

1 It should be noted that, for a long time (perhaps as early as 1947 and constantly modernized since), the United States, the United Kingdom, and other English-speaking countries have had in operation a global electronic communications surveillance system (Echelon) with highly sophisticated intercepting capabilities. Nevertheless, if Echelon is as good as it is believed, one cannot help but wonder why, for instance, the FBI constantly asked the federal government and Congress for more snooping powers much earlier than September 2001, claiming that it risked being outsmarted by criminals with advanced encryption software.

2 According to the "Opacity Index," developed by economists at the consulting firm PricewaterhouseCoopers, the United States has a very low score (36 out of a 1–100 ranking), indicating a high degree of transparency. The index is available from <www.opacity-index.com/> [February 19, 2004].

3 As explained earlier, whether they belong to a company, an organization, or a person, domain names are the "trademark" of the Internet. They are the way a product or information can be easily located on-line.

4 Chamorel (1994:77) observed that with the possible exception of Canada, "the United States probably has the most decentralized political system among the major industrialized democracies."

5 "Powers not delegated to the United States by the Constitution ... are reserved to the States, or the people."

6 Before the arrival of telecommunications, however, the Radio Act was approved immediately after World War I and the telegraph industry was well established even before then.

7 The 1996 act also contained provisions for illegal transmissions via computer of obscene and indecent material to minors, which would constitute the basis for the passing of the 1996 Communication Decency Act (CDA).

8 The DES worked with algorithms based on 56 bites, that is, 2^{56} possible permutations.

9 In both incidents, it was more a case based on appearance rather than substance. The first event was popularized by Cliff Stoll, who was the actual "chaser" of the West German intruders. The second episode was never extensively investigated, but it appears that the Iraqis turned down the offer, thinking it was a hoax.

10 This decision was unquestionably in accordance with the guiding principles of the Clinton Doctrine as outlined in the 1994 National Security document ("A Strategy for Engagement and Enlargement") which called for the promotion of free market democracy abroad.

11 Exceptions include Japan and the Scandinavian countries, where the telecommunication industries are so crucial for those countries' economies that serious disruptions in those industries would severely compromise their national security.

12 See the Pew Internet & American Life Project reports (2000, 2001). EPIC also has a web page with links to several opinion polls on Internet issues conducted since as early as 1990, available from <www.epic.org/privacy/survey/> [February 6, 2004].

13 Since 1998, the DOC has granted blanket exceptions for certain countries and uses (e.g. banking and financial services). Only a handful of countries on a "black" list are completely banned from the export of strong key encryption software (being "sponsors of terrorism," i.e. Iran, Iraq, Libya, North Korea, Sudan, Syria, and Cuba).

14 The provision for the V-chip was contained in the 1996 Telecommunication Act.

15 EPIC opposed the enactment of CALEA in 1994 and participated as a party in the FCC proceeding, arguing that many of the FBI standards went beyond the scope of the legislation and threatened communications privacy. The full text of CALEA is available at <www.epic.org/privacy/wiretap/> [March 18, 2004].

16 Indeed, a federal report (available from the EPIC website at <www.epic.org/privacy/wiretap/stats/1998-report/>) showed how, in 1998, interception by federal and state law enforcement officers went up by 12 percent and 24 percent respectively.

17 Republicans are considered to be traditionally suspicion of "too much government."

18 These different players had different agendas. Civil liberties NGOs worried about the FBI or the NSA, while the private sector was more concerned with regulating authorities.

19 The leading position of the DOC in the domain name dispute was due to the fact that it basically inherited the "root" (that is, the core of the domain system) from the National Science Foundation network (NSFNET). The NSFNET, in turn, had taken over the management of the Internet from the Department of Defense's ARPANET.

20 According to the World Wide Web Virtual Library, safety-critical systems are those computer, electronic, or electromechanical systems whose failure may cause injury or death to human beings (such as an aircraft or nuclear power station control instruments); available at http://foldoc.doc.ic.ac.uk/foldoc/foldoc.cgi?safety-critical%20system [February 3, 2004].

21 The Morris Worm (it was long debated if it was a worm or a virus) was created in 1988 by Robert T. Morris, a graduate student at Cornell University. It was not supposed to be a malicious piece of software and Morris spoke of an experiment gone awry. Nonetheless, Morris was the first person convicted under the criminal code for a hacking offense (Hafner and Markoff, 1995).

22 Ironically, the DOJ was the counterpart to Microsoft in the 1999 antitrust case against the software giant, thus siding, in this case, with civil liberties NGOs.

23 Carnivore is FBI-developed software (basically a "sniffer") that, placed in specific routers, monitors Internet traffic in clear, searching for keywords, and copying suspect messages.

24 Executive Order 13010 of July 17, 1996, available from <www.ciao.gov/resource/pccip/eo13010.pdf> [February 9, 2004].

25 At the end of the 1990s, the list of special US government agencies earmarked to monitor the Internet or protect the NII was rather long. In addition to the FCC, the NTIA, and CIAO, there was the Federal Networking Council (FNC), the DOC Information Infrastructure Task Force (IITF), and many others. In 2002 several of these organizations were incorporated into the Department of Homeland Security.

26 For a chronology of where the expression "electronic Pearl Harbor" comes from, see the Crypt newsletter available from<www.soci.niu.edu/~crypt/other/harbor.htm> [February 11, 2004]. See also Giacomello (2004).

27 In a DoS attack, the machine targeted is submerged with an overwhelming number of requests, which, eventually, lead to a complete blockage of the machine itself.

28 A chronology of how the story developed is available from <http://sun.soci.niu.edu/~crypt/other/eligib.htm> [February 11, 2004].

29 Interview with John Pike, Washington, DC, July 15, 1999.

30 "Script-kiddies" is a derogatory term to describe young adults with enough computer skills only to download software programs that other, more knowledgeable programmers wrote, and to use then to bother users and system administrators on the Internet.

31 Paradoxically, the RAND Corporation recommended the US Air Force not to modernize all communications nodes and to avoid full connectivity, since the old USAF communication system was robust and unfamiliar for cyberterrorists and hackers (Arquilla *et al.*, 1999: 81). Most of the documents still available on information operations focus on defense, how weak the NII was, and what was necessary to do to protect it. Nothing is said by the DOD or other federal agencies about how much damage the United States would be able to inflict to the information infrastructures of other countries.

32 Interview with Wayne Madsen, Washington, DC, July 16, 1999.

33 To defend the right of people to free speech, ACLU has also made cases for the Ku Klux Klan and neo-Nazi groups. The ACLU website is at <www.aclu.org>.

34 The EFF website is at <www.eff.org>.

35 The ISOC website is at <www.isoc.org>.

36 The Computer Professionals for Social Responsibility was one of the first American NGOs concerned with the development of growing reliance on computing power by the US military. Since its inception (1981), the organization has pursued this goal, also becoming more and more involved with the future of computer networks. The EPIC website is at <www.epic.org>; see also <www.cprs.org>.

37 EPIC surveys on cryptography have been used in Chapter 2 of this book.

38 EPIC proudly states that it has "no clients, no customers, and no shareholders."

39 The CDT Web site is at <www.cdt.org>.

40 The NCL also founded the Alliance against Fraud in Telemarketing and Electronic Commerce.

41 Their website is at <ftp://ftp.csua.berkeley.edu/pub/cypherpunks/Home.html>.

42 The OSI website is at <www.opensource.org/index.html>.

43 The GILC website is at <www.gilc.org/>.

44 In that year, the National Science Foundation stopped the funding of NSFNET, heir of ARPANET, and then the main backbone of the Internet.

45 Clever children (who often know their computers much better than their parents) could make Surf Watch ineffective. The presence of filtering software did not diminish the importance of responsible parenting.

46 The full text of the Supreme Court decision is available from <www.ciec.org/SC_appeal/ syllabus.shtml/> [February 13, 2004].

47 The take-off of 2004 presidential candidate Howard Dean was entirely due to the large support he was able to harness early from enthusiastic Internet users.

48 Summaries and figures on these polls are available from the EPIC website at <www.epic.org/ privacy/survey/> and from the CDT website at <www.cdt.org/privacy/survey/findings/> [February 14, 2004].

49 "Privacy" is definitively culture-specific, as the differences between Europe and the United States show, including the dispute on how American companies should behave with regard to the treatment of the personal data of Europeans, after the EU Directive on Personal Data Protection entered into force in October 1998 (Directive 97/66/EC).

50 COPPA requires websites to get parental consent from visitors age 12 and under before using their personally identifiable information for any secondary purpose, while COPA (Children's Online Protection Act) created a national "harmful to minors" standard for speech on the Internet. I am grateful to Ari Schwarz of CDT for clarifying the differences between COPA and COPPA.

51 Federal agencies support 910 major databases (General Accounting Office, 1990, quoted in Diffie and Landau, 1998: 137). With regard to the Internet, however, it seems that the private sector will rapidly close the gap. In fact, Double Click, an Internet advertising company, may have tracked as many as 90 million US households, mostly through "cookies." Furthermore, Double Click planned to match this information with data from other sources to create more precise customer profiles (matching names with commercial preferences) that could be "sold" to third parties. EPIC filed a public complaint against this plan and on March 2, 2000, Double Click announced its intention to abandon the plan. Double Click was later awarded the "Big Brother Award" that a committee of privacy NGOs gives once a year in April. The FBI and NSA had also won the prize.

52 In 2000, when the on-line company eToy failed, and had to sell its customer list (which contained names of parents and children, and credit card numbers), considerable concern arose within public opinion. In the end, Disney bought the list and destroyed it to show that it cared about children' and parents' privacy.

53 9/11 is how Americans now prefer to call September 11.

54 O'Harrow (2002) provides a very detailed account of what happened in those weeks.

55 For more details about the DHS, see White House (2002).

56 This passenger information includes among other things, name, address, flight number, credit card number, and choice of meal.

5   *Das Netz über Alles*
Germany on-line

Deutschland Vorn im Internet!

(Initiative D21, 2000)

"Ist Deutschland fit für die digitale Ära?"[1] the German magazine *Der Spiegel* inquired in March 2000 (p. 7). To external observers it indeed appeared that Germans had literally "fallen in love" with *das Netz* ("the Net"). With the exception of the Scandinavians (who are in a league of their own), Germans have been among the most active surfers on the Web, possibly preferring contents in the German language. Germany is unmistakably in the group of the world's technological "leaders." In 2000, T-Online, the Internet access provider owned by telecom giant Deutsche Telekom AG (DTAG), was the world's second-largest ISP and the most visited site of the home market (*The Economist*, 2000a). In 2001, DTAG itself entered the American mobile market and was named "Europe's biggest telecom company" by CNN (2002a). In 2002, Germany ranked number 18, after Switzerland, in the Network Readiness Index (out of 75 countries) and number 11 (out of 72) in the Technology Advancement Index of the UNDP Human Development Report of 2001, just next to Singapore and before Norway. In 2003, the top-level domain for Germany (dot.ude) was the fourth most frequent country domain on the Web,[2] and the International Telecommunication Union (2003a) placed Germany in the group of countries with the highest Digital Accession Index.

These notable results are the consequence of an impressive, conscious digitalization effort by the whole of German society and economy, planned and executed through a coordinated action by the government, private industry, schools, and the media. It is the traditional logic of German orchestration and consensus among social and economic actors, with a whole new goal, namely bringing Germany into the information age and the new economy. Crucial to this endeavor is not only the full backing of the SPD–Green cabinet, but even the enthusiasm of Germany's industrial colossi. In Germany's corporatist democracy model, institutional actors (i.e. trade unions, industrialists' associations, consumers' groups) have fairly good access to federal and local governments and legislatures. Once consensus is reached among all these players, it endures, and the resulting policies are highly likely to be implemented. Two examples of this condition are Initiative D21 and the ICANN At-Large membership. The former case is a coherent project of the federal government and the private sector to boost IT education in schools and society in general. In the latter case, mainly thanks to the publicity given to the event by Spiegel Online (May 2, 2000), a considerable number of Germans registered for the election of the new Board of Directors of ICANN, the organization that is responsible for domain names.

Lijphart (1999: 177) ranks Germany mildly low in his index of pluralism. Although contemporary Germany is no longer a corporatist country as it was until the 1990s, Germany's domestic interest configuration still shows a tight coordination among interest groups. During the Cold War and the reconstruction of Germany, the federal government (Bundesregierung), the private sector, and strong trade unions cooperated tightly to produce a stable and robust economy. National security was strictly a matter for NATO. After 1989, cooperation between the three players (the government, business, and trade unions) deteriorated. The government is wary about letting the private sector into national security, although it is also perfectly aware that, when it comes to Germany's NII, like all other advanced countries, there is no other alternative. Controlling the Internet for the federal government is mostly protecting the NII, with a few considerable exceptions in monitoring content. Internet stakeholders (the government, the ICT sector, and civil liberties NGOs), however, still debate the typology and dimension of cyber-threats. According to the Working Group on Infrastructure Protection (AKSIS), ICT business executives preferred low government intervention in the NII and were skeptical of cyberterrorism (Wigert, 2004e). A simulated cyber-terrorist attack in November 2001 (CYTEX) highlighted weak points in the NII but also confirmed the skepticism (Hutter, 2002). Under these circumstances, even if the Red – Green cabinet had been inclined to do so, any attempts at forcing a strong securitization move would have failed.

With the backing of at least a portion of public opinion, the government deems it necessary to prevent the diffusion of neo-Nazi propaganda, Holocaust denial, and hatred speech or child pornography on the Internet. German civil liberties NGOs have, to some extent, opposed these policies, but they too support banning child pornography. Neo-Nazi material is more controversial, however, since civil liberties activists tend to think that, albeit despicable, it too should be protected by freedom of speech. Since the collective guilt for the past is still very strongly felt in all segments of German society, resistance to these policies has also come from American NGOs, on the basis that freedom of speech also applies to hatred or Nazi material on-line.

September 11 inevitably affected Germany's approach to the Internet. However, the attacks on New York and Washington in 2001, and those on Madrid trains in 2004, did not change the German view that terrorism is "a crime" (Katzenstein, 2003), not a military endeavor. It follows that cyberterrorism is also a crime and should be dealt with by law enforcement agencies. In doing so, the federal government signaled that it would hardly try to securitize the issue of Internet control and the protection of the NII. All in all, in January 2002 the German Parliament, the Bundestag, passed an anti-terrorism law that allowed intelligence and law enforcement officials to access digitally stored traffic records but *not* Internet data retention. German ISPs cannot retain data on what their subscribers do when they are on-line. After the bombing of Madrid in March 2004, European leaders agreed to look into this matter, under the existing EU privacy guidelines, but Germany and the Scandinavians remained adamant (BBC News, 2004c). Even before the Madrid bombings, according to Reporters Sans Frontières (2003), about twenty civil liberties and privacy NGOs had condemned the tendency to increase surveillance that the Council of Europe Convention on Cybercrime (signed in November 2003 and in force in July 2004) authorized. The treaty should help advanced, industrialized countries that are highly dependent on computer networks to fight criminality as well as terrorism on the Internet.

Like many other democracies, Germany faces a difficult digital challenge. It wants to remain the most technologically advanced country in Europe, protect its information infrastructure, respect freedom of speech, and defend users' privacy and decency. But it also wants to show that it is not going to forget its past and that freedom of speech cannot become a justification for hatred or Nazi nostalgia, or a loophole for child pornography. Furthermore, the number of stakeholders in society (and in the ICT sector in particular) is considerably greater than in the past. Nevertheless, all the main actors – the federal government, the private sector, and the public – seem to share a remarkable similarity of what the Internet evolution should be.

Europe's technological giant

Germany's telecommunications history does not differ much from that of Italy or other continental European countries. A "natural monopoly," telecommunication services had been highly regulated by German governments. After the war, West Germany rebuilt its telephone system as a public service, as the property of the Deutsche Bundespost (the Federal Tele-communication and Postal Service). Article 87 of the West German Constitution explicitly affirmed that the management and regulation of telecoms were reserved to the state. Furthermore, the federal government's traditional concern for maintaining the consensus of all the economic and social actors inevitably required state monopoly for services and oligopoly for equipment (Natalicchi, 2001). The long process of reform and, later liberalization took place in three stages (Werle, 1999).

The first phase (Poststrukturgesetz or Postreform I) took place in 1989–90 and established three separate operational units for the provision of postal services (Postdienste), banking services (Postbank), and telecommunications services (Telekom) (Werle, 1999). The Bundespost became a holding company. After German reunification and Deutsche Telekom's need for capital and entrepreneurial autonomy to build a modern telecommunications network in the former East Germany, the German Parliament (the Bundestag) approved Postreform II in 1994 (Natalicchi, 1996; Werle, 1999). In this phase, all of the three former branches of Bundespost became independent joint stock companies, but the federal government maintained control of the majority of shares well after 2000. The final stage, Postreform III, was the Telecommunications Act (TKG), voted for by the Bundestag in July 1996, to replace the old Postgesetz. A revision of the TKG aimed at assuring fairer competition for non-German ICT companies began in 2004.

As in other European countries, the opening up of the German market to European competitors required the establishment of independent authorities with the power to regulate market competition. The TKG thus established the Regulatory Authority for Telecommunications and Posts (Regulierungsbehörde), and ended the telecommunications network and phone services monopoly by January 1998. The Regulatory Authority has information-gathering and investigative capabilities as well as a set of sanctions. It cooperates closely with the Federal Cartel Office (Bundeskartellamt). The Federal Cartel Office is another independent high authority, earmarked with the application of federal laws against the limitation of competition. However, the exact realms of competence of the Cartel Office and of the Regulatory Authority have never been laid out. Since the telecom sector has been a "natural monopoly" for years, and, thus, a predictable target for antitrust actions, disagreements and diversity of interpretations between the two agencies have been the rule.

A remarkable case in point of how that wave of liberalization has changed Germany's telecom and multimedia industry has been the outcome of the Vodafone–Mannesmann case.[3] Here, the British mobile phone group Vodafone Airtouch launched a 124 billion euros bid for its German rival, Mannesmann, in a hostile takeover at a time when such actions were practically unknown in Germany. Mannesmann fought back, supported by the press and also by Chancellor Schröder. The BBC (2000b) described the federal government as openly hostile to the takeover. After an initial bitter battle and under the pressure of Mannesman's many non-German shareholders, the two companies agreed to a merger at the beginning of 2000, creating the world's largest mobile operator. This event occurred against the opposition of the German press and government. The takeover of Mannesman, as *The Economist* (2000c) noted, was a coup that blew Germany's market for corporate control wide open. Given these circumstances and the fact that the last phase of liberalization of the telecom sectors only began in 1996, it is impressive that, by 1999, Germany had one of the most liberal regimes by European standards (Natalicchi, 2001).

The Internet (and, more generally, computer networks) came to the attention of the general public in two major instances, in the late 1980s and again much later in 1996. In the late 1980s – more exactly between 1986 and 1989 – the topics of hackers' break-ins and espionage began to appear in the West German press. West Germans came late to computer hacking, that is, only in the early 1980s, with the Chaos Computer Club (CCC) being founded in 1984. The CCC was "chaotic" only in name, since the club was "the very picture of meticulous organization, with a hierarchy of officers and sub-officers" (Hafner and Markoff, 1995: 156). With their left-wing sympathies, and their Hacker Ethics manifesto, CCC members somehow fascinated the West German public. The CCC wanted to increase public awareness about new methods of gathering personal data and to expose how outside intrusion could compromise federal computers. CCC members were exposing how people's data were not protected. Many Germans looked sympathetically at the "technological wunderkinder of Chaos," as a symbol of harmless dissent in West Germany (Hafner and Markoff, 1995: 158).

The CCC received particular notoriety in 1984 when some affiliates showed the media how easy it would be for them to collect money from a bank using the federal postal payment system. The CCC thus convinced many Germans that their accounts were "helpless victims in the hands of electronic hoodlums" (Hafner and Markoff, 1995: 158). In 1987, news came out that CCC associates had penetrated NASA computers, forcing NASA to admit the intrusion.[4] Nevertheless, when in 1989 a group of young West Germans, loosely associated with the Club, admitted they had broken into US computers for the Soviet bloc, the West German public was shocked. The revelation also enraged the CCC's leaders, who feared the Club could acquire a bad name.[5] Eventually, three individuals loosely associated with the group were indicted and tried in 1990, but the sentence was rather lenient. However, all that they had sold to the Soviets was freeware or innocuous information. These highly publicized events have given the hackers' community in Germany a considerable, albeit controversial, popularity. The Chaos Computer Club has become "an icon" in cyberculture, to the point that it can present itself as "a galactic community of human beings" of all ages, genders, races, and social positions, demanding "unlimited freedom and flow of information without censorship." The current spirit of the CCC seems more in tune with the many computer civil liberties groups that are now active in the United States, than with the unconventional attitude of its beginning.[6] Recently, it has even taken up "lobbyist work" domestically as well as internationally.

The last moment of celebrity for the CCC and an eloquent instance of Germany's new boldness in Internet matters was the German participation in the first (and only) election of the new ICANN board of directors. ICANN began in February 2000 to inconspicuously prepare for the election by calling for "voters" from five geographical "regions."[7] Most European Internet users did not know about the initiative until May 2000, when Spiegel Online decided to publicize and promote the event with weekly coverage. Spiegel Online even interviewed several candidates.[8] The idea was tremendously successful. In the end Europe had almost 36,000 applicants (more than any other region except Asia), 57 percent of whom were Germans.[9] Not only were the majority of European candidates Germans, but the three with most support were all Germans. Two of these candidates had a strong "civil society background" (which is why they were endorsed in first place) and stated that they wanted to represent the Internet's ordinary users, not the corporate world. The most popular candidate was Andy Mueller-Maguhn, speaker of the Chaos Computer Club. He was ultimately elected to the post of European representative at ICANN. The new board, apparently, would have real decision-making authority within ICANN. Furthermore, given ICANN's control of domain names, the board could have had significant power on shaping the future of the Internet. That impression quickly faded away, leaving elected board members and "registered" voters very disappointed. It was a "public relations failure" for ICANN.

In Germany, the other foremost moment of Internet notoriety was the case of the Internet service provider CompuServe, in the mid-1990s. In 1995, the German authorities decided to take strong action against the proliferation of pornography and neo-Nazi propaganda on the Internet, and in December of that year Bavaria's law enforcement officials searched CompuServe's offices. Bavarian prosecutors found examples of child pornography and other illegal images through the network. The then head of CompuServe Germany, Felix Somm, was charged with consciously allowing that material to reach CompuServe's customers. Despite the fact that, in 1997, the Bundestag had passed the Multimedia Law, which implied that ISPs were not responsible for on-line contents, in May 1998 a Munich court found Somm guilty for complicity in 13 cases of distributing illegal pornography. The court declared that Somm had failed to block CompuServe customers' access to those sites, thus allowing child pornography to be sent across the network. Somm received a two-year suspended jail sentence and a 50,000 euros fine. CompuServe tried to avoid further prosecution in Germany by stopping access to 200 message boards, and announcing that it would install screening software to avoid the recurrence of such circumstances. CompuServe customers did not approve of such decisions, accusing the ISP of "censorship."

The sentence was highly criticized inside and outside Germany. Jörg Tauss (SPD), later chairman of the Bundestag committee on the new media, called the decision "a catastrophe." The then CDU technology minister declared that the development of the Internet in Germany must not be held back (Wired News, 1998). In the end, in November 1999, the appeal high court of Bavaria ruled to reverse the guilty verdict against Somm. As a *Wired* reporter wrote (Hudson, 1998), the case was so convincing that even the prosecution did an about-face and pleaded for Somm's acquittal. Civil liberties organizations greeted Somm's exoneration as a victory for freedom of speech on the Internet. German public opinion did not like to be seen as undermining fundamental human rights. In all likelihood, German judges took into consideration such views. However, public concerns for human rights provide only a partial explanation for the final ruling. The German telecom market is one of the largest in the world and the richest one in Europe. Suddenly, Germany's trade and diplomatic partners might view Germany as a technophobe, Internet-resistant, rigid society, at a moment when the country was undergoing a critical shift from the industrial to the information age. Such a perception of Germany could have disastrous economic consequences. The "high-precision technologists" of Europe (as Germans like to be regarded) viewed this prospect as unacceptable.

In addition to the Telecommunications Act (TKG) and the Multimedia Law, the Digital Signature Act (SigG) was the third key law affecting the Internet in Germany adopted in the late 1990s, before the SPD – Green coalition came to office. The SigG established a uniform legal framework for digital signatures. A digital signature is a seal affixed to electronic data which certifies the owner of the signature key and the integrity of the data. The signature key certificate is awarded to individuals by a certification institution, recognized by the Regulatory Authority for Telecommunications and Posts. The Authority first licensed two certification institutions (Deutsche Telekom and Deutsche Post) to provide nationwide services under the Signature Act. Five more service providers then accepted the common technical standard for signatures required by the Act. The SigG was a "technical law," whose purpose was to provide the conditions for a secure infrastructure for the use of digital signatures in Germany.

The technology adopted for digital signatures is based on public key cryptography. The BSI, the Federal Office for Information Security (an NSA-type government agency), conducted the technical studies on reliability and security of digital signatures. The BSI's setting of the technical standards for this law was to deeply affect the future development of the Internet (and the dependability of the German NII), because of the law's reliance on public key cryptography. Founded in 1991, the BSI had its first moment of popularity at the end of 1999 when it was preparing to counter the Millennium bug. Since then, the BSI has enhanced its authority in several technical security aspects of Germany's ICT sector. BSI established the federal CERT in September 2001, which since then has become a focal point for the security of the NII.

Two other significant factors that might have consequences for the protection of Germany's NII as well as government control have been the division of competencies between the federal government and the

Länder, and the growing structural inadequacies of the German educational system. The former problem is critical because both federal and state governments have competency in regulating media and broadcasting. More precisely, the federal government awards licenses and regulates telecom services, while the *Länder* have authority on media and broadcasting. Overlaps and administrative conflicts have already been rather common, and they are likely to be even more numerous, given the processes of merging multimedia and the Internet. Since both sides tend to define their jurisdiction extensively, "new problems concerning the jurisdictional confines of the federal government and the *Länder* governments have emerged" (Werle, 1999: 120).

The structural rigidity of Germany's educational system, which is also divided between federal and state level, was another obstacle. Many Germans had criticized the system in the past for its slowness in adapting to the transformations in society and then in the economy (Koch *et al.*, 2000). Such failures could be fatal for Germany in the case of ICT and the Internet. *Der Spiegel*, on its cover page of March 27, 2000, referred to it as "the digital education catastrophe." The federal government has addressed this problem as a top priority and, through Initiative D21, has tried to provide every pupil with a laptop and draw the attention of new generations toward ICT. Deutsche Telekom echoed the proposal of wiring all schools by 2001. Such solutions (e.g. the necessary training of computer-literate teachers) take a long time to be implemented, however, while the German government and industry want to be identified as the leading European actors for electronic commerce and ICT.[10]

The relaunch of the German economy in 2000 was planned on the joint effects of government support, biotechnology research, and the Internet. Deutsche Telekom had gladly echoed and championed the federal government's intention of making Germany one of the leading Internet countries by the end of 2000. Last but not least, Schröder's government had hopes that bringing Germany quickly into the information age would also have fostered the economic development of the former East German *Länder*, particularly in those areas (such as around Jena) that seemed already technologically more prepared. The German strategy for success was thus based on a twofold approach: reinforcing those areas in which Germany already has a comparative advantage, and entering and consolidating those fields that are essential for the future development of the Internet.

Telecommunications and the new media really did give the left-wing German cabinet a lucky start. For a moment, it seemed that the promises of the new economy and the information age could become true for Germany. In August 2000, the federal government launched the auction for the third-generation mobile phone licenses that would make the Internet truly mobile. The auction ended with record takings for the government: the combined value of the bids was more than 50.5 billion euros. The total amount was higher than many (including the bidding companies themselves) expected, even higher than the already rich auction that the British government had launched in April 2000 (Woodall, 2000). The burst of the dot.com bubble in 2001, September 11, and the long structural recession that followed shattered Germany's (and Europe's) hopes for a quick recovery. More importantly, many Germans realized that ICT and the Internet would not be the goose that laid the golden eggs, but there would be high costs associated with being a member of the information society.

Protecting Germany's NII and Internet control

Before the Red–Green coalition came to power, Chancellor Kohl's conservative cabinet mostly worried about child pornography and Nazi propaganda. Because of the country's past, in 1998, Kohl's cabinet was ready to issue a "telecommunications surveillance order" requiring ISPs to build monitoring capabilities that would affect users' privacy (Hudson, 1998). The plan eventually aborted but it was a clear sign of the federal government's "Internet Angst." From the start, Gerhard Schröder's SPD – Green coalition cabinet (which took office in 1998) tried to distinguish itself from its conservative predecessor, by looking more "Internet-friendly." The new coalition wanted to show a positive attitude to ICT, emphasizing economic benefits for Germany from moving into the information economy. Such a "positive" attitude toward the Internet did not mean, however, that all German ministries and under-secretaries of the coalition were at ease with the Internet. Indeed, only a few in Schröder's coalition government were Internet-savvy (Fischer, 2000). Among those few, the most notable representative was the Green Party's leader and Foreign Affairs Minister, Joschka Fischer.

The SPD–Green government saw the CompuServe case as a "bad start," which it intended to correct. The new attitude of the modern left-wing cabinet should be "no unnecessary regulation" and "the government should promote the Internet."[11] A new package of economic, training, and technological measures aimed at moving Germany into a front-runner position in the international information society was planned by the coalition. The federal government's program was published in 1999.[12] At first, the federal government intended to focus on "basically everything": education, development, democracy, art and culture, special groups (such as women and senior citizens), consumers' protection, copyrights, and taxation.[13] The federal government wanted to promote multimedia technology in education, link schools to the Internet, put computer networking and new technologies in universities and vocational training, develop a legal framework for telecommunications, competition and cartel legislation, and so on.

The left-wing cabinet recognized that achieving those goals would be practically impossible in the short run. Nevertheless, the federal government still decided to cope with the many technical and legal problems associated with the diffusion of the Internet in a distinctively holistic manner. Data protection, cryptography, digital signature were all considered as different parts of the same challenge. Hence, they had to be tackled with consistency, and with particular attention to their interdependent effects. One of the government's first moves for the protection of Germany's NII was to reaffirm that there would be no limits to the use of strong encryption software in Germany. Internet security represented one of the crucial pillars on which the new economy was to be based. The federal government reckoned that the global network was bringing in an entirely new dimension of business and competitor espionage. Moreover, the lack of security in ICT was causing damage worth billions of euros every year at the expense of the economy and jobs. A widespread use of strong encryption software was the right solution to these problems.

Not content with allowing free use of encryption software for individuals, the federal government actually took a considerably different stance on cryptography than the US government, by providing a substantial research grant for open source software[14] to independent software developers. In November 1999, the federal government awarded roughly 170,000 euros to the German UNIX Users Group (GUUG) to help it enhance a program known as GNU Privacy Guard. This program is an open version (freeware) of the widely popular PGP. The United States had lobbied the Germans to restrict that technology for fear that criminals and terrorists might use it. The German federal government went ahead with the decision, emphasizing the need to protect electronic commerce and private communications against those very same criminals and terrorists.

Germany decided to intensify research on free source software (including the popular Linux operating system) to decrease the reliance on only US-made software, after rumors that some of the Microsoft software had been compromised by US intelligence services. In 1997, for instance, the Swedish government was astounded to learn that the version of Lotus Notes that they were using came with a "key escrow" feature that apparently made it easy for the US government to read documents. Moreover, Microsoft was said to have hidden a "NSA-key" instruction into the encryption interface for its software (cf. Levy, 2001).[15] Although these rumors were never proved, and both IBM (owner of Lotus) and Microsoft have always strongly denied any such possibilities, expectations for increasing security through the development of open source software have since steadily grown.

Germany also decided to become a leader in the encryption software business. According to the GUUG, Germany has in fact replaced the United States in the field of cryptography. For the Electronic Privacy Information Center (EPIC, 1999a: 53), "Germany has been at the forefront of countries opposing restrictions on encryption. It has been a counterbalance to US efforts to promote key escrow and international restrictions."

"No restriction" on use, and support for Germany's encryption products, has remained the mainstay of the federal government's official policy on encryption, even after September 11 and the increased attention that German law enforcement agencies devote to potential targets of terrorist attacks. Well before September 2001, even the "Internet-friendly" SPD – Green cabinet realized that neglecting the protection of the NII for an advanced country like Germany might have disastrous consequences. In line with the view of many other countries highly dependent on computer networks, the federal government considers as "critical" for the NII the following sectors: (a) banking and finance, (b) communications, (c) energy and utilities, (d) public administration, (e) public health, (f) rescue services, and (g) transport (Wigert, 2004e). The federal government also stressed the importance of equipping the administration with the modern electronic facilities for the conduct of its relations with the public and companies. The plan was to develop practical, short-term actions that would allow on-line tax declarations, telework in municipal administrations, and elections on the Internet. Within this framework, a new communication link was established between Bonn and Berlin, under the expert supervision of the BSI. The link now represents the essential technical platform for the rationalization of the work of the government.

Like all other OECD democracies, Germany views some degree of Internet control as necessary to protect their NII. Like other fellow Europeans, Germans have tagged along a distinctively different path from the United States, viewing the security of the NII as a task truly for law enforcement agencies, more than as a new mission for military or intelligence services. For the Germans, attacking the NII is "a crime," just as terrorism is a crime and not an act of war, even after 9/11 (cf. Katzenstein, 2003). In the late 1990s, alarmed by the report of the US President's Commission on Critical Infrastructure Protection (PCCIP) and the Y2K bug, the German federal government began to ponder about Germany's own dependability on critical infrastructures. As a first step, in 1997, the federal minister of the interior established an inter-ministerial working group (AG KRITIS), which undertook the first evaluation of the infrastructure sector in 1998. AG KRITIS found that awareness of threats varied considerably from agency to agency and that there was a strong reluctance to reveal known infrastructure vulnerabilities. These findings were further confirmed by the CYTEX simulation of November 2001 (Hutter, 2002).

Following the CYTEX exercise, Germany engaged in numerous other initiatives to increase the protection of its NII, including the inter-ministerial campaign "Sicherheit im Internet" ("Security in the Internet"), to increase awareness among the public and companies, and the creation of the "Secure Internet" task force. Furthermore, several government bodies (including the Bundeswehr, the German army) began to systematically analyze their information infrastructure and publish their studies (Bruno, 2002).

The federal ministry for economics and technology, along with 40 trade associations and private companies, launched the "Partnership for Secure Internet Business," specifically tailored to promote security as a quality factor in the electronic business area. These actions highlight the priorities of the SPD–Green coalition for securing the country's NII. Nevertheless, as of 2004 and almost three years after September 2001, a comprehensive policy document for the protection of Germany's NII was still lacking.

What stands in the way of government control

As is common in democracies, Internet stakeholders in Germany are the federal government, the ICT private industry, and civil liberties NGOs (the latter include consumers' organizations and trade unions, the former "counterculture" users' groups such as the Chaos Computer Club). NGOs are important for the distribution of technical information. The federal government considers the protection of the NII a necessity, but it is also aware that a securitization of the NII and of the Internet could lead to violation of freedom. Securitization would also collide with personal privacy, which Germans greatly value.

The support of consumers' organizations is also crucial. In fact, consumers' protection is taken extremely seriously in Germany. Two of the best known of such organizations, namely the Stiftung Warentest (an independent institute for carrying out comparative product tests and surveys on service) and the Association for Consumer Protection (Verbraucherschutzverein) were born in the sixties. The Warentest provides, among other services, links to web pages on secure electronic commerce and other consumers' organizations. Unlike the United States, where the US federal government and the private sector have a "love – hate" relationship, or Italy where the private sector is simply happy to follow the government's lead, in Germany there is an stable, "institutionalized" state – business relationship. In Germany, the federal government and the private sector have agreed to coordinate their efforts to put the country within the small group of advanced countries that can shape the future of the Internet. Initiative D21, ("Germany's largest public – private partnership") is a typical case in point.[16]

The D21project originated with IBM Germany at the end of 1998, when it became evident that in ICT Germany was falling behind the United States and other OECD countries. The federal government joined forces with ICT companies and D21 can now count on almost 300 members from all spheres of business, politics, and society. It represents the most noticeable instance of the coordination of forces and resources from different social, political, and economic actors to achieve the goal of "digitalizing" Germany. The SPD–Green cabinet is highly involved in the initiative. Chancellor Gerhard Schröder is himself on the advisory board. If D21 is a prototypical public – private, consensus-based initiative so often associated with the cultural image of democratic Germany, the obstacles that the federal government faces in defending the NII and modernizing the country's economy are also prototypical of the highly sensitive, contemporary Germans. The first of those obstacles is to make freedom of speech and neo-Nazi propaganda coexist.

Freedom of speech is strongly protected in Germany. Article 5 of the German Constitution unambiguously guarantees liberty of expression for all citizens, within the limits established by laws approved by the Bundestag. The same article states that there is no censorship. Despite these premises, the definition of freedom of speech indicates a considerable conceptual divide between Germany and the United States, and generally, between the latter and Europe at large (Corriere.it, 2004). Websites promoting hate or containing Nazi material that are considered protected by the free speech Amendment in the United States are outright illegal in Germany.[17] In addition to child pornography, Kohl's cabinet worried a great deal about neo-Nazi propaganda on the Internet. Now the issue of neo-Nazi propaganda is demanding attention from Schröder's coalition as well. In the last few years, neo-Nazi activists have coordinated their movements at the international level through the Internet (*The Economist*, 2000e). The US-born "Blood & Honour" group claimed to have operational members in Germany (apparently in Berlin), Scandinavia, Britain, and other countries (Kleffner, 2000).[18]

Reference to Nazi ideology has begun to appear on web pages actually based in Germany, and not simply downloaded or mirrored from sites in the United States. For instance, in August 2000, a user registered the domain name "www.heil-hitler.de" with the Berlin ISP Strato (which managed more than a million names). After the news appeared in the media, Strato unilaterally decided to cancel the registration of that domain. Although no content was on that website, Strato declared that such action meant "entering a new legal territory" (*Tageszeitung*, 2000). In fact, ISPs are not required to actively monitor what users register as domain names. The German government called for an effective and multilateral approach to tackle the issue of hate and racist material on the Internet. For instance, in June 2000, at a conference in Berlin on hate speech on the Web, the then German justice minister confirmed the principle that "what is forbidden offline must be forbidden online" (quoted in Wired News, 2000). Global rules against hate speech on the Internet and strong self-regulation by web companies should be the solution. At the same conference, Abraham Cooper (associate dean of the Los Angeles-based Simon Wiesenthal Center) remarked that the explosion of extremist websites in the United States proved the need for action. Hate websites had grown from one in 1995 to over 2,000. Despite the gravity of the situation, the federal ministry of justice admitted that the goal of international regulation was a long way off and that it was particularly difficult to establish a dialogue with the United States (cf. Corriere.it, 2004).

Unsurprisingly, the federal government was caught in a dilemma: how to isolate the channels of diffusion of racist and hate propaganda on-line, without hindering the expansion of the Internet in Germany. In the effort to curb neo-Nazi activities, the Berlin mayor (CDU) urged the federal government to consider measures to restrict the right to demonstrate (Gessler, 2000; Maschler, 2000) and use the network for communication. The federal minister of the interior, Otto Schily, also demanded that the neo-Nazi Nationaldemocratische Partei Deutschland (NPD) be banned. The German Supreme Court, however, rejected those demands. Had the constitutional court agreed, it would have been the first such instance in Germany in the last fifty years. The Red–Green coalition was uneasy about the situation because it could create a serious precedent to limit the rights to demonstrate for other causes or hamper freedom of speech.[19] Because of its past, Germany is highly sensitive to allowing unrestricted hate speech whether on-line or off-line. Understandably, a certain type of free speech evokes memories that many Germans and Europeans find very hard to bear. At the same time, the German government was uneasy about forbidding a specific group of its citizens from freely expressing their controversial views about "politics."[20]

Most Germans, however, do *not* see their freedom of speech diminished if their government wants to block hate and racist websites. Although there is disagreement about possible solutions, the majority of Germans do think that something should be done about the neo-Nazi problem. Civil liberties NGOs and the majority of Internet users tend to be more liberal than the average German and thus have more mixed feelings about whether neo-Nazis (albeit loathsome) should be guaranteed the right to speak or not. Internet stakeholders seem to share these concerns, and there is some consensus on limits to racist and hate propaganda on-line. It is worth noting that opposing Nazi propaganda tends to find German public opinion quite unanimous, while other freedom of speech topics are more controversial. For instance, in 1996 the conservative government decided to discontinue the website of the extreme left magazine *Radikal*, on the premises that it promoted political violence. The ISP that hosted the website complied. Left-wing groups and the CCC protested strongly against this act of censorship, although many Germans seemed to approve the decision.

As in many other instances, international control over Internet content regimes could be an effective answer to this problem. However, agreement on the definition of "hate" or "racism" would be hard to reach. Germany, France, and the United States, to name just three of the world's most advanced democracies, have difficulties in working together on this issue. Blocking websites or canceling neo-Nazi domain names might have some effect in Germany. Most Europeans shared Germany's opinion that European governments have a duty to stop hate speech and neo-Nazi propaganda. This was the reason why EU members decided to sign a protocol attached to the COE Cybercrime Convention that would allow police forces to take immediate action against racist and hate speech, whether on- or off-line. The Convention entered into force in 2004, and so did the protocol, but it is difficult to judge how effective it will be. In fact, European neo-Nazi groups may base their material in the United States.

Because of their experience with Nazism and later with the pervasive presence of the East German secret police during the Cold War, both East and West Germans are sensitive to the issue of free speech, but there is another issue that is taken equally to heart in Germany – privacy. The importance that Germans attribute to personal privacy has hindered Germany's protection of its NII more than once. But the German public is not likely to change its attitude. Privacy is valued by all Internet stakeholders. In the past, civil liberties (including data protection commissars) and users' NGOs and ICT firms have usually met requests by federal and local law enforcement agencies for more monitoring powers with resistance. The right of the German people to their privacy is explicitly guaranteed in the Basic Law. Article 10 states that the privacy of letters as well as the secrecy of post and telecommunications are inviolable, and those restrictions may only be ordered by law. The main legal basis for protection of personal data is the Bundesdatenschutzgesetz (BDSG), that is, the Federal Data Protection Act finally approved by the Bundestag, after several revisions and amendments, on May 18, 2001. The BDSG specifically states that the purpose of the act is to protect the individual against his right to privacy being impaired through the handling of his personal data. In addition to that, each *Land* has its own state law on data protection that is drafted along the lines of the BDSG.[21] After adopting the BDSG in the early 1990s, Germany remained, for some time, one of the few Europeans countries that did not implement the EU Directive on personal data protection (96/45/EC). Nevertheless, the prevalent German jurisprudence emphasized that the BDSG should be interpreted according to the EU Directive.

The 1996 Telecommunications Act asserted the secrecy of telecommunications and the prohibition on interception. The provisions applied to telecommunications companies that gathered detailed data on location of users and traffic. These data could be collected, processed, and used only for the proper functioning service offered (Art. 89).[22] Moreover, the Multimedia Law stated that personal data concerning the process of retrieval, access, or any other use had to be deleted immediately after termination, insofar as any further storage was not necessary for billing purposes. Last but not least, to further strengthen the protection of individual privacy, as in other EU countries, independent data protection agencies (Datenschutz) have also been established in all the *Länder* as well as at the federal level. These agencies are competent for violations of privacy committed by public administration bodies. The private sector is self-regulated, but it has to follow, naturally, the guidelines of federal (BDSG) and state laws.

Generally speaking, the principle regulating the government's or law enforcement agencies' access to personal data is that of "principle of necessity." The police, under warrant, can have access to personal information of a specific individual (or individuals) but only when the person is clearly identifiable. Investigators could not ask, for instance, for the monthly record of phone calls of an entire building or apartment block. Officers should specify exactly who the suspect to be monitored is. In 2000 and 2001, G8 governments discussed at length how long those data should be stored and made available to law enforcement officers without reaching an agreement. At first, in the aftermath of September 11, to demonstrate their support for the US-led war on terrorism, European governments announced their willingness to store data on traffic for at least a year or longer. Europeans, however failed to implement that and other measures (such as the European warrant) and found their faults exposed when Madrid suffered the train bomb attacks in March 2004. Despite the Madrid bombing, Germany, along with Sweden and Denmark, kept opposing the proposal that all countries should have minimum standards for the retention of sensitive data, such as mobile phone and Internet logs (BBC News, 2004c).

In the second and third layers of the telecommunications system where content is carried, data are differentiated, hence it can be distinguished which communication belongs to whom. Germans regulators have been able to insist that rules should be strictly followed in these layers. However, the first layer (the transmission layer) is a noteworthy exception. In the transmission layer, bytes carrying contents and bytes carrying addresses are all intermingled, making any distinction impossible. By analyzing the pattern of communication traffic, however, it is possible to pinpoint the exact location of people communicating and to follow their movements. At this level, law enforcement agencies do not need a warrant to access the data. This is an area of ongoing conflict between the data protection commissioners (who would like to apply this pattern only to heavy crime) and the police forces who would rather maintain the status quo.[23] With current portable phones it is possible to pinpoint the exact location of a person within an error of one meter. Inevitably, after September 11, the German ministry of the interior has been able to win more support in the government and the Bundestag to grant that the monitoring capability that German law enforcement agencies currently have on layer one will be retained.

Another potential point of controversy is the conduct of foreign companies when it comes to gathering personal information about German consumers. German companies do not come under the scrutiny of data protection agencies, but they are obliged to comply with German laws. Companies also have their "in house" data protection commissioner.

Theoretically, foreign companies that are not physically resident on the territory of the Federal Republic are not legally compelled to act in accordance with German privacy laws. Foreign companies could gather data about German citizens and just sell the data. Most foreign companies, however, are eager to do business in Germany or have German associates.[24] Hence, it is important for those companies to show consideration for German laws, and most foreign companies adhere to German rules as a sign of respect for their business partners.

The German attitude toward legislation on the treatment of personal data is stricter than that of the United States. In the United States, company self-regulation is the rule, and individuals are not even informed that data about them are being collected. There are also differences among fellow EU members, although the EU Directive (96/45/EC) on personal data protection provides a common framework. The German position on privacy, for instance, is different from Italy's. In Italy the treatment of personal information is generally allowed with the consent of the selected person. In Germany, the handling of personal records is in general forbidden, with the exceptions established by the law. There are, finally, more complications for the federal government when it has to strike the delicate balance between protecting the NII and controlling content. Whenever the German government takes a decision that might have even minor consequences on civil liberties, it has to do so knowing that the decision will be judged on the background of Germany's past, at home, but, even more so, abroad. This was the case, for instance, in the dispute with the Church of Scientology.[25] Another telling example of this difficulty was the much publicized "green card."

The federal government's green card initiative was intended to heighten Germany's position in the global ITC competition by granting a special working permit for non-German ICT specialists. Officially, the green cards would be available to all non-EU individuals, including, for instance, Americans or Canadians. But the federal government was mostly keen on attracting highly qualified computer scientists from developing countries, in particular India (Baldas, 2000). Locally and internationally, the scheme met considerable difficulties and criticisms.[26] In fact, the same people that the program was supposed to attract could easily obtain jobs and working permits in the United States. Top-notch computer scientists saw the United States a challenging and rewarding place. The German media pointed out that Indian and other non-European software wizards "turned up their noses at Germany's blandishments," and said that if they were going anywhere "it would be Silicon Valley" (*The Economist*, 2000d: 32). Germany is a strong, modern democracy that has come a long way from its xenophobic past. But the perception of increasing activity of neo-Nazi groups in Germany and the belief that a mild racism is indeed rooted in German society contributed to the poor results of the green card plan, which was finally abandoned. Potential candidates from India and other places continued to view the United States as a more open, non-discriminatory society, especially in comparison with Germany. September 11 and the consequent toughening of the visa process for the United States changed these perceptions. A growing number of foreign ICT specialists (especially from Asia) decided that it was more prudent to remain in their own countries (and "telework" from there).[27]

Conclusions

Post-war Germany has been characterized by a low level of social diversity and by an economy based on "social consensus" that required the tight cooperation of companies, trade unions, and the government. More recently, this socio-economic structure has become more complex. The number and diversity of stakeholders in the society has grown. The level of pluralism has increased but has not produced a fragmented and more antagonistic situation typical of highly pluralistic societies like the United States. The ICT, the NII, and the evolution of the Internet in Germany have all reflected these transformations. The Vodafone – Mannesman case, for instance, has been a watershed and a culture shock for the whole of German industry, traditionally aggressive abroad but consensus-seeking on the home, market. It signaled that social consensus and the prestige of the old industrial tradition clearly were no longer enough to guarantee a successful performance in the information age. Given open competition, the German telecom industry has begun this transformation. Mannesmann is one successful example of an engineering company that has become a leading telecom giant. Deutsche Telekom is a dominant telecom carrier in Europe that has been expanding globally. DTAG's foreign acquisition policy, however, has been criticized as "strategically bold, but tactically naïve" (*The Economist*, 2000a: 68), exemplifying how even the German telecom industry is still in the process of learning its trade in a liberalized world.

Observers familiar with German economic behavior and traditions (coordination, consensus, and a broad effort of government and social and economic actors) would consider the D21 initiative a predictable German response to the digital challenge of the information age. The "Partnership for Secure Internet Business" followed the same logic as D21, but was more specifically tailored for ICT business security. The federally funded Open Source Privacy Guards project (GNUPG) is another sign of Germany's articulated response to the Internet challenge. Within this program, the task of developing secure public key encryption software is left to a loose community of programmers and users, typical of many Internet undertakings. Uniting corporate business and open source software developers may be a masterful tactic that should reward Germany with considerable benefits. Germany has also retained its very liberal regimes on cryptography. In Germany, as in other European countries, the ICT private sector and civil liberties and users' NGOs supported the unrestricted use of encryption software. The German federal government never tried to securitize the issue.

German institutional actors have been more efficient at circulating relevant information among them than their counterparts in the United States, Italy, and other countries. Individuals have to rely more on non-institutional sources, like the media, of which there are plenty. Since control on content may affect freedom of speech, privacy and protection of personal data, and, less directly, electronic commerce and the information economy, it is not surprising that the Germans are sensitive about these "exceptions." At times, this state of affairs generates hot debates among the public. Overall, if the position of the SPD–Green cabinet has been fairly progressive on issues such as open source and encryption, the position of the German government on other topics (like racist material on the Web) is more controversial. The SPD–Green coalition has displayed a determination to protect the NII. The federal government, on the other hand, has been reluctant to increase Internet control. The government has realized, at the same time, that the German public does want content control to hinder the diffusion of Nazi propaganda, Holocaust denial, hate speech, and/or child pornography. The process of achieving consensus has been long, but, as expected, once reached, policies have been adopted and are being implemented with mixed success. Germany's Internet enthusiasm has matured within a consensus-oriented, traditional alliance of private business and government, with the addition of civil liberties NGOs and consumers' and users' groups. These conditions have allowed Germany, despite a "bumpy" start and disagreement among stakeholders, to acquire a relatively liberal regime on Internet control.

For national security, Germany's position is considerably different from that of the United States and closer to other European countries. Internet security is definitely one of the problems that demands the constant attention of the federal government, but the "national security" issue has hardly emerged in the case of Internet control. The Red–Green cabinet never tried to securitize Internet control or encryption software. Fighting terrorism remains a law enforcement enterprise. Even after September 11, in German eyes, fighting terrorism still "required intense international collaboration in multilateral institutions" (Katzenstein, 2003). The Madrid bombing attacks of 2004 did not change the German attitude, as the German reluctance about retaining telecommunication logs for a long time demonstrates. The lesson of Germany's past does not seem to wane. The German government views the implementation of the information society and the protection of the NII as being achieved only by liberalizing telecommunications, limiting Internet control to the most critical cases (child pornography and hatred speech), and, more generally, by showing a "positive" and engaging attitude to ICT, even in the "war on terror."

In the United States, protecting freedom of speech has, in the past, hampered the efforts of law enforcement personnel in this fight. The

American public has now accepted limiting civil liberties for security concerns. For the moment, other democracies (including all the Europeans) have moved in the same direction. After September 11, Germany, like all fellow EU members, signed the COE Cybercrime Convention and showed an unmistakable commitment to fighting terrorism alongside the United States. Nevertheless, Germany, dependent as it is on computer networks, has not fallen into the trap of wrecking civil liberties the way in which another fellow European country, the United Kingdom, has done. Protecting the NII remains a goal for the federal government, but censorship and control do not need to increase and securitization has never been an option. It remains a mission for law enforcement, not the military, and it should be accomplished with the consensus and cooperation of the ICT private sector. In this field, Germany, like the Scandinavians or the Netherlands, certainly has an edge. More importantly, the large majority of the German public seems to share the federal government's general attitude to the Internet. And even the majority of liberal German Internet users do not appear to be truly far away from that position.

Notes

1 "Is Germany in shape for the digital age?"
2 Internet Software Consortium, "Distribution of Top-level Domain by Host Count," January 2003, at <www.isc.org/ds/WWW-200301/dist-bynum.html> [January 25, 2004].
3 The evolution of the cellular phone market is significant for the Internet (especially in Europe), because the next generation (the third) of wireless phones will offer reliable Internet access, thus turning e-commerce into m-commerce (mobile).
4 Before the news came out, CCC leaders informed the BfV (Bundesamt für Verfassungschutz), the federal office for the defense of the constitution (Hafner and Markoff, 1995:199). The BfV, anticipating a conduct of law enforcement agencies that would become typical in many similar cases almost anywhere, simply did not know what to do.
5 Cliff Stoll (1989) has elegantly presented the whole story seen from "the other side" (that is, from the person who discovered and pursued the break-in). Stoll's book has become a classic of cyberculture.
6 The highly informative Club website is available at <www.ccc.de> [January 20, 2004].
7 The "regions" were Europe, North America, Latin America, Asia and Pacific, and Africa. ICANN hoped to register between 5,000 and 10,000 voters. In the end, more than 158,000 people had applied, and over 50 percent were verified (i.e. their e-mail address was matched by, and verified through, a physical postal address). According to the organization, it was "an overwhelming success," although one may wonder if ICANN has really been pleased with being confronted with such a large number of users, instead of the small technical group approach so typical of the past. The website archive for the election is available at <http://members.icann.org/index.html> [January 20, 2004].
8 The Spiegel Online archive is available at <www.spiegel.de/archiv/> [January 20, 2004].
9 This figure represents "unverified" voters, that is, individuals who submitted on-line applications but did not complete all the steps of the procedure. 21,600 voters were from North America (19,500, or 90 percent from the United States), and 93,800 from Asia and Pacific (the calculations are based on figures available at the ICANN archive). Candidates had to be "endorsed" by registered voters. This evaluation was based on candidates who received the highest numbers of endorsements. The high numbers of German voters and

candidates, however, should be explained not only by the attention given by the German media, but also by the fact that Germany is Europe's largest country. In all the other regions, winners came from large countries with many voters, i.e. Brazil, the United States, South Africa, China, and Japan.

10 Interview with Hans Jörg Denhardt, director of company activities with federal and regional governments, IBM Germany, Berlin, June 28, 2000. Denhardt also remarked that while it was perfectly acceptable for Germany to be seen lagging behind the United States, it was hard to accept for Germans to fall behind other European partners.

11 Interview with Bundestag member Jörg Tauss (SPD) and Andreas Schaal, Federal Ministry of Economics and Technology (Bundesministerium für Wirtschaft und Technologie), Berlin, June 26, 2000.

12 The document that summarized the measures was, meaningfully, entitled "Information and Jobs in the Information Society of the Twenty-first Century."

13 Interview with Jörg Tauss.

14 Open source software means that the source code of programs is publicly available and can be modified by developers other than the ones who wrote the software originally.

15 Lotus was used by the Swedish parliament and the military. BSI has routinely cooperated with the NSA on problems related to protecting communications.

16 The website of D21 is available at <www.initiatived21.de/>.

17 On this topic, the best portal is "Hate Watch" at <www.hatewatch.org/frames.html> (August 1, 8, and 21, 2000). Excellent examples of pro-hatred and pro-Nazi websites are collected, including <www.americannaziparty.com>, <www.adolfhitler.com>, or <www.theneworder.org> to name just a few. While these websites contain only neo-Nazi propaganda, Hate Watch has also links to white supremacist, racial discrimination, anti-gay, anti-Semitic, etc., sites.

18 On its web pages, the neo-Nazi group used to call for the battle against the "Zionist Occupation of Government."

19 These facts happened in the summer of 2000 in relation to the decision of the NPD to march through the Brandenburg Gate on January 19, 2001, Holocaust Memorial Day. The words of a spokesperson for the Trade Union Association showed what many Germans thought about such an event: "In 1933 the SA marched through the Brandenburg Gate. And in January 2001 we should see the NPD march in? No way!" (Gessler, 2000: 19; author's translation). In the end, the government decided that it had no legal basis to prohibit the march as an expression of freedom of speech and the NPD was authorized to carry on its rally (but not through the Brandenbug Gate). Attendance was very low.

20 *The Economist* (2000e: 17) noted that to uphold freedom of expression, as Germany was committed to do, also meant to uphold the freedom to offend "however vile that may be."

21 The law for the state of Berlin, for instance, was approved by the local senate in 1995.

22 The federal and local organizations entitled to demand information on telecommunication traffic are (1) courts, public prosecutors' offices, and other judicial authorities as well as other criminal prosecution authorities, (2) federal and state police forces for purposes of averting danger, (3) customs investigation offices for criminal proceedings and the Customs Criminological Office, and (4) the federal and state authorities for the protection of the Constitution (e.g. BfV and BKA), the Federal Armed Forces Counter-Intelligence Office, and the Federal Intelligence Service (Bundesnachrichtendienst, BND).

23 Personal conversation with Hansjürgen Garstka, Data Protection and Information Access Commissioner of the State of Berlin, in June 2000.

24 See, for instance, how key Internet companies like Yahoo!, Amazon, or Google have been eager to establish German branches (the dot.de) of their business.

25 In 1997 the government, with a large backing in the media, decided to curtail the activity of the religious group Scientology, accusing it of being a money-making structure. In this case, much of the rage against this action was generated in the United States where the group was born and where it benefited from the protection granted to all religious

organizations. Germany was accused by many in the United States (including various Hollywood stars) of reverting to its Nazi past. The large majority of Germans, however, did support the federal government, believing that the issue had nothing to do with religious matters but rather with fraud and exploitation of weak individuals.

26 In the early 2000 regional elections, the North Rhine-Westphalia Christian Democrats used the slogan *Kinder statt Inder* ("Children instead of Indians") to call for investing the money allocated for the green card program to train German pupils in software skills at school, rather than using it to attract IT professionals from India (Koch *et al.*, 2000: 41; *The Economist*, 2000d: 32).

27 Several foreign science and technology students, stranded from American universities because of visa requirements, have increasingly been offered places in Australian, British and, ironically, German universities.

6 "*Internet per tutti!*"
Italy's elusive information society

> The development of the Information Society is a major goal of the Italian Government.
>
> (Massimo D'Alema, former Italian Premier, February 1999)

For a long time, "cabinet instability" has been almost a hallmark of modern Italy. There have been more than fifty governments since World War II, with an average tenure of less than one year. Several authors (Koff and Koff, 2000; Pasquino, 2000) noted that part of the problem with the executive branch lies with the fact that the constitution does not clearly spell out the functions of government. Under these conditions, the prime minister becomes a "limited leader," and the formation of a government can be a very complex matter. As a welcome change for Italians, the situation has, somehow, stabilized toward the end of the 1990s.

Between 1996 and 2004 there have been only four governments holding office, with some cabinet reshuffling. In 1996, the center-left *Ulivo* (Olive Tree) coalition won the general election. Its acclaimed leader, Romano Prodi, promised that his government would last the full term. In 1998, premier Prodi lost to a vote of confidence, and was replaced by Massimo D'Alema (of the Democrats of the Left, the heirs of the Italian Communist party) who also promised that his government would endure until the end of its term. In April 2000, following a serious defeat in local elections, Giuliano Amato, a former Socialist and a professor of constitutional law, replaced D'Alema.[1] Amato also promised he would lead his government until the general election scheduled for 2001. Thus, the *Ulivo* coalition that had guaranteed the Italian electorate that its government would, at last, follow the example of other European countries and last the full five years, was shattered after two years, its leader Prodi removed (to the new post of EU Commission president) and replaced by a premier who, at the general elections in 1996, did not even run. Instead of the promised one government for the full tenure, Italians had to cope with three cabinets, which was a marked improvement, but still a far cry from the praxis of other advanced democracies.

Much as in the United States and other EU countries, all political parties before the 2001 elections courted Italian Internet users, who were (mostly) the young, educated, and interested.[2] They were also more willing to volunteer for campaigns and to vote. The Internet was the focus of attention of the right and the left alike because the center-right leader and Italy's media mogul, Silvio Berlusconi, had an immediate and clear personal interest in the convergence of media, telecom, and the Internet.[3] The incumbent center-left government, on the other hand, had hoped, to no avail, that a good performance of the new economy (with lower unemployment and rising GNP) would help defeat the Berlusconi coalition. In fact, in May 2001 the center-left coalition was soundly defeated by the center-right alliance led by Berlusconi.

In an effort to trim down Berlusconi's media supremacy before the general elections of 2001, the center-left coalition had enacted the equal access law during the previous year. The law imposed an equal "quota" of political commercials on all TV broadcasters (private and public alike) for all political parties. As a consequence of that law, the center-right alliance could not take advantage of the privileged position of its leader, Silvio Berlusconi, by flooding all the private television channels with political spots for his alliance. The Internet was exempt from this limitation but it did not have any major impact on the final political outcome.[4] Nevertheless, Berlusconi business strategists and advisors realized that the network had become an important element of the media world and thus it should be included in all the future plans of Italy's media and entertainment conglomerate. Several acts of the Berlusconi government now point in that direction.

Judged by Italian standards, the governments that have ruled Italy at the turn of the century have been alluded to as exemplary long-standing governments (Koff and Koff, 2000). Nevertheless, the electorate still perceived all of them (with no exception) to be so entangled in the coalition partners' petty in-fighting that they gave the image of being feeble, shaky, and about to be replaced (Pasquino, 2000). They were seen as paternalistic and aloof as all the governments before them. Berlusconi's cabinet, with all its emphasis on being "new" to politics, was no exception. On the one hand, scholars writing about the composition of modern Italy's governments fear that what they write today will no longer be (literally) the case by the time they publish their analysis. Ironically, some features seem to remain the same, or "to change without change," as Giuseppe Tomasi di Lampedusa masterfully put it in his book, *Il Gattopardo*.

Before the privatization of the 1990s, Italian politics was a strong presence in the telecom sector. Many government parties saw such an opportunity as a useful economic base for their political activities. Despite this strong interference, the Italian government had less direct control over public telecoms than in other countries. The bureaucratic elites who ran the telecom companies had vested interests in maintaining autonomy from the government, while recurrent government crises prevented continuity of policy action in the modernization and reorganization of public telecommunications (Natalicchi, 2001). The Italian case provides a valuable contribution to the generalizations of this study. Italy's structurally "weak" governments represent a remarkable juxtaposition to the United States' and Germany's traditionally more stable governments. The Italian state also has a tradition of intruding into the economy. For a long time, most political parties (with the exception of the extreme right and left) and their large apparatus of middle-men and intermediaries have operated to extract maximum benefits from such situations.

To some extent, Italy's malaise is common to most of Europe. Attitudes toward information and communication technologies, for instance, are quite similar. As early as the mid-1980s, European leaders realized the importance of the telecommunication sector and that the United States and Japan were making impressive gains in it (Noam, 1986). Despite the self-interest of bureaucracies, the bureaucratic and hierarchical style of decision-making, the short-term interests of domestic manufacturers, and scientific nationalism, by the end of the 1990s the Europeans had caught up in most areas of telecommunications. Italy ranks 26 in the Network Readiness Index (out of 82 countries), after France and before Spain and Portugal. It ranks 20 out of 72, just next to Spain and before the Czech Republic), in the 2001 Technology Achievement Index (UNDP, 2001). Finally, Italy ranks 22 among 178 "economies," according to the ITU (2003a) Digital Access Index. These are the ICT figures of a post-industrial, modern OECD country, struggling to join the top group, as a "potential leader." Italy is still an elusive member of the world information society.

Lijphart (1999: 177) in his classification of democracies puts Italy within the "pluralist" group (along, for example, with Spain). This position classifies Italy as a low-corporatist state (but less than France) where, before the reforms of 1994, all major parties participated in the policy-making process. Thus, Italy now has relatively few formal access points to the executive but substantially more informal ones, thanks to the experience with the trade unions and other grass-roots political organizations. Nevertheless, individuals and civil liberties NGOs should overcome considerable obstacles to have policies modified. Within the ICT sector, independent businesses promoting open source software find it difficult to break the bureaucracy's traditional inertia, which prefers to rely on Microsoft products, while the once publicly owned telecom sector has retained reliable contacts with the government. Last but not least, the current premier, Silvio Berlusconi, a business tycoon, has conflicts of interest between his institutional role and the future of his media empire. This is the state of affairs as the Italian parliament is making strategic decisions about digital and satellite television and the development of broadband.

When it comes to shaping national security policy, much as in Germany, Italian governments have always made it clear that policy belonged strictly to the "public" sphere and that the intervention of the private sector should be limited to the defense industry. With the end of the Cold War and the privatization wave that has touched all advanced economies, this unofficial, yet strict, policy has relaxed. Nonetheless, the vast majority of Italians, like most Europeans and the Japanese, still tend to believe that national security policy is a job for the government. Despite the positive experience with partisan warfare during World War II, Italy never seriously considered a Scandinavia-style "total defense" option, even in the most dangerous moments of the Cold War. It is not surprising that the necessary public–private partnership to protect the national information infrastructure has emerged only slowly and reluctantly.

As a latecomer to the Internet and ICT in general, Italy has quickly recovered ground. For instance, virtually every Italian has a cellular phone. The social acceptance of the Internet, however, is still a work in progress. Italians at large are troubled by child pornography, cybercrime, and terrorism, both domestic and international. They worry (although not for the reasons that the media world would like them to) about intellectual property rights because they fear that they would pay for CDs and DVDs. They somehow feel uneasy about the loss of privacy, but issues such as protection of the NII or free speech (let alone "technicalities" like open source software or cryptography) leave them nonplussed, if not aloof. This scant popular support and the low level of pluralism leave the few watchdogs (users' and civil liberties NGOs) with a difficult job. Italy is still an elusive member of the information society. Italians love to communicate (as their culture and traditions show) and love the "outer shell" of technology. They would buy the latest ICT gadgets, but, on average, are not interested in knowing what complex systems make those gadgets work. Above all they do not want to be told how vulnerable and fragile those systems may be, that their country is highly dependent on computer networks, and that being a member of the global information society has costs in addition to advantages.

Italy, the Internet, and the information society

Consistent with its historical tradition, the Internet was introduced in Italy by scientists in the 1980s, and, more precisely, by nuclear physicists, whose field has a strong historical heritage of research and innovation. Nuclear physicists were the first in Italy to think in terms of developing a scientific knowledge network, and thus created the INFNet[5] in 1980 to link all the nuclear physics institutes, locating the main node in Bologna (Siroli *et al.*, 1997). In 1988, the ministry for universities launched the Group for Research Network Harmonization[6] with the goal of integrating INFNet with other Italian research networks.

For a long time, the Internet was an almost exclusive domain of scientists and researchers. The Internet was not, however, Italy's only packet-switching network. Telecommunications were a state monopoly and thus, in 1986, the telephone company SIP (Società Italiana per L'Esercizio Telefonico, forefather of today's Telecom Italia) and the ministry for posts and telecommunications launched their proprietary packet network reserved predominantly for business users. With this initiative, SIP/Telecom Italia intended to extract maximum advantage from its monopolist position that allowed it to offer high value-added services to the business sector, providing only a basic telephone service to the rest of the country. SIP/Telecom Italia fought a hard rearguard battle to defend its monopoly until 1995–1996, when it was finally privatized. Given that market forces were virtually absent from the telecom policy process (Natalicchi, 2001), the success of this operation can be ascribed entirely to the pressure of the European Commission and the work of the Italian Antitrust Authority.[7] Telecom Italia and its cellular phone associate, TIM (Telecom Italia Mobile), still have the largest share of the fixed and mobile telecom markets, followed by Infostrada and Wind. Telecom Italia is thus one of the crucial counterparts of the government when it comes to telecom and the Internet in Italy.

In the spring of 1999, Olivetti took control (51 percent) of the incumbent operator, Telecom Italia, and, at the same time, it sold Infostrada to Mannesmann (BBC News, 1999). Five years earlier the company itself as well as Italian public opinion would have considered such an occurrence impossible. In spite of the fact that Telecom Italia had been privatized, the new management has ruthlessly taken advantage of the still quasi-monopolist position of Telecom Italia in the local call market, disappointing many users who had hoped that privatization would end the state's involvement in the telecommunications market. Moreover, while claiming to be like any other telecom carrier, Telecom Italia used its dominant position in local calls to boost its business as the major Italian ISP. Several ICT businesses (from small ISPs to large telecom carries), consumers' organizations, and civil liberties NGOs have been battling against Telecom Italia's monopolist position, demanding more competition and greater transparency for tariffs. Ironically, Telecom Italia undertook another battle against government interference in the telecom sector. The center-left government, after the privatization of Telecom Italia, tried to remain neutral, but in 2000 Wind and Infostrada appeared to be vulnerable to a takeover, and Enel (the half-privatized energy provider) took over both telecom companies. Hence, the government reentered the telecom sector via the back door. The anti-Telecom Italia front harshly criticized this move.

Liberalization of the telecom sector was a necessary step for the diffusion of the Internet in Italy, but was not sufficient. The Prodi government was the first to recognize, in the mid-1990s, the potentialities and problems associated with the country's increasing dependence on computer networks. It thus established, in February 1999, a study group ("a permanent workshop") open to public institutions, businesses, unions, universities, research institutes, associations, etc., with the goal of monitoring and promoting ICT developments to benefit Italy. The most crucial problems for

Italy were extensive computer illiteracy (including insufficient knowledge of English), lack of attention by local authorities and municipalities (with a few exceptions like Bologna), and cultural conservatism in the productive system (industry, credit, finance).[8] The center-left cabinet recognized that extensive investments in human capital and infrastructure would be necessary for Italy to become a fully-fledged member of the global information society.

Among the activities targeted to improve the quality of human capital were a better computers-to-students ratio, mobility of researchers to industry, better coordination between private and public research, and spin-off of research for companies. Training in ITC for unemployed or unskilled workers and new growth opportunities for southern Italy were also high on the government agenda. The main financial source for these initiatives should have been a percentage of the expected profits (between 20 and 25 billion euros) from the auction of licenses for the third generation (3G) of mobile phones in the fall of 2000 and EU funds. In addition, Telecom Italia would have been able to complete the upgrade of the communication network, as previously agreed with the government. All these prospects resulted in bitter disappointment for the center-left government and the public. The EU has indeed allocated substantial funds for ICT infrastructure and research, but Italy has always been rather inefficient at spending EU funds and this proved to be the case also with ICT.

The auction did not produce the expected results for the government. The Italian government hoped to imitate the successful auctions of Germany and Britain, albeit on a smaller scale. At the end of October 2000, after only a few days of auctioning, five licenses were awarded to five of the six participants (one of the contestants withdrew) for slightly over 12 billion euros. It was a serious blow for the Amato government, which was highly criticized by the opposition and by the international press for not considering other auction cases that had disappointing results.[9] Last but not least, Telecom Italia claimed that the cost of the 3G license had been high and that it would slow down considerably the plans to modernize its infrastructure and to wire up "the last mile" for broadband access.[10]

Only a minority of the population still owns a personal computer. Even in 2002 (that is, after the spreading of the "Internet mania") less than one Italian out of four was classified as a computer user, according to the ITU. Internet users have been an even tinier minority, despite claims to the contrary. In the same period, among the various attempts to address the problem of the skepticism and aloofness of Italians toward the computer, the center-left government launched the "PC for students" project. Within this framework, students entering secondary schools are given the option of purchasing computers at subsidized prices. Later, the Berlusconi government also adopted a similar initiative. In both cases, however, the impact was minimal because those students who were interested in ICT already had their computers but could not exchange them for new ones, while those who were not interested bought the computers and left them unused on their desks. Computer illiteracy among students was a problem, but computer illiteracy among teachers was an even bigger problem.

If Italy undoubtedly sits at the bottom end of Europe's most computerized countries, Italians are among the top countries in the area of portable phone usage. Basically the whole Italian population (according to ITU, 93.87 percent in 2002) uses cellular phones. Only Scandinavians are more eager users. The monopolist telecom company introduced car phones in Italy at the beginning of the 1990s, targeting business customers. Despite their cost, they proved to be a considerable success. Soon it began to commercialize cellular phones, whose popularity dwarfed car phones. Business customers were fond of the new communication device, and cellular phones quickly became a fashionable status symbol among non-business users. The "exclusivity" did not last long, and cellular phones turned out for Italians to be the most popular invention for communications since the telephone itself. Telecom carriers and national and EU regulators realized the potential almost simultaneously. Consequently, as the offer from state phone companies attracted more and more customers and telecom became the market for the 1990s, their monopolies started to be questioned at the EU level, allowing new and aggressive competitors into the market. Italians have fallen in love with cellular phones for various reasons. Economies of scale have allowed for lower tariffs and diversified offers while the demand has grown steadily.

Taking advantage of prepaid cards and falling prices of handsets, parents have discovered an attractive way of keeping in touch with (and keeping track of) their adolescent children, who have become adept at instant messaging (SMS) to communicate with their peers. The boom in cellular phone use was not paralleled by an increase in Internet usage by the larger public. The cost of local phone calls, the lack of cable television (which helped the spread in the United States), and a generally, lukewarm attitude toward computers all contributed to keep the level of Internet growth below the other large EU countries. European telecom carriers hoped that by putting the Internet on third-generation cellular phones, they would soon take Europe to the level of the United States and help fill the ICT gap (*The Economist*, 1999b). Those hopes scarcely materialized, especially in Italy.

Italy's attitude toward controlling the Internet has been a rather "benign" one compared to that of the United States, even before September 2001. Like other fellow EU members, Italy's attitude was of apparent laxity and *laissez-faire*. This was, however, due more to a lack of understanding of ICT in general and the Internet in particular than for any other reason. Experts had long warned that Italy was slowly but inevitably becoming a country highly dependent on computer networks (Cammarata, 2004). The spread of the Internet among the public at, large in addition to positive returns (e-commerce, new revenues, etc.), would have also raised the risk factors for the whole of Italian society. But the government and the bureaucracy seemed very slow to focus on this trade-off. Furthermore, to realize the benefits of the Internet the government had to convince public opinion. To achieve such a goal, the political elite had to stress the positive and downplay the negative of the Internet.

In the early 1990s, the Italian public considered the Internet to be synonymous with "child pornography." Popular reactions, encouraged by sensationalist journalists, obliged governments to take action at national and EU levels. The scarcity of computer-literate people was among the reasons why the Internet was mostly seen as a tool for child molesters. When the perception (fuelled by government enthusiasm and news from the United States) that the Internet was a sort of economic miracle began to spread among the larger public, the initial "Internet-phobia" was followed, in 1999–2000, by the "Internet mania." Words like new economy, net-economy, Web, and Internet entered the daily vocabulary of most Italians. Obviously, going from little public knowledge to a frenzied and emotional popularity, the diffusion of the Internet in Italy yielded some questionable outcomes. The D'Alema cabinet reacted enthusiastically and (apparently) eagerly to intervene in this new "area of competence." Among other things, it nominated an ad hoc Internet undersecretary and proposed the creation of a "state portal" that would have been free for small and medium-size enterprises.[11]

Part of the government's eagerness was understandable. Between 1999 and 2000, Italy's media, stock market investors, bankers, and ordinary citizens caught the "new economy" craze. In mid-2000 there were dozens of trading operators, and several thousands trading accounts in banks. In newspapers and on television commercials the Internet and the new economy were endlessly promoted. To achieve spectacular performances on the Italian stock exchange, companies included the words "Internet," "Net," or "Web" in their trademarks. As a government official put it, "Everybody started lecturing about the Internet. Journalists and business people, who a year earlier had no idea of what the Internet was, began to explain what the new economy was."[12] Several government reports concluded that the new economy would be one of the most outstanding economic opportunities for Italy. The new economy bubble burst in 2000. September 11, 2001, crushed what hope was left that the frenzied period of stock exchange speculation and apparently unlimited growth would soon come back.

During the period of the center-left coalition (1996–2001), serious structural obstacles were never overcome, despite high expectations that the Internet would become a mass phenomenon in Italy (Caravita, 2000) or that new cellular phones would bring the Internet to millions of Italian phone enthusiasts. In July 2000, not one single Italian location was mentioned in the ranking of the world's forty-six "venture capitals" prepared by *Wired Magazine*.[13] In the same year, not one of the ten world ICT "colossi" listed by the Italian newspaper *La Repubblica* was Italian (Zampaglione, 2000: 38).

Only Britain (Vodafone), Germany (Deutsche Telekom), and Finland (Nokia) represented Europe. Much to the disappointment of Internet-enthusiast policy-makers, a considerable number of companies still considered electronic commerce to be "a waste of time, a game, or, at the most, the illusion of being part of the global market."[14] A year before September 11, the prestigious economic newspaper *Il Sole 24 Ore* (2000a) continued to forewarn its public about Italy's abysmal performance. Italian banks simply persisted in viewing home banking as a public relations exercise.

If the dot.com bubble bursting took many Italians by surprise, many had remained skeptical that the Internet could change the rules of economics or bring Italy into the information society overnight. What happened in Italy seems really to support Gadrey's (2003) argument that the new economy was a myth mostly developed through the discourse of politics and the media. The dot.com demise and the NASDAQ crash figuratively put an end to the early period of Internet growth in Italy and also to the political experience of the center-left coalition. The Berlusconi government had a different view of the media and the Internet, but it had to start from where the opposition left to bring Italy fully into the information society.

The NII and what Italy controls on the Internet

Although Italian politics had long been involved with the national economy, until the 1990s privatization the telecom sector was seen as marginal because it could hardly provide revenues and power. Past Italian governments considered national security and public order the exclusive domain of the state. The telecom monopolist (controlled by the minister of treasury) might be called in for wire-tapping or in a supporting role when required. Political leaders could not even conceive that, one day, the technical expertise of private businesses, individual groups, and associations would become absolutely necessary to guarantee those public goods. In these respects, the arrival of the Internet and the country's growing dependence on computer networks have been a true watershed for Italy's notion of the state's role and responsibilities.

Currently, the country's main public ICT concerns are child pornography and children's safety on-line, cybercrime (frauds, scams, gambling, and money laundering), and terrorism (Strano, 2002; Vulpiani, 2002). Business people have long been aware of the economic damage caused by viruses and worms, unauthorized access, or vandalism. It was mostly bored kids in search of a challenge that were accountable for those damages (Ardù, 2000). Intellectual property rights are a more recent add-on, since the entertainment and music industries undertook several initiative in the United States. National security is hardly mentioned and neither is the protection of the NII. As of 2004, there is no specific state agency to protect the NII, but only attempts at coordinating different committees, within the ICT sector representatives and government officials. Privacy and freedom of speech are, to some extent, of less importance to the government, although the delicate balance between free speech and racist ideas does emerge in the debate on how to fight cybercrime. Here Italy's position is much aligned with that of the other EU partners, and the Berlusconi cabinet signed the COE Convention on Cybercrime in November 2003. Public plans or documents on possible threats to the NII have been scarce and the debate on the media has been nonexistent. The department of civil defense has studied the problem of a collapse of sections of the NII and rehearsed possible remedies, but it is reactive, not proactive, and it has no assignment in the protection of the NII.

Italian policy-makers and state officials have been distinctively known for their inability to include individuals and associations (with the exception of political parties) in the management of public goods and the economy.[15] The business sector itself has never been good at presenting an independent (let alone antagonistic) position to the political elite, thus reinforcing the opinion that running the country and the economy was a job best left to professional politicians. After World War II, EU membership and the unabated influence of American business culture have helped Italy to mildly correct some of these problems (and thus make Italy more modern). But "old habits die hard," and despite the fast-paced nature of the Internet and its grass-roots users, some of the old rigidities of Italian bureaucracy reemerged. An example of the cultural inability of the political elite and of the business establishment to manage the unusual occurrences of a modern country was the controversy over the country's top-level domain. Since the mid-1980s, Italy's top-level domain (dot.it) has been administered by the National Research Council (CNR), following an agreement with the Internet Assigned Names Authority (the forebear of today's ICANN). The registration law excluded individuals from holding domains and the CNR had to operate mostly with universities and a few large companies. Only individuals with a tax registration number (thus having the legal representation of a firm) could acquire a domain.[16] Despite these restrictive procedures, the percentage of registered domains grew considerably in the period 1994–2000.

In the midst of the Internet frenzy, the government decided to liberalize the rules for domain names: the tax registration requirement was lifted and it was possible for an individual to register more than one domain. The registration authorities had only to verify that the required names were available. Once the media received the news a rush to register names ensued, including "domain-grabbing" acts.[17] Some of the domains involved names of politicians who urged the government to intervene. Hence, the government announced a bill to regulate anew the ownership of domain names. If Parliament had passed the bill, however, it would have contradicted ICANN's first-come-first-served rule. Ultimately, the first-come-first-served rule was preserved and the protection of well-known names and brands was left to the civil code.[18] In this instance, the "self-governance" spirit of the Internet was, generally speaking, preserved. Nevertheless, the core of the problem was that some cabinet members were convinced that the only solution was a national law, not governance (seen as inefficient). Users' groups and civil liberties NGOs opposed the move. They claimed that it was unnecessarily complicating matters and increasing government control and that, evidently, the policy-makers could not grasp the technical structure of the Internet. The private sector sought contacts with both parties, showing a preference to "cosy up" with the government, with the hope of winning a better deal.

Much as in the United States case, the outcome of the domain name dispute could have cast its shadow over the Internet's future development in Italy. In the former case, the provisional convergence of "hands-off" government policy with business interests and NGOs' support led to establishing the only real governance body, ICANN. In Italy that synergy never materialized, not even temporarily. A certain animosity prevailed among civil liberties NGOs and users' groups, typically mistrustful of the government, while the private sector seemed more interested in doing business the "old way," namely appeasing the government. This lack of cooperation between users, NGOs, and the private sector only reinforced the wariness of all players when it came to other essential issue areas.

While the number and functions of ministries involved with the task of protecting Italy's NII may vary from cabinet to cabinet,[19] the operative institutions that are assigned to the task can be clustered into three main categories: public administration service and utility providers, law enforcement agencies, and defense. The former group is the largest and it includes both government bodies and private organizations. The government's main tools are the National Center for Information Infrastructure in Public Administration (Centro Nazionale per l'Informatica nella Pubblica Amministrazione, CNIPA) and the authority for communications. The center was established in 2003 (although its predecessor was founded as early as 1993) with the mission of standardizing PA networks and implementing the digital signature and other e-government initiatives (to improve the overall quality of PA services).

Another decisive area where CNIPA has played a primary role is in authorizing "trusted third parties" (mostly banks or financial institutions) that could supply official digital signatures to individuals (electronic documents with digital signatures now have the same legal validity as hard-copy documents). As part of its effort to protect the NII, in October 1999 CNIPA's predecessor published a very detailed ten-point guideline about how system managers in the PA (and, indirectly, in the private sector as well) should conduct themselves. The goal was to achieve a standardized defense, but the effort was short-lived owing to the inertia of many civil service officials and the lackadaisical attitude of private businesses.[20] A noteworthy law enforcement instrument that is hosted at CNIPA is the anti-cybercrime group (Gruppo Anticriminalità Telematica). Supposedly, this anti-cybercrime group should draw together the most skilled personnel from all law enforcement agencies.

The authority for communications (roughly equivalent to the American FCC) was established in July 1997 and operates in the telecommunications market and in audiovisual deregulation. Among others, its tasks include providing oversight security of communications, regulating relations between operators and consumers, and promoting integration of national networks with international ones. There is, thus, considerable overlapping between the authority and CNIPA. Although a technical institution like the latter, the authority has some policy-making functions that make it more prominent than CNIPA. It oversees, in fact, the development of satellite and digital television, ensures equal political access to the media and protection of minors, and protects intellectual property rights. Digital television is a fundamental issue for prime minister Silvio Berlusconi, who has tried (with mixed success) to guarantee particularly favorable conditions for his media empire.

The protection of minors using the Internet is a major concern in Italy. It is the main justification that law enforcement officers use for monitoring websites and Internet communications, and for cracking down on improper operations in this area. There, law enforcement officers usually receive widespread public support. Last but not least, the Berlusconi cabinet has followed United States practices to ensure copyright protection and to target piracy. Law enforcement officers have intensified their efforts against those copying software and downloading music. These activities are popular with young users, who now face criminal charges. To fight cybercrime and terrorism on-line, the ministries of interior and of justice set up two inter-ministerial groups, one on information networks security and the other on cryptography. These groups are hosted at the ministry of communication. The working group on network security regularly gathers together 15–20 experts form the ministries of interior, justice, industry, communications, the anti-Mafia national directorate, the postal police, the communications authority, and the National Research Council (CNR). The working group on cryptography includes, among others, specialists from the ministries of interior, justice, communications, the authority for privacy protection, and the CNIPA.

The postal police, a specialized branch of the Italian national police, was established in 1981 to safeguard postal and telecommunications services. It became further specialized in March 1998, as the postal and communications police. The branch coordinates the operational activities of various field offices, conducts analysis of high-tech crime, and defines the appropriate countering strategies. Within the organization, the investigative division staff plays a key role in researching and investigating computer crime, especially related to electronic commerce and Internet fraud. The territorial organization of the postal police includes 19 field offices and 76 postal police sections located in the principal Italian cities. The legal basis for the activity of law enforcement agencies is the computer crime law of December 1993, which defined new offenses and made more investigative tools available to police forces by amending and adding new provisions to the Italian Penal Code and Penal Procedure Code.[21]

The law on computer crime marked a period of time in which technical advice to legislators was probably sketchy and the implementation of the law has turned out to be "unnecessarily complicated" (Corasaniti, 1998: 137). When the law was first enacted, in the mid-1990s, police investigators confiscated all the objects related to computers from suspects, including the mouse pad (cf. Ciccarelli and Monti, 1997). They ordered the termination of all the activities of unaware ISPs that had been used by suspects, thus depriving other baffled users of their legitimate Internet access. Knowledge-able observers noted that these operations should be performed by properly trained personnel (Corasaniti, 1998; Vulpiani, 2002). Things should have improved since then. Nonetheless, although the ministry of interior asserts that the personnel of the investigative division is now highly skilled with specific legal and technical knowledge, even in the late 1990s the Italian police were still seizing every item.[22]

Another important police branch assigned to monitoring Internet activities is the Guardia di Finanza (GdF), under the authority of the ministry of finance.[23] One of its areas of competence is fighting software and audiovisual piracy. In the spring of 2000, the GdF special unit for fiscal crimes produced a report highlighting the major crimes that are likely to occur on-line (various types of fraud and money laundering). After the US Congress passed the Digital Millennium Copyright Act in 1998, the EU (also lobbied by the entertainment industry) followed suit with a directive that obliged all member states to take appropriate measures to fight violations of intellectual property rights.[24] The GdF was thus instructed to increase its efforts to stifle software piracy and pursue illegal file sharing on the Internet. The GdF has exclusive jurisdiction in this area of cybercrime.

Conspicuous for its absence in these inter-ministerial groups (and in the whole debate on NII and Internet control) is the ministry of defense (MOD). The explanation is straightforward: to date the MOD (and the cabinet itself) does not believe that the threat of information warfare through the Internet is a "clear and present danger." They believe that extensive cybercrime could be a problem, but that is still the domain of law enforcement officers, not the military.[25] For the first time, Italian troops participating in the peace-keeping operation in East Timor in the spring of 2000 could rely on the Internet for communicating with Italy, mostly for personal communications. Since then, this practice has become common among military personnel of several advanced countries involved in active operations, such as in Afghanistan in 2002 and Iraq in 2003.

In 2002 the MOD began to consider the Internet not only for self-promotion of the armed services (especially to attract volunteers), but also as a functional tool (Ministero della Difesa, 2002). By 2003 the ministry developed its own network (Defensenet), which was linked with the PA unified network (managed by CNIPA) for unclassified information. The MOD used Defensenet to build a secure intranet for war-fighting applications. The Italian army has its C4IEW (Command, Control, Computers, Intelligence, and Electronic Warfare) units, based in Anzio, near Rome.[26] However, as of 2004, the Italian MOD has not published any document on the armed forces doctrine to conduct information operations or protect the NII.

Major development programs in the area of information operations in Italy are planned in cooperation with other European and NATO partners. There seems to be no concern among the Italian military that the United States is the undisputed information superpower, and that, if information superiority were mismanaged, it would cause a serious backlash against the United States. The consequences for Italy, the reasoning goes, would be far less dramatic. Overall, it seems that Internet security and protection of the NII in Italy is almost exclusively synonymous with fighting cybercrime. Terrorism is the one area in which one would expect greater involvement of the armed forces. Yet there is little evidence that cyberterrorism may be a cause for concern for the Italian defense forces. At the end of 2003, a report by the Italian military intelligence service did point out that the country infrastructures (water and energy distribution) could be a target for al-Qaeda operatives (Sarzanini, 2003). However, they believe that terrorists would attack these infrastructures with traditional explosives, not digital tools. The Internet was also central but only for perception management purposes, namely propaganda and psychological warfare.

The military and law enforcement agencies view terrorism the same way. Italy has long experienced both international terrorism and domestic extremism (on both left and right). In the past, extreme-right terrorists targeted both people and some transportation infrastructures (trains), whereas extreme-left terrorist groups almost exclusively targeted specific individuals. The former killed many more innocent bystanders. The best-known terrorist organization in Italy was the Red Brigades, which were active in the 1970s and 1980s. After a long hiatus, the Red Brigades resumed operations in the late 1990s and did use the new ICT for communications between themselves and with the media (CNN.com, 2002b; Vulpiani, 2002). The terrorists, however, were not particularly adopt at using these technologies and their attempts actually backfired and provided the police with clues and information (Fusani, 2003b).[27] Neo-fascist organizations use the Internet for their propaganda as do extreme-left and anarchist groups. Law enforcement officers actively monitor their websites, and find that anarchist groups' websites are more "dangerous." The reason is that the Red Brigades may have supporters in anarchist groups who are part of Italy's anti-globalization movement (Bonini, 2003). The mostly young anti-globalization movement is very active on-line and has a loose, networked structure, but there is no evidence that it has ever tried to launch attacks on the NII or even government websites.

The watchdogs that stand in the way

At first glance, the overall number of Italian Internet users runs in the millions and seems truly remarkable. A closer look, however, reveals that those "millions" include individuals who browsed the Internet only once and then decided that it was not worth their time and attention. Are those millions all Internet stakeholders? Are their voices heard concerning how much control of Internet content is justified so that the state can protect the NII? The answer to both questions is negative. The majority of the Italian public hardly thinks about freedom of speech and the Internet. Sporadically, they tend to be nervous about their privacy on-line and are afraid when they hear news about child pornography. Recently, many Italians have learned that terrorists may wreak havoc on the country's infrastructures, but they do not know how likely this is or doubt it could happen (finding valid information and diversity of opinions on these issues appear arduous). What is problematic is that even educated Italians are not accustomed to check for multiple sources. Overall, the vast majority of the public simply does not bother to acquire information on topics that it considers marginal. Hence, despite the growing availability of the Internet in Italy, the issue areas of Internet control and the protection of the NII are still debated only among a relatively small group of more or less well-informed actors, the few watchdogs.

The alliance of those who oppose the expansion of government control on the Internet in Italy resembles similar coalitions elsewhere in advanced countries. The major divergence is the position of the private sector. Europe as a whole is characterized by a close (and frequently very cordial) relationship between businesses and governments. In Italy, that relationship is not only close, but the business sector is very considerate and forthcoming toward the public administration and policy-makers. The period of telecom privatization was crucial because private investors were very competitive vis-à-vis the government. But that was the exception, and since then businesspeople have gone back to the traditional way of appeasing the government. In Italy the most distinctive example of the alliance between the private sector and civil liberties NGOs is the battle over the use of encryption software, or the cryptowars.

Without the availability of encryption software, it would have been impossible to implement the March 1997 law establishing the legal validity of electronic documents and the digital signature. This software was likewise indispensable for all e-government projects (launched by the G8 countries in the mid-1990s) and for the protection of personal data. The specific problem for Italy was that, while there was no prohibition of access to strong encryption software, there was also little awareness among Internet users about why cryptography should be important to them. Had the government tried to change the legislation, it would have been more difficult to organize a grass-roots opposition. It also seemed unlikely that a bureaucracy usually "deaf to its clientele" (Koff and Koff, 2000: 152) would release its control of encryption software that was turning out to be a source of prestige and influence. At the same time, law enforcement agencies tried to convince the government that wireless communications should use only those encryption codes that law enforcement officers could easily break.

Unrestricted access to strong cryptography was essential for all these projects (such as digital signature and e-government), but it was also essential to make electronic commerce a reality for Italian customers. As in many other countries, civil liberties NGOs and the ICT business sector joined forces to resist any government attempts at restricting individual access and use of encryption software. They succeeded. Strong cryptography in wired communications remained freely available and was never restricted in Italy. Even the PA contributed to this effort by publishing security guidelines based on encryption software and public key cryptography. Before encryption became part of off-the-shelf products, law enforcement agencies could, at least, monitor the encrypted communications of organized crime (even if they could not decipher than) to see who talked to whom. Now, law enforcement officers argued that, with the greater availability of strong public key encryption for individuals, it was increasingly difficult to distinguish between the messages of law-abiding citizens and those of drug dealers.

Advocates of control aggressively clamored about the increasing risk of criminal and immoral pornographic use of computer communications due to the availability of encryption software. The outcome of the debate on free cryptography was substantially different. ICT companies integrated encryption in many of their products so that they would be viable for electronic commerce and users would feel secure, but the police made sure that those companies would be able to assist police officers if needed. If access to encryption remains freely available, most of the merit goes to the few civil liberties NGOs (like ALCEI) that struggled to turn that into a right for Internet users. It is significant that after September 11, although law enforcement monitoring of computer communications has increased, no police officer or policy-maker has asked to turn back the clock of cryptography to the early 1990s.

The period between 1994 and 1996 was particularly crucial for Italy since, like other European countries, in addition to the privatization of telecom, the Internet was expanding to a larger audience and there was growing media attention. The media, however, consistently portrayed "hackers" (or any gifted Internet user) in a negative manner. Ciccarelli and Monti (1997) identified three main periods in the first ten years of the Italian hackers' movement. The years from 1988 to 1993 were a sort of "golden age," because the relatively small community of hackers could roam freely on the undersized but open networks. Most hosts were universities that were not concerned with security but interested in sharing research.

The second period, 1994–1995, is known, among Italian hackers, as "the busting." The sudden notoriety of the Internet in the United States had drawn the attention of the media principally to child pornography, and a baffled public demanded some response. Thus, law enforcement officers and the judiciary heavily investigated the hackers' scene. Inexperience and ignorance of technical matters among police officers and judges was high and a proper legal framework was missing. Excesses and mistakes happened. Finally, in 1997, there was the "new generation" Internet, with an increase in users and the arrival of the private sector. This progression shows how, in the absence of a proper legal framework and public awareness to overcome their technical deficiencies, law enforcement agencies could have simply asked for and obtained more control of the network.

Local administrators in a few municipalities were among the first laypersons who recognized the Internet as a new tool for providing public access to information. In 1995, Bologna was the first Italian city (the second in Europe after Amsterdam) to implement the idea of a "civic network"[28] (Iperbole), which allowed all residents quasi-free access to the Internet, and of "cyberdemocracy." Had the project of civic networks been fully understood, it might have met stronger opposition. But arguments against providing free Internet access were indeed few. The project was relatively cheap and promised to win Bologna prestige (Tambini, 1998). The non-hierarchical, non-profit, and "young" nature of the Internet appealed to left-wing activists who enthusiastically embraced it, with long-term visions of "tele-referenda and tele-polls."[29] Furthermore, civic networks should have been the ideal substratum over which grass-roots movements of Internet users and consumers could have thrived. Such movements could then have provided a greater counterbalance to government efforts to increase Internet control. Yet, these bottom-up movements never materialized.

Civic networks could also have lured the adolescent Internet business sector (especially ISPs) into an alliance to resist interference from the central government. This prospect never occurred either. The example of Bologna was followed by other municipalities, with varying degrees of success, but when large numbers of ISPs began to offer services and high-speed access at discounted prices, the main *raison d'être* for the civic networks disappeared. Even Bologna's Iperbole (by far the most successful example) reached only 17,000 subscribers (out of a population of nearly 400,000) in the middle of the Internet craze in 2000. Soon Italy's civic networks had to embark on search for a "new identity." Pressed by private ISPs that offered better Internet access, they had to shift their mission from providing plain Internet access to offering content services. This was an early form of e-government, but without financial assistance from the national government. The private sector, far from cooperating, accused them of unfair competition and tried to put them out of business. After the center-right coalition won the 2001 election, the Berlusconi cabinet showed no interest in connecting with the existing civic networks and launched its top-down plan for e-government.[30] For all practical purposes, the experiment with civic networks terminated there.

Social, pacifist, and anti-globalization movements have looked with interest at the experimentation with civic networks. Such movements have logically adopted a grass-roots approach to setting up a "social network" of websites that offer unorthodox ideas and counterculture-style chat rooms for sympathizers (cf. Keck and Sikkink, 1998).[31] Many older leaders of those movements had experienced something similar with independent radio broadcasting during the 1970s and had a very positive attitude. Law enforcement agencies, however, fearing that there could be linkages made between these movements and left-wing terrorism, watched those websites closely and often proceeded to seize them. Movement members consider these actions purely as a form of censorship.[32] Pacifists and anti-globalization protesters have also shown little inclination to connect with more "traditional" civil liberties and users' NGOs. While interested in promoting their political ideas, they have fought what they consider government censorship in isolation but have been hardly present in the dispute on privacy protection.

Privacy and censorship (which is the other side of the "free speech" coin) have been the traditional rallying calls for civil liberties organizations and users' groups. On the Italian political scene, the oldest Italian NGO tackling civil liberties and electronic communications is the Association for Free Electronic Communication, ALCEI, which was established in July 1994 by a group of electronic communications users.[33] The association (roughly similar to the American Electronic Frontier Foundation, EFF) is funded entirely through members' fees and has no corporate sponsors. The association's philosophy can be summarized in the words of Andrea Monti (a lawyer and its president), "The Internet brings out the attitudes of many governments toward civil rights." ALCEI's actions have consistently appeared to be well informed and competent.[34] In 1999 the Internet Society, a historical organization for the Internet, also established an Italian chapter.

Among the watchdogs, somehow ironically, there is the Authority for Privacy Protection, a state institution that has often collided with the government about Internet control. The last of the independent agencies to be established, the authority is now led by one of Italy's leading experts on privacy rights, Stefano Rodotà. The agency finds its rationale in two EU directives on personal data protection and two articles (14 and 15) of the Italian Constitution.[35] The agency's main mission is to guarantee that the treatment of personal information by the PA and private business is fair and on a "strictly necessary" basis. Personal information may be processed by those who gathered it only for the purpose for which it was gathered (for instance, the identification of participants registered for a conference) and only after the specific person has provided his or her explicit permission. After the bombing of Madrid in March 2004, when a renewal of requests for more surveillance on the network emerged, Rodotà explicitly opposed the idea of increasing Internet control. He argued that the downside of further Internet control (such as discovering the information source of a journalist) as well as other electronic measures, like biometrics, to fight terrorism eroded personal privacy in a manner that only autocratic regimes could afford (Martirano, 2004).

The existence of specialized agencies to protect personal data, especially in Europe, has been a consequence of the rising number of people with access to computer networks. Every time users log on the Internet, they leave an electronic trail behind them. The capability of matching huge amounts of information stored in different databases endows those who manage those databases with unprecedented knowledge and power. States as well as companies run these mega-databases. The various European authorities have the technical and legal skills to monitor and fight abuses, although not always successfully. For instance, in February 2000, the European Parliament asked the privacy authority to provide its opinion on the Echelon intelligence organization. However, after September 11, inquiries about Echelon have declined. Last but not least, the privacy authority is a member of the controlling committee on Europol, the European organization that coordinates national law enforcement agencies within the Schengen area. Without that committee, Europol would have no political supervision.

After September 2001, the job of all privacy protection agencies in Europe has undoubtedly worsened. Nonetheless, the situation of privacy protection in Italy, as well as other EU members, is far from being as dramatic as it could have appeared only a short time after that tragic date. Users' and civil liberties NGOs feared that, despite the watchdog role of the privacy authority, Italy would soon be engaged in the debate on the balance between liberty and security that quickly spread across the United States. Italy was not alone in fearing that evolution, since most Western-style democracies were in the same situation. National and international users and civil liberties NGOs have criticized attempts to strike a delicate balance because of their privacy-endangering potential, and there is scant evidence that they have been effective in the fight against terrorism (Provos and Honeyman, 2002; Schneier, 2003). Protecting personal privacy or enhancing security ultimately depends on which elements a government and its constituency value as more important. After September 11, the latter has prevailed among many of the members of the information society. Italy, the aspiring member, could only follow suit.

Conclusions: the elusive information society?

On the night of Sunday, September 28, 2003, the whole of Italy was struck by a complete blackout. The primary cause was a trivial accident (a fallen tree on a crucial power line in Switzerland), but there was a domino effect of human mistakes amplified by the structure of the system. There were fortunately no fatalities or major damage, but if it had been a Monday morning at 11 a.m., the effects would have been substantially different. Although it was not an act of terrorism, it taught the Italians how fragile their NII could be. In many ways it was a sour "welcome" to the information society.[36]

Before September 11 and the dot.com bust, stakes in the new economy were so high that the Italian government would do nothing to undermine the diffusion of the Internet, and ICT in general, among the population and shatter the expected economic returns. Security was a minor issue, mostly of concern to computer experts, and to some sections of law enforcement and the judiciary. The perceptions that "the sole information superpower" (the United States) may take unfair advantage from its hegemonic position have been rather unfounded for the Italian government (both the current and the previous one). Like the American and other European counterparts, Italy's executive branch is fully convinced that electronic commerce and the Internet are indispensable for a post-industrial, service-oriented economy like Italy. But unlike most Americans, Italians at large do not yet seem convinced that that status comes with costs. Even if the public became more involved in the debate on protecting the NII (thus pressuring policy-makers, for instance) and the government more forthright on the real situation of Italy's NII and the measures to defend it, many structural problems would be unlikely to simply disappear.

There is, for instance, the die-hard habit of many governments, including Italy's, of hiding or minimizing dangers and risks. If the Bush Administration's indispensability has been accused of being too secretive, Berlusconi's government has an excessive fondness for putting down risks so as not to distress the electorate. Avoiding panic is a duty for a government, but shunning public debate and accountability is a different matter for any democracy. In Italy, a large number of members of Parliament, of local administrations, of political parties, and of PA officials still have only a poor understanding of ICT. This is a generational change that will take some time to complete. It is not only the older generations, however, that have trouble with comprehending what it entails to be a member of the information society. Italian users, most of whom are very young, show an abysmal lack of interest. This was the case during the 2000 election of ICANN's board of regional directors, when the government, business associations, and the media began to advocate Italian membership only in mid-July 2000 (the deadline was July 31). Only a very few users bothered to register for the election.[37] Furthermore, according to the research institute Censis (2003), the Internet is popular among the young (58.7 percent), but even more popular are television (94.6 percent) and the cellular phone (93.7 percent). Hence, even in 2003, almost one out of two young individuals between the ages of 14 and 30 still did not use the network. Among adults (over 30) the figures are even lower.

On the surface, the Internet stakeholders are the same as in other parts of Europe or the United States, namely civil liberties NGOs, consumers' and users' groups, the ICT industry, and the cabinet. But their relationships are different. The few NGO watchdogs have only a few institutional access points to policy-makers. Many young people in the social movements are only marginally attracted to the "traditional" issues involved with Internet control (and not at all with NII protection). The business sector prefers to appease the government and work with and not against it. If one adds to this picture a distracted public, who should be the primary stakeholder in the NII security and Internet control in a democracy, and a premier who has a private interest in all the media, it is hard not to think of Italy as *still* an elusive member of the world information society. Hence, if membership is elusive, Internet control also is elusive. It might be that the country will have to learn the "hard" way, through blackouts and failures of critical systems, what that membership truly entails.

Notes

1 Under the D'Alema government, the prime minister's office applied for membership of the World Wide Web (W3) Consortium. The membership was later completed by the Amato cabinet, in May 2000.

2 The first Italian party to be on-line was the *Radicali* (the Radical party). The Radicals (who, in Europe, are roughly equivalent to American liberals) were the first to value the Internet as a communication medium. Their website <www.radicali.it/> is extremely informative. *Radio Radicale*, their radio station at <www.radioradicale.it/index.shtml>), has its own CNN-style website (also of high quality).

3 True to an American-style "hands-off" approach, the center-right alliance indicated in its political program that "the Internet should be left alone" (*The Economist*, 2000h: 41).

4 During the same electoral campaign Silvio Berlusconi's party, *Forza Italia*, had a poster that read "Le Tre 'I': Inglese, Internet, Impresa" ("The three 'I's': English, Internet, Enterprise"), which would be the goal of tomorrow's Italian schools.

5 Istituto Nazionale di Fisica Nucleare (National Institute of Nuclear Physiscs).

6 Gruppo Armonizzazione Reti di Ricerca.

7 The privatization campaign for telecom services was the first successful battle of the Antitrust Authority. The Antitrust (whose long-time chairman was former premier Giuliano Amato) was established in Italy in October 1990 and was the first of the Italian regulating authorities modeled along the American experience. The competencies of the agency include bank mergers and acquisitions, cartels and monopolies, and, more recently, e-commerce and Internet business. The fact that in other instances of the liberalization of public utilities the Antitrust has been less successful has not diminished its prestige.

8 In August 2000 an Internet consulting firm, Forrester Research, explained the slow Internet adoption in Southern European countries (France, Spain, and Italy) as a hindrance due to "Latin culture and climate" (that is, sunny weather causing people to stay and shop outside and unfamiliarity with new technologies). The press release is available from <www.forrester.com/ER/Press/Release/0,1769,377,FF.html> [January 30, 2004].

9 Customers were also extremely slow to switch to the new 3G mobile phones when they began to appear on the Italian market in 2003. Italian customers (particularly young ones) use their

phones to exchange text messages in addition to calls, and the fact that 3G phones could send pictures did not seem to them a compelling reason to switch to more expensive handsets and services. Telecom companies have hence planned a smooth shift first to 2.5 generation phones and then to 3G ones, in the meantime offering new services.

10 The "last mile" is the distance between the local switching point and the private user. Broadband access is a relatively minor problem for businesses, which are generally willing to sustain the expenses. Such a cost, however, discourages private users from requesting broadband access. Consumers think that the wiring up of their building and houses should be done by telecom companies. The main owner of the physical infrastructure, Telecom Italia, asserts that it is not a public service provider but a private company that acts only when it is profitable. With neither users nor the carrier willing to sustain most of the cost, a deadlock has ensued and the diffusion of ADSL services in the country has been extremely slow.

11 The right-wing opposition and bipartisan experts criticized the proposal, which did not have any value added for many firms who already had their web pages, and it put advertising companies (which could not offer their products "for free") at a disadvantage. Most importantly, the ministry of finance, the portal administrator, did not have its own network infrastructure, but it had to rely on its usual provider, the former monopolist Telecom Italia. The ministry would then give public money to a private company without fair competition.

12 Interview with Giuseppe Rao, head of the Forum for the Information Society, Rome, May 3, 2000.

13 Europe's "Silicon Valleys" seemed only to be near Stockholm, London, or Helsinki. Milan, Turin, and Ivrea failed to meet the magazine's criteria, namely, proximity to universities and research centers, presence of large companies providing marketing skills and economic stability, residents' propensity toward entrepreneurial risks, and availability of venture capital (Hillner, 2000).

14 Survey conducted by George S. May International on 350 Italian entrepreneurs (quoted in *Il Sole 24 Ore*, 2000b: 12).

15 In all fairness, the D'Alema government did try to cast the image of being a more Internet-friendly administration, characterized by genuine enthusiasm among its team of independent experts, and the awareness of participating in a truly innovative experimentation for Italy (Caprara and Picci, 2001).

16 As in the rest of Europe, tax registration numbers are usually owned by businesses or professionals for tax requirements.

17 "Domain-grabbing" (or "cybersquatting") is the US definition of the act, by an individual or a group, of registering a large number of domains of famous trademark names, with the goal of reselling them to the original companies or well-known personalities; e.g. juliaroberts.com or madonna.com (for a while a pornographic website) were true instances.

18 It would thus not be possible for an early comer to register the domain www.fiat.it or www.ferrari.it because well-known names are already protected by the civil code.

19 Currently, in addition to the ministry of interior, there are the infrastructure and communication ministries. The defense ministry does not appear to be involved "on the front line."

20 The guidelines were not readily implemented in the whole administration and, at the end of May 2000, allegedly Brazilian crackers penetrated the websites of the communication authority and of the ministry of communications (Cammarata, 2000). The full CNIPA document (in Italian) is available from <www.cnipa.gov.it/site/_contentfiles/00464500/464511_quaderni_2.pdf> [January 27, 2004].

21 Law enforcement officers consider unauthorized access to a computer equivalent to "trespassing." Among others, the offences include unauthorized access codes for computer or computer communications systems, stealing codes, passwords, or other means to access a

computer telecommunication system protected by security measures, the obligation for safeguarding against malicious software programs, computer frauds, etc.

22 In June 1998, on a judge's warrant, the Bologna Postal Police seized the server machine of the non-profit provider Isole nella Rete, depriving ordinary users — mostly oblivious of the circumstances — of their Internet services for days. The justification for the seizure was the legal action taken by a travel agency for "continuous defamation" by a left-wing activist group using the server to urge the boycott of the agency for providing travel to Turkey, a country commonly known for disregarding human rights. The machine remained for days at the police offices. When it was returned, the provider recommended all the users to change their passwords since it could not guarantee that unauthorized individuals had not accessed their files. Several articles on the case are available (in English and Italian) from the website of the organization at <www.ecn.org/inr/nodo50/inr.html> [January 25, 2004].

23 The GdF is the approximate equivalent of the US Internal Revenue Service (IRS).

24 According to the BBC (2004a), Italy has the highest level of film piracy in the western world.

25 The Carabinieri are the exception to this rule because they have also a military police function.

26 Some details on C4IEW units and organization are available from <www.esercito.difesa.it/root/Sezioni/Sez_organizzazione.asp> [January 30, 2004].

27 In April 2003, Italian law enforcement officers could not break the encrypted filed of an apprehended terrorist and they asked the FBI for help. The FBI could obtain encryption keys from Microsoft and Psion for "national security" needs. However, the FBI did not consider the Red Brigades a threat to the United States and it did not proceed. The Italian police had to work on evidence of unencrypted files, which was nonetheless abundant (Fusani, 2003a).

28 Reti Civiche. Bologna took advantage of having a local administration recognized at the national level for its efficiency and openness. The rumor according to which civic networks in left-wing cities, such as Bologna, had been an attempt at balancing the predominance of right-wing parties in other media, has not found support. In fact, the Democratici di Sinistra, the major party of the left (and for long the dominant party in Bologna), became intrigued with the Internet long before Forza Italia, Berlusconi's party, did.

29 For instance, Francesco Rutelli, former mayor of Rome, was the leading candidate of the left-wing coalition for the 2001 elections. He presented himself as very much in the mould of Bill Clinton and Tony Blair, that is, vigorous, outgoing, modern-minded (*The Economist*, 2000g).

30 Traditionally, Italy's most efficient local administrations had long been associated with the left, in general, and the Communist and Socialist parties in particular (Putnam, 1993). The center-left coalition had its own plan for e-government which was presented to the press in mid-June 2000. The plan would have allowed the government, within ten to twelve months to call for improving the efficiency of the public administration, integrating different administrative services offered to the public with maximum access to information for the public. The estimated cost would have been 690 million euros. The process had barely begun when the Berlusconi government came into office and revised the plan.

31 An example is the independent media center "Indymedia," available at <http://italy.indymedia.org/> [February 2, 2004]. Indymedia Italy is part of the larger news network Indymedia that is active in various countries (including the United States).

32 For instance, see another such case involving again Isole nella Rete, available from <www.tmcrew.org/sequestro.html> [February 1, 2004].

33 Associazione per la Libera Comunicazione Elettronica. The originating event for ALCEI was continuous action by Italian police forces against BBS (bulletin board systems) providers, under suspicion of offering pornographic material. ALCEI is also one of the founding members of the Global Internet Liberties Campaign, which coordinates international initiatives for Internet civil liberties.

34 ALCEI has very close ties with one of the most informative websites for laws and commentaries on the information society in Italy, Interlex. The URL is <www.interlex.it>.

35 Directive 95/46/CE (October 24, 1995) on personal data protection and Directive 97/66/CE (December 15, 1997) on the harmonization of EU member countries' legislation on personal privacy. Since its approval, 97/66 has been a topic for negotiations and discussion between Europeans and Americans. The former wanted US companies treating data on EU citizens to abide by the EU directive, while the latter refused. The "safe harbor" proposal was a result of the negotiations, but the problem is far from solved. However, after September 11, the United States insisted that all European commercial carriers that fly to the US should provide details about their passengers, or be denied permission to land. European privacy protection authorities protested, but the US government refused to reconsider that policy and carriers had to comply.

36 The only services that worked were those that could rely on back-up power (hospitals) or were not "on the network." Local and national radio stations worked, but the Internet did not (cf. Cammarata, 2003).

37 The Italian participation in the "At-Large" membership (only 1,670 "unverified" applicants) became an issue only after government, associations, and business realized that by July 2000 only a few hundred Italian users (including the author) had bothered to apply, compared with tens of thousands of Japanese, Chinese, Americans, and Germans (Mola, 2000).

7 Conclusions
Digital winners, virtual losers

> Internet *is* for everyone – but it won't be unless *we* make it so.
> (Vint Cerf, co-founder, Internet Society, and co-author of TCP/IP)[1]

Where do we stand now?

In August 2000, *The Economist* (2000f: 9–10) assessed the early period of the "Internet's coming of age." The Internet's days as a predominantly scholarly research network were over, and it seemed to be omnipresent in people's lives, finances, and entertainment. The British magazine entitled its review "What the Internet Cannot Do." As with all new technologies, a wave of public enthusiasm and hope had greeted the Internet in the early 1990s. Many optimists foresaw the Internet preventing wars, reducing pollution, and fighting inequality. Some authors had ventured as far as predicting the Internet as the end of the nation-state system (Naisbitt, 1994; Burton, 1997) or the beginning of a new brave "wired world" (Burton, 1997). That optimism and those predictions now seem far-fetched after the dot.com bust and September 11. For a start, they could never have been fulfilled, as they set the bar of expectations too high for the Internet. Yet the network has changed the way of doing business, communications, culture, and even international politics. It has done so in ways so subtle that we cannot even realize now that these changes have so much become part of our daily routines. There have been winners and also losers. So, what happened?

From the beginning, the ability of governments to enforce their boundaries has been central to sovereign statehood (Saurin, 1995). Furthermore, the degree of control that they exercise over the state frontiers has always constrained their policies and practices (Anderson, 1996). As long as information was written on paper that had to be carried by human beings, the degree of control was high, but the progressive "dematerialization" of information has undermined the absolute physical control over a finite area (Anderson, 1996). Broadcasting, whether by radio or television, has moderately weakened the states' critical prerogative of granting legitimate access to their territories (Krasner, 1995). Normally, firms may enter the market without the approval of governmental authority. The telecommunications industry, however, has traditionally been "character-ized by entry controls" (Stone, 1997: 14). The Internet is part of telecommunications, but also of the media, the distribution grids, and so on. In many ways, the Internet is the quintessential part of the whole ICT world.

The most important outcome of such a situation was that national governments became only *one* of the Internet stakeholders as ICT firms and civil liberties NGOs joined in as the new stakeholders. These three players struggled against one another or joined forces (as in the accidental alliance of ICT firms and NGOs in the cryptowars) to shape the various policies of Internet control. The multiple ways in which the three stakeholders cooperated or impeded each other in the same country depended on three factors: (a) the *domestic structure* of the country (whether it was a democracy or an autocracy), (b) the *domestic interest aggregation* (whether the country was more corporatist or pluralist with multiple access points), and (c) how much the executive *securitized* the debate on Internet control. This first section will examine these factors further ahead.

As more and more users went on-line, national governments became aware that the Internet might introduce information into their territories over which they have limited or no control. That information might affect the attitude of their citizenry vis-à-vis the political and economic structures of their state. Under these conditions, the set of reactions from national authorities has ranged from mild concern to suspicious alert to outright severing of connections, often depending on which government branch is in charge of Internet control. Given the organizational and cultural obstacles posed by establishing an international regime of regulation over the network, and the increasing accessibility of the Internet, governments had little alternative but to embark on the technically more costly and difficult operation of setting up national rules for control. These projected or actual national dispositions greatly diverged in terms of the extension and intrusiveness of control and of the topics covered by them.

This state of affairs was the result of the fact that the Internet came together unplanned, almost accidentally. The first stakeholder (the govern-ments) could do little to alter its given technical nature. That was the exogenous variable, outside the governments' reach. They certainly had more leverage to affect and control the behavior of the other stakeholders, such as the ICT private sector and users' and civil liberties NGOs. So, why do governments want to control the Internet and where do we go from here? In addition to summarizing the main findings of the case studies, this concluding chapter looks at possible future avenues of research for the Internet and ICT in international relations.

The nature of the Internet meshes communications and the NII. The two functions are mostly indistinguishable. These conditions prevented the emergence of a hierarchical structure, with no specific center managing the network.[2] At the same time, protecting the NII is a priority for national security, therefore governments have to ensure a certain level of control to fulfill this goal. The first key element for my analysis was the *domestic structure* of the countries that practice Internet control. Are they democracies or autocracies? Currently, advanced democracies (the OECD club), along with their national ICT sectors, own the largest portion of the world's information infrastructure. For them, protection comes understandably before content control. Some authors (Kehoane and Nye, 1998) have argued that democracies fare better in the information society then non-democracies because the former can "take more information" without their social fabric being disrupted. In fact, abundant information produces a multitude of informed actors who, in turn, multiply the levels of bargaining and further subdivide the issue areas. Such an outcome is certainly not efficient, but it is unquestionably consistent with the decision-making process in democracies.

For autocracies it is the other way around. Autocratic states control communication content by default and then are concerned with NII assurance because their share of the global information infrastructure is smaller than that of democracies. However, this situation may change as countries like China or Malaysia increase their portion of the global information infrastructure. One function (control to protect the NII) may easily "creep" into the other (controlling the contents of communications or censorship). The control of certain themes (e.g. neo-Nazi propaganda) might find ample support among the public, and even the majority of users, as in the case of Germany, France, and other European countries. The public would see that control as "legitimate." Both autocracies and democracies might use the rhetoric of "threats to national security" and securitization to partially justify their control. Again the distinction between democracies and autocracies is important. In the latter, the other stakeholders (ICT firms and users' and civil liberties NGOs) have multiple access points to influence policy-making. This is not the case in autocracies where the governments can cajole the ICT sector onto their side and simply push around or ignore civil liberties NGOs. Many autocratic governments actually label civil liberties NGOs and human rights groups as threats to national security. This state of affairs makes studying why democracies want to control the Internet more intriguing and meaningful.

What then would explain differences among democracies? The second key element is hence the *domestic interest aggregation* or how the three main stakeholders find synergies, act together, or resist each other to pursue their own specific interests. The level of pluralism (Lijphart, 1999) denotes the corporatist nature of a democracy. In corporatist democracies (such as Japan, Austria, or Germany) the stakeholders are more likely to look for consensus on what on-line issues should be controlled and how to fight, for example, cybercrime and cyberterrorism. Corporatist democracies also tend to have very codified (both formally and informally) access points to the state apparatus, that is, the bureaucracy, government agencies, the legislature, and so on. Among pluralist democracies like the United States, the United Kingdom, and Canada, lobby organizations and civil society NGOs constantly try to create more access points.

Whenever the accidental alliance of ICT sector and civil liberties and users' NGOs was formed, it proved to be a formidable opponent to governments' policies to raise Internet control, as the case of the cryptowars clearly demonstrated. The ICT sector could be a formidable opponent since it owns the largest share of the NII in OECD democracies and electronic business in the United States, which is estimated to be around US$ 120 billion in 2004 (*The Economist*, 2004b).[3] More services are now the key Internet strategy to assure customer satisfaction and include, for example, greater care for personal privacy. This is the outcome of civil liberties NGOs' campaigns to alert users and companies to the importance of this issue. Thus a synergy between the stakeholders emerged.

The other important reason why the accidental alliance was a remarkable challenge for governments was that information asymmetries did not work this time. In fact, information asymmetries worked against national governments, which normally benefit from them. As Milner (1997) noted, information distribution asymmetries influence domestic as well as foreign policy decisions and both create political advantage or penalize certain actors. In the struggle over Internet control, however, the ICT sector and civil liberties NGOs could master technical and legal information far better than government officials could ever hope to do (cf. Keck and Sikkink, 1998: 18–22.). Last but not least, the assurance of the NII requires the full participation of the ICT sector and some democratic governments have even started to recognize that recruiting expert users' groups (and even some civil liberties NGOs) to that goal would be a very sensible policy.

Autocratic governments have a simpler life. As China and Singapore demonstrate, autocracies also want to spread out the Internet, build their own version of the information society, and collect the economic benefits of the Internet. They enjoy centralized state structures which allow fewer access points to political leaders. Within the country, the number of "arguing actors" is also smaller. However, those governments ponder, how many people should be allowed to have access? Should they be only the politically reliable ones? How much, and what kind of information, would companies really need? The list of questions could go on considerably. For the time being, autocracies can centralize Internet control, restrain users, and resist pressure from interest groups. There is no guarantee that once the numbers of users in autocratic states is as large as the Internet public in industrialized democracies, autocratic governments can maintain the same efficiency and intensity of control. Such circumstances will make for an interesting test of the theses presented in this work.

To explain why national governments want to control the Internet, this work has considered the three predominant approaches in international relations theory, namely realism, liberalism, and constructivism. Liberalism belongs to the rational choice meta-theory, like realism, while constructivism, according to many authors (Adler, 2002; Fearon and Wendt, 2002), is its own meta-theory that can be used to answer research questions. Apparently, because the Internet and the NII are enmeshed and the latter needs to be protected anyway, some degree of control is thus necessary and that seems to favor a realist explanation of the research question. In fact, this account disregards not only that there are differences between autocracies and democracies, but also that the different aggregation of interests in democratic states determines what level of control and the issues to control. This aggregation of interests is, in turn, decided by how the three main stakeholders (governments and their agencies, ICT firms, and civil liberties and users' NGOs) may join forces or be in opposition to each other. Then, the different types of democracies channel policy changes proposed by the stakeholders through diverse access points.

Liberal theory is definitely rich on these points, but the issues of national security and protecting the NII seem firmly within the realist domain. Here, the third important factor of this research emerges, namely the move *to securitize* Internet control. As Buzan *et al.* (1998) observed, when government actors securitize a certain issue, this issue is taken out the public's scrutiny. There were several attempts at securitizing control of the Internet, which were partially justified because of the need to protect the NII. The most notorious securitization move was to attempt to ban encryption software products from individual use. However, sometimes the "security argument" does not prevail and the accidental alliance through technical skill and political clout brought securitization to a standstill and actually reversed it. In other instances of securitization, national governments have had more success, although, in democratic countries, civil liberties NGOs have stressed the importance of protecting freedom of speech and have attracted the attention of ICT firms on the need to secure individual privacy. Depending on the access points and level of pluralism, NGOs have been able to generate synergies with the private sector and may have staved off control policies. The problem of Internet control in democracies has not been settled once and for all. It still is an ongoing process where governments try to meet the demands of law enforcement and intelligence officials, business people, and civil liberties activists, most of the time producing unsatisfactory compromises.

A summary of cases

The choice of countries for the case studies was determined by several reasons. First, the chosen countries are all democracies. For the moment, in fact (aside from few a autocratic states such as China and Singapore), only advanced democracies face three potentially conflicting goals: (a) exploiting the opportunities of electronic commerce, (b) safeguarding national security (both internal and external), and (c) preserving the privacy and freedom of speech of their citizens. The stakeholders representing the socio-economic interests of (a) and (b) (such as users' and civil liberties NGOs, ICT companies, and business associations) have at times joined forces to form powerful, albeit unofficial, coalitions. Such an outcome has been manifested in the United States and, to a lesser extent, in Germany and Italy. The national security interests are embodied by law enforcement and intelligence agencies (in all three countries) and defense departments (predominantly in the United States). Under autocratic regimes, the government stakeholder does not have to win over the other major players. Second, according to various indexes, all the countries in the sample are "ICT leaders" and are in the OECD club, which *de facto* owns most of the Internet. As democracies and shareholders of the global information infrastructure these countries have large responsibilities with regard to other non-members. How these democracies control the Internet as infrastructure will foster the growth of electronic business, and how they control Internet content will be an example of which other countries will take note. Hence, as the "top of the class," the way those countries act and plan to act is remarkably significant for the issue of Internet control, now and for quite some time in the future.

Overall, the thirteen countries surveyed in this work can be clustered into four, somehow overlapping, sets, depending on the agreement/disagreement they showed on the diverse issues that entail Internet control. First, all countries consider cybercrime a serious threat to the NII and to the expansion of electronic commerce. At the same time, all countries strongly feel that free speech cannot be used to defend child pornography. This could be called the "law enforcement is necessary" set. At the same time, although all the countries agree that international terrorism should be defeated, they have mixed reactions to cyberterrorism, which some governments consider an imminent threat whereas others are less inclined to belive so. Second, there is the set of mostly EU member states that believe that fighting hatred/racist speech and neo-Nazi material on the network might justify some limits to free speech and whose constituencies are willing to accept a higher degree of Internet control to eliminate such aberrations. This would be the "limits to free speech" set. The United States starkly stands out with its willingness to accept that even hatred speech might be protected by the First Amendment. Finally, there is the small set of those who believe that cyberterrorism is a clear and present danger and that the protection of the NII is also a mission for the military. This set, the "cyberwar ready," includes the United States and Israel and also France, Canada, and Australia.[4]

The fourth set, the "total defense," is also small and consists of those countries that have long conceived defense as a comprehensive concept that encompasses military defense, law enforcement, participation of the private sector, and public support: Finland, Switzerland, and Israel.[5] If, as it seems, the fight against international terrorism and cyberterrorism increasingly requires the cooperation of the private sector, countries like Finland, Sweden, and Switzerland will be far better off in that fight than countries like the United States. The Scandinavians and the Swiss developed policies of total defense during the Cold War, which allowed them to muster the support and resources of the *entire* society, economy, and public opinion to defend their neutrality. They thus presented the Soviet Union with a credible deterrence. These countries could easily revert to those plans and experiences, if pressed on cyberterrorism. The United States seems to be leaning toward the adoption of similar policies for terrorism and to protect the NII. For a country like the United States, however, with its open society, checks and balances, and multiple access points, to pursue a total defense-like policy would imply tremendous cultural and organizational changes. Such a policy, even if adopted, would probably fail to be implemented or it would be implemented half-heartedly, or Americans would find it so alien to their culture and mind-set that they would simply refuse to comply.

Realists would argue that, because of its position in the world, the United States must be concerned with Internet threats, while Japan, Canada, Italy, Germany, and other Europeans could overlook them. However, such an argument would too easily dismiss that all these countries are OECD members and therefore, as advanced economies, they are all highly dependent on computer networks and the NII, perhaps not as much as the United States, but considerably more than several other countries.[6] Moreover, it would be plainly wrong to say that countries like Finland or Japan are not as dependent as the United States. Were these countries to ignore cyber-threats that the US seems to be taking seriously, one could only conclude that they would be doing a lousy job of protecting the security of their infrastructures. Cybercrime is, in fact, considered a credible risk by most of the countries, which have acted accordingly, adopting several countermeasures, but only within the scope of normal law enforcement jurisdiction. That was the approach of several members of the Council of Europe Convention on Cybercrime. Fighting cybercrime is crucial to securing the NII, and the German, Italian as well as American governments know full well that if individuals perceive the Internet as an extension of "Big Brother," they will never embrace the network *en masse*.

The United States is a society-dominated structure, with powerful interest groups, as well as the foremost "national security" state of all three cases. In addition, it is still the "number one" country on the Internet, for network traffic and content produced. Much like transnational alliances, intra sectorial alliances can quickly be established there. Access to government, legislature, and bureaucracy is ample. Owing to these conditions, however, alliances of interest groups influence policy for brief periods, before new coalitions emerge and the focus of government and groups shifts to new issues. Information (particularly on domestic issues) is distributed quite evenly; individuals can thus rely on plenty of independent sources. Albeit in a class of its own when it comes to waging military computer network operations, the United States is no longer the undisputed number one ICT country, having been surpassed by the Scandinavia countries and, in certain areas, by Japan or other countries. Nonetheless it is still undoubtedly the *primus inter pares* and one of the countries that relies the most on computer networks and is thus still highly vulnerable.[7] Logically, the US federal government is concerned about the protection of its NII and what economic and social consequences a serious disruption of them would entail, and it is raising the budget to protect those infrastructures. In the aftermath of September 11, the protection of the NII was placed at the top of the national security agenda (a further move of securitization). The cost, namely increased control on information content, was at first deemed acceptable by the executive, the legislative branch, and the public at large.

September 11 strengthened the argument of the US national security community and partially won over the ICT sector. Nonetheless, after the first "rally around the flag" moment, it remains to be seen how far the commitment of the ICT industry will go in making security a valuable features of their products. If that is the case, it will be more due to the growing demand for electronic commerce than from the perceived benefits of "national security" (although it would be hard to have ICT firms admit that). A large part of the American public only partially accepted the thesis that the Internet can pose a threat to national security. A certain degree of skepticism remained even after September 11, when Americans increasingly wondered whether reduction of civil liberties was unjustified. This was the case, for example, of the Total (later Terrorist) Information Awareness (TIA), which was then abandoned by the executive branch. The TIA was intended to collect huge amount of personal data on Americans and foreigners alike. The tendency of expanding control through extensive database searches (data mining) has only slowed down but, in all likelihood, will not go away.[8] Nevertheless, American civil liberties NGOs seem determined to continue their role as the government's "watchdogs" thanks to their impressive grasp of technical and legal information that only ICT companies could surpass.

Germany is a democratic corporatist model. Socio-political actors (whether the federal or local governments, trade unions, industrialists' associations, etc.) slowly build consensus on specific policies within the system. The process obviously takes considerable time and, more often than not, the outcomes are compromise solutions. Nevertheless, once consensus is reached on some issues, it endures, and the deriving policies have a high likelihood of being implemented. Information is disseminated among the institutional stakeholders, which tends to exclude individuals. These, however, can easily fall back on several independent sources. In Germany, enthusiasm for "das Netz" stemmed from a joint coalition of government and business in the traditional consensus-oriented fashion. Indeed, the private sector has taken the initiative, asking for government support from the very beginning. The civil society (represented by educational organizations and schools) quickly joined the effort.

The Red–Green alliance made it clear that if Germany truly wanted to move into the information age, it would be a "collective mission" that could not afford to leave behind the many computer-illiterate members of society. As expected, the consensus-building process has taken time, but once accord was reached, all of German society now seems committed to that goal. The Internet as a threat to national security is the last thing German users, industry, and the federal government would believe. An important variation in this case was the freedom of speech issue, which, for well-known historical and cultural reasons, Germany has been obliged to address by increasing the limits to neo-Nazi material and hatred speech.

In the ICT world, Italy is a latecomer, much like Spain or France. Despite their instability, Italian governments have had a long tradition of intervention in the economy (as its record of privatization and liberalization clearly showed). Policies are the outcome of compromises within coalition governments, and are based on the mutual exchange of political favors ("I'll scratch your back if you scratch mine," or *do ut des*). However, certain long-term policies (such as intervening in the economy) have not been dependent on the specific government but have been followed by most executive branches. Only in the last ten years, and thanks to EU pressures and initiative, has the process of privatization begun, albeit slowly. Access to government and the legislature is mediated by a full array of middle-men and intermediaries, both inside and outside the state bureaucracy. Information is obviously filtered by these intermediaries for their own ends. Independent sources abound, but relatively few individuals avail themselves of them. Among Internet countries, in Europe and elsewhere, Italy is a latecomer that has quickly recovered many positions.

Until 1998–1999, managing the Internet in Italy was basically left in the hands of mid-level bureaucrats, inexperienced police officers, and judges. Enthusiastic ISPs and users' groups often operated in ignorance of what the status of legislation on the network was. The few, filtered access points to the government and the legislature made the situation worse. The Internet did not belong to high politics or serious business circles. In the last years of the past century, big ICT companies and the government came almost simultaneously to the conclusion that Italy risked failing to construct the information society and was being excluded from the benefits of the new economy. Despite a consolidated image of a "weak government," Italy's executives have endorsed several steps to spread the use of the Internet, particularly among students and pupils – although the current situation is still far from satisfactory. Italian political parties, after long-standing disinterest, have all embraced the Internet, much like their counterparts in Germany and the United States. However, viewpoints on what are the necessary steps to spread the Net in Italy frequently diverge.

Much like other ICT leaders, the legal framework for the growth of electronic commerce is constantly evolving in Italy. Access to broadband, intellectual property rights, and the need for greater reliability of the NII are the latest issues that the executive branch has to address. Given Italy's past of public intervention in the economy, one might have expected more "activism" by the Italian law enforcement (especially the internal revenue police) in controlling Internet content. There have been instances of abuses by law enforcement officials, and of incompetence by some judges, but these have been few, certainly not more than anyone would normally anticipate in such a state of affairs. Some of those occurrences of judicial incompetence could have been prevented had state authorities been more willing to tap into the technical skill of users' and civil liberties NGOs. Overall, Italy acted on Internet control like Germany, its other European partners, Canada, and Japan, awaking late to the need of its dependence on computer networks more than in the United States, Israel, or Switzerland. In accounting for these differences, "past institutionalized practices and different conceptions of self and other" matter considerably (Katzenstein, 2003: 773). Overall, the Italian government has retained a relatively low level of control on Internet content while trying, at the same time, to improve the assurance of the NII.

While cybercrime (and, to a lesser extent, cyberterrorism) and the need for assurance of the NII to foster electronic commerce elicited interest in the European, Japanese, and Canadian authorities, concerns for other cyber-threats to national security were definitely not on the agenda. Overall, most states have preferred a more relaxed attitude about Internet control, national security, and the NII. On the one hand, states accept the argument that civil liberties NGOs and users' groups make (at times with the backing of the ICT sector): that the network is an "improbable" threat to national security. On the other, the securitization argument, and the discourse that national security professionals tried to present in countries other than the United States, were unconvincing and therefore failed.

Where do we go next?

Do these findings have long-term impacts on the field of international relations? As this work shows, the answer to that question is yes. We can see the three key themes characterizing the work of scholars on the Internet: the emergence of "grass-roots foreign policies," a further expansion of what "national security" means, and the struggle toward an international information regime. Several authors have already begun to confront these themes (for example, Mayers, 1994; Arquilla and Ronfeldt, 1997; Keck and Sikkink, 1998; Denning, 1999; McCaughey and Ayers, 2003), while Buzan *et al.* (1998) have already convincingly argued that the concept of national security is long due for redefinition and "rejuvenation."

Although they will not bring about the ultimate demise of the nation-state, computer networks have joined the many other factors (e.g. finance and trade, tourism, the environment) that have changed the domestic organization of the state, its foreign policy, and also its perception of national security. At the same time, states can still greatly influence the future development of the Internet (as information content and infrastructure). Some states could do more than others, but this is hardly a novelty in world politics. As the nation-state has adapted to other challenges, it seems it may also learn to adapt to the Internet. Internationally, states have already seen their freedom of action somehow diminished (Denning, 1999). As Keck and Sikkink (1998) noted, NGOs working on human rights or environmental issues have found an excellent tool in the Internet to keep contact and organize actions such as the boycott of the Multilateral Agreement on Investments or the WTO Seattle meeting of December 1999. Old-style, inter-state diplomacy has thus become harder to accomplish without being under real-time monitoring by NGOs with Internet access. Computer networks enable network-based organizational structures of the new international actors, be they human rights NGOs or terrorist organizations. These features are bound to increasingly influence world politics and if they have some bearing on foreign policy, they also inevitably intrude on the realm of national security policy.

When governments decide to apply "national security" to the Internet, they are attempting to secure exclusive authority over, at least, certain areas of the computer network. The nature of the Internet, which does not allow differentiating between information as content and information as infrastructure, partially explains governments' efforts. The distinction between Internet content and Internet infrastructure, however, is more germane for democracies than for autocracies. Autocratic states control content *and* infrastructure, as a matter of national security. Policy-makers around the world put protecting the NII at the top of their national security policy list. With that prioritization comes a certain degree of control over the network. If a government is democratic, control intended for Internet infrastructure may, or may not, spill over into certain socio-cultural content issues, may, or may not, find the support of the public and of the civil society at large. But if the state is autocratic, then the government simply follows the "standard operating procedures" of autocracy, and puts control over content and infrastructure alike.

National governments have shown that economic gains from Internet growth should overcome, at times, even national security, as the cryptowars demonstrated. Policy-makers are convinced that, at least for the time being, expected economic gains from the diffusion of the Internet are more probable to occur than are foreign attacks through the network. Indeed, in 2004, *The Economist* (2004b: 9) forecast that the potential of electronic commerce was "bound to be even greater than in the past few years." The British magazine went on to note that the two key steps to achieve that outcome were to continue broadband expansion and make the Internet safer for business transactions, which also means a better assurance for the NII. Governments are now concentrated more on maximizing the gains than reducing the risks, as demanded by their national constituencies, and are still rather oblivious to what other actors do in the international arena. Now governments (including, or perhaps especially, the democratic ones) demand that, to foster the security of computer networks, the private sector should undertake more responsibilities, and a growing number of firms seem to conclude that it is time to shift their interest coalition closer to government. The same developments have been noted by other observers (Bessette and Haufler, 2001).

As governments digitize their activities, the organizational structure of states will change. Will governments have to learn how to defend "their" cyberspace? This change may well result in a major watershed for the discipline of international relations, which have long been based on the territorial sovereignty of states. Moreover, when researching the effects of the Internet on world politics, scholars will have to progressively abandon the artificial partition between domestic and international levels of explanation. In cyberspace, in fact, this distinction is already meaningless. At the same time, by increasing the reliance of their economies and societies on computer networks, countries also increase their vulnerability to malicious computer attacks. Several governments still seem to be oblivious to such risks. These governments prefer to concentrate only on the fact that economic returns outweigh the risks of vulnerability.

In both the issue areas of Internet control and protection of the NII, all Internet stakeholders (national governments, ICT companies, civil liberties, and users' NGOs) have long developed international ties with their counterparts in other countries.[9] Is then an international regime on information infrastructure possible or even desirable in the near future? The two major obstacles to the creation of international agreements establishing an information infrastructure regime have been the reluctance of the United States to back such initiatives and the cultural sensitiveness that the Internet seems to provoke in various countries. International frameworks, such as the United Nations or the ITU for instance (Ferguson, 1998; Cogburn, 2004), for such a treaty are already available. But, so far, the main obstacle has been for governments to decide whose legislation standards should be adopted. Should it be the Western legal standards? Should there be room for cultural exceptions? Even Western countries could not agree on the definition of many crimes (cf. Corriere.it, 2004). Criminal categories are so tightly associated with a country's society, culture, and tradition that even among countries with fairly similar features such as Western industrialized democracies, it would be very hard for governments to strike common ground.

Within the group of Western OECD countries, there are considerable differences, for example on the treatment of personal data (more strictly regulated in Europe) or in defining free speech (which the United States traditionally characterizes more broadly than Europe). Other important dissimilarities have emerged on the issue of taxation. The United States would prefer, more generally, little or no taxes on the Internet. Private sector "self-governance" should also be preferred, which, for Americans, means that businesses should be left to regulate themselves, while the market should set prices and priorities for Internet use. The Europeans have a more consensual approach. To some extent, Europeans would like to see their governments more active in managing the network. Divergences of opinions are also present among the Europeans themselves and should not be underestimated.

The circumstances described above apply entirely to international treaties, signed by national governments, at times within the framework of international government organizations. In addition to cultural, legal, and political differences, another important reason why governments have not yet finalized international agreements on the Internet is that, in the past, states have excluded NGOs during negotiations for telecommunication treaties. NGOs have been able to secure support by a large number of individual users and, at least for some issue areas, the backing of private industry. Thus, the absence of NGOs at international conferences is even more startling. Furthermore, civil liberties NGOs, through their members, could provide a highly knowledgeable presence. Because of their technical proficiency, NGOs could convince users and ICT companies of the validity of their requests. This state of affairs began to change with the ITU-sponsored World Summit on the Information Society held in Geneva in December 2003, where the presence of NGOs was not only accepted but actually encouraged. This outcome was possible because civil liberties and users' NGOs had been able to develop informal, but strong, epistemic communities (Cogburn, 2004). These communities were hence repositories of priceless technical and legal knowledge.

National governments have nonetheless continued their practice of negotiating treaties on information infrastructures and computer networks without any consultation with the NGO stakeholders, especially if those treaties have direct relevance for post-9/11 national security. The Council of Europe Convention on Cybercrime is such an example. The convention was redrafted several times, as member governments jostled to agree on such definitions as "computer crime" or "unauthorized access." The last draft was approved in August 2001 by member countries of the Council. Given the relevance of the topic, Canada, Japan, South Africa, and the United States had also been actively participating in the negotiations.[10] In fact, the FBI had contributed considerably to the drafting. After September 11, the draft was quickly approved in Budapest in November 2001. But it took three full years to have five members of the convention to ratify it. Furthermore, none of those that ratified it, as of 2004, were EU countries or other advanced modern countries such as Japan or the United States.[11]

Although the convention entered into force in July 2004, it is still unclear how the most important countries (the United States, the big EU states, and Japan) will actually apply it since none of them had ratified the treaty before it actually entered into force. Subsequently, Japan and the EU countries had rushed to approve the convention to show the United States their commitment to the war on terror. The United States, however, was quickly shown to favor a unilateral approach to fighting that war and feared being hindered by European and Japanese extensive regulations on business practices and responsibilities. On the other hand, the Europeans and Japanese were put off by the disinterested attitude of the Americans. The Europeans in particular thought that the convention was too weak in stopping hate or racist speech on the Internet, and thus proceeded with approving an amendment to help tackle the problem of hate speech. The Americans, who did not want to further inflame the issue of free speech in their own country, were happy to steer clear of the amendment. Given the lack of support, it is unlikely that the convention will represent a watershed in international cooperation on the regulation and assurance of computer networks worldwide.

A more comprehensive international regime for the Internet would have to take into account the distant views of additional countries with quite distinct religious, cultural, and historical values. Such circumstances would further hamper reaching a multilateral agreement on how to protect the world's information infrastructure or controlling computer networks more efficiently at the international level.[12] A functioning Internet international regime would have to win the support of users' and civil liberties NGOs. With the notable exception of the World Summits on the Information Society of Geneva (2003) and Tunis (2005), the possibility of comprehensive international treaties on information infrastructures has been, at least temporarily, taken off the states' international agenda. National governments have been left with little alternative but to continue with their national approach to Internet control, trying to foster regional cooperation like the OECD countries have done.

Since "e-commerce takes off" (*The Economist*, 2004b: 9), with its hopes of economic, human, and social benefits, no government wants to be left out. At the same time, as all technological innovations before them, the network and ICT (such as digital cameras and webcams) will continue to provoke cultural and behavioral changes in many societies, particularly in the long term. Not all these changes will be welcomed by all the governments, especially in autocratic states. China and Singapore are still textbook examples. Both will continue to promote the diffusion of the Internet, while still controlling content information (suppressing undesired material such as the websites of some newspapers and magazines) and infrastructure information. If those countries become more democratic, it will be worthy of note to see whether they move their control from content to infrastructure, as true democracies are expected to do. All in all, policy-makers worldwide are still torn between expected benefits and drawbacks, the "negative" and "positive" sides of the Internet. In most cases, political leaders will simply react to the stimuli, trying to please public opinion, law enforcement, and business communities with their often competing and sometimes irreconcilable agendas. The Internet of 2005 is considerably different from that of 1995, but the "digital challenge" (accepting the network with all its pros and cons) will continue to puzzle Internet stakeholders for many years to come.

It is fair to presume that international relations scholars will have their hands full in studying the impact of computer networks and ICT on world affairs in the next few years. National security, information operations and cyberterrorism, foreign policy and cyberactivism, electronic commerce, globalization and "connectiveness" (Barnett, 2004), epistemic communities, and international information regimes will be the main functional areas for scholarly investigations. The most difficult challenge, however, will be for IR theories to integrate problems such as the fading distinction between the domestic and international levels of analysis, the appearance of more non-state actors, and the impact that fast-circulating ideas and perceptions will have on the culture of politics. Which of the three main school of international relations will best integrate and explain these ontological challenges? This long path of investigation has just begun.

A slightly normative ending

In the end, with Internet control, the ICT revolution, electronic commerce and all the "cyber hype," who will be the digital winners and virtual losers? The Internet, like any other technology, was (and is) fundamentally neutral, as James Rosenau (2001) pointed out. It can be used to improve peoples' lives, through spreading education and telemedicine, or to ruin them, through serving gamblers, pornographers, and drug dealers. Where do all these conflicting circumstances leave stakeholders when coping with the network? This situation implies that extrapolating from the past may help discover who the digital winners and virtual losers will be. If Barnett (2004) is correct, globalization should benefit the economy and societies of all those "connected" countries that communicate and trade with each other. Quite interestingly, the Internet is one of the least controversial symbols of globalization, cherished by anti-globalization activists and Wall Street bankers alike. It is only fair to say that humankind is instinctively fond of the Internet and wants to fully embrace it. But a large portion of humanity is still a virtual loser with no access to the network. Furthermore, even those in the developed world could become virtual losers if control moves from infrastructure to content, with less personal privacy, less freedom of speech, and more "Big Brothers."

Complexity and intricacies abound in working with the network. The same civil liberties organizations that demand "hands-off" policies regarding free speech on the Net call for governmental regulation when on-line privacy is threatened by the industry's own hands-off, self-governance policy. The fact is that political leaders, lawmakers, scholars, and users will keep facing thorny issues about the Internet. Although it is problematic to assess the validity of the statement that democracies can "take more information," it is appropriate to expect democratic countries to behave correctly when dealing with the Internet. These states indeed have a "moral imperative" to defend users' privacy, freedom of speech, and free choice. If democratic governments impose too many limits on the network, non-democracies will see themselves even more justified in enforcing their own national standards of control.[13] Clearly, free speech cannot be completely unrestricted and personal privacy can be breached to collect criminal evidence. These actions, however, should be made obvious in a few clear, unambiguous, and specific legal guidelines. National governments should enforce these guidelines without exception.

Given the meshed (communication/infrastructure) and multi-level (domestic/international and public/individual) nature of the Internet, governments' recourse to the all-encompassing notion of "national security" will not disappear. The Internet, the argument goes, has made national computer networks more vulnerable, and has thus put national security at risk. The prohibition by the US federal government on exporting encryption software (claiming that it was a breach of US national security) was all but an example of those improper limits, and an escalation in the level of Internet control. The evaluation of malicious attacks on national information infrastructures should also become more sober, and based on a more convincing substantiation of actual damage than currently exists.

While some of the Internet's features, such as freedom of speech, mostly require passive protection (that is, "do not increase censorship"), other attributes such as individual privacy demand positive, active engagement (that is, more guarantees) by democratic governments. In fact, government agencies have not been alone in collecting information on users; private Internet companies have been even more active and even less accountable.[14] In this situation, more involvement by democratic governments seems inevitable. These governments should restrain both public and private actors that aim to gather information on individuals, and set forth the precise, unambiguous circumstances in which collecting information should be allowed.

To fulfill that mission, democratic governments should begin by agreeing on the definition of issues such as "privacy." If the private sector consumers' organization and users' and civil liberties NGOs are actively involved in the process of creating an international regime, the chances for success will be higher. Moreover, as it seems that the European view of privacy is currently more far-reaching than the American one, Europeans should take a lead in this new issue area, namely "international privacy." Another easy step in this direction would be to sign a treaty between the United States and Europe on banning child pornography on their territories.[15] These countries have similar views on protecting children, and thus some common ground could be found. Once this goal is achieved, it would be possible to move step by step to reduce on-line crime. The guiding principle of these agreements, however, should be to regulate as little as possible, protecting individuals' rights, and set out clearly the criteria followed to determine this level of Internet control.

The number of studies analyzing state behavior on the Internet from a comparative perspective or the impact of computer networks in international politics is now gradually increasing. But what are the critical problems that scholars will have to face to better understand the Internet's socio-economic impacts and how these impacts may change international politics? Here I want to highlight some of the possible problems for future research in this field. First of all, there is the fundamental problem with the quality of data available on the Internet. It is not that there are too few data—there are too many. Some of those data, however, are of dubious quality, while others can be only partially useful to scholars. In this work I have tried to avoid figures as to the numbers of users, web pages, traffic, etc., as much as possible because the pace with which these data change is breathtaking. By the time a book on a topic like Internet control is published, those figures should already be updated. More research is then needed in comparing the different sources, methods, and elaboration techniques of data on the size and attributes of the Internet (Giacomello and Picci, 2003). By assessing quality and presenting findings to the academic community and the general public, Internet scholars can make sure that the scope and explanatory power of future research on the topic will increase considerably.

Second, as more and more countries go on-line, and more governments have to face common Internet dilemmas, it will be interesting to assess the differences between democracies and non-democracies. Currently, this differentiation is arduous to make, since the Internet is still mostly a venture of the "OECD club" of industrialized countries. Would an OECD-imposed international regime on Internet content be accepted? May democracies still claim the moral "high ground" of human rights, universal access, and freedom of information for all? May democratic governance become the rule on the network? If democracies truly display a more positive behavior toward on-line privacy or freedom of speech than non-democracies, it is nonetheless still unclear *how far* democratic governments are willing to go to protect those rights. Estimating their attitudes in these respects would also provide interesting findings about how solid the social fabrics of many democratic societies are. The ICT sector will play a crucial role here. That role will imply that concepts like individual privacy and even freedom of speech should become an integral part of business and corporate ethics.

Third, the Internet will force extensive reorganizations of governments' structures and functions. This restructuring will affect the size, and therefore government officials should be able to offer faster and cheaper administrative services to their public. These are just some of the anticipations for e-government. More importantly, the restructuring will have effects on jurisdictions and competencies of the states' various departments and agencies. Some national governments have already begun "outsourcing" their traditional task of protecting and modernizing information infrastructures to private industry. On the other hand, in several countries, the military already mostly relies on commercial computer networks (off the shelves) for at least some of their communication traffic.

Several of the case studies in this work have revealed another key feature of this in-flux situation: the blurring of jurisdictions within the same governments. Most governments used to have fairly precise (and jealously defended) institutional boundaries among their branches. Now e-government has obliged government agencies and bureaucracy to increase cooperation and learn to communicate more efficiently. Similarly, there used to be a clear-cut division between competencies in domestic or foreign matters, which has now mostly disappeared. The epitomes of this change are the NII and the Internet where economics, culture, and national security are all blended together. The problem is more severe for many democracies, which usually have institutional limits and constitutions that are harder to bend or modify, for instance, in the separation between civil and military spheres.

The multiple access points and the multiple stakeholders (in lieu of the state supremacy over all other interests) also contribute to make the problem of Internet control more complex for democracies. But that is the price that true democracy pay, while phoney democracies or autocratic states are not affected. Governments, whether democratic or autocratic, will have to learn how to cope with overlapping administrative responsibilities, not only domestically but also internationally, since their national laws on the Internet may have an impact on other states as well. The cases of ICANN functioning on American laws and the EU Directive on personal data affecting American businesses and European and American copyright laws hampering research on open source software in developing countries are just three such instances.

No longer only geeks, scientists, or freedom of speech advocates, the new users/consumers are less ideological, more "local." They also want security *and* freedom. In the end, all revolutions become establishment and the Internet is no exception to that rule. The network will not "eradicate all the world's problems." But it has changed businesses' operations and governments' policies, empowered grass-roots groups, and facilitated peoples' communications. When, in 1993, the Irish rock band U2 with their song *Stay* somehow mocked satellite television because it let us "go anywhere,"[16] perhaps they should have also poked fun at the Internet, which has truly made the world smaller. Who knows where we are going next?

Notes

1 "The Internet is for Everyone," Computers, Freedom, and Privacy Conference on April 7, 1999, available from <www.isoc.org/isoc/media/speeches/foreveryone.shtml> [May 19, 2004].

2 A significant example of this case is the utter failure to substitute the TCP/IP, created by researchers working on connecting networks, with the OSI (Open Systems Interconnection) protocol by the International Standards Organization. OSI came to be regarded by Internet "free-thinking" users and scientists as a top-down imposition by an intergovernmental institution that had no part in creating the network.

3 Ironically the wild estimates of the 2000–2001 Internet frenzy did materialize, not in 2002, after the dot.com, bust but only in 2003 (*The Economist*, 2004b).

4 The United Kingdom was not examined here but would also fit in this set.

5 Sweden could be another country for this set.

6 In cyberspace, industrialized democracies are somehow more equal than in the real world, i.e. they are all increasingly dependent on computers and computer networks. Their economies could never survive without computers and their networks. Paradoxically, developing and underdeveloped countries are even more penalized in cyberspace than in the real world, because they are not as "computerized" as industrialized countries (thus they are not as vulnerable), but they need to become so if they want their economies to grow (thus they will become more vulnerable).

7 Because of the way the Internet was first developed, most of the Internet traffic goes through router computers on US soil. This is an impressive opportunity for US intelligence services to monitor information content traveling to different parts of the globe, but it is also a tremendous responsibility for the security of the world information infrastructures, because blows to those routers on American soil would have repercussions far away from American territory. Another example of the still great influence that the United States possesses in the world of computer networks is the fact that even Tim Berners-Lee, the first inventor of the World Wide Web, had to move to the United States from the CERN in Geneva to continue his research (the W3 Consortium at the MIT) or that ICANN, the domain name system governance body, operates under Californian laws.

8 See, for example, the US General Accounting Office (2004).

9 For instance, governments try to fight cybercrime (the FBI and NSA are cooperating with their counterparts in other democracies); companies such as Yahoo, eBay, or Amazon now have branches located in countries other than the United States; and users' and consumers' NGOs have coordinated their actions, as has been done by the Global Internet Liberties Campaign which has a large membership of NGOs.

10 Many non-EU European countries such Russia and Turkey are full members of the Council of Europe.

11 As of 2004, President Bush urged Congress to ratify the treaty. However, American civil liberties NGOs opposed ratification and Congress seemed somehow sympathetic to the NGOs' argument that, if ratified, the convention could undermine freedom of speech in the United States.

12 The bulk of Internet traffic as well as websites and host computers are in OECD countries, which might well decide to implement an "OECD regime," at least for the time being. This action, however, would simply enrage non-OECD countries, which would feel excluded from cyberspace even more and would probably start calling OECD members "on-line imperialists."

13 For instance, it would be all too easy for the Chinese or Saudi Arabian governments to point out that not even human rights champions like Western democracies can take unrestricted free speech or comprehensively protect personal privacy.

14 At least (and with many exceptions) in democracies, intelligence and law enforcement services respond to political leaders who are accountable to parliaments.

15 The EU itself is considering a number of "regional" (i.e. intra-EU) agreements such as on e-commerce or illegal and harmful contents on the Net, or intellectual property rights.

16 *Stay (So Far, So Close!)*, music and words by U2, Island Records, 1993.

Bibliography

Abelson, H. *et al.* (1998) "The Risks of Key Recovery, Key Escrow, Trusted Third Party and Encryption," Digital Issues No.3, Washington, DC: Center for Democracy and Technology.

Adler, E. (2002) "Constructivism and International Relations," in W. Carlsnaes, T. Risse, and B.A. Simmons (eds), *Handbook of International Relations*, London: Sage, 95–118.

Agnew, J. and Corbrige, S. (1995) *Mastering Space: Hegemony, Territory, and International Political Economy*, London: Routledge.

Alberts, D. (1996) *Defensive Information Warfare*, Washington, DC: National Defense University.

Allison, G. and Zelikow, P. (1999) *Essence of Decision: Explaining the Cuban Missile Crisis*, 2nd ed., New York: Addison-Wesley.

Anderson, C. (1995) "The Accidental Superhighway: A Survey of the Internet," *The Economist*, July 1.

Anderson, K. (2002) "US 'Fears al-Qaeda Hack Attack'," BBC News, June 27, available from <http://news.bbc.co.uk/1/hi/sci/tech/2070706.stm> [February 17, 2004].

Anderson, M. (1996) *Frontiers: Territory and State Formation in the Modern World*, Cambridge, UK: Polity Press.

Ardù, B. (2000) "Italia, allarme hacker: minacciano la Net economy," Repubblica.it, June 1, available from <www.repubblica.it/online/tecnologie_internet/sicurezza/sicurezza/sicurezza.html> [January 31, 2004].

Arena, K. and Ensor, D. (2002) "U.S. Infrastructure Information Found on al Qaeda Computers," CNN.com, June 27 available from <http://edition.cnn.com/2002/US/06/27/alqaeda.cyber.threat/index.html> [February 17, 2004].

Arquilla, J. *et al.* (1999) "Networks, Netwar and Information Age Terrorism," *Countering the New Terrorism*, MR-989-AF, Santa Monica, CA: Rand, available from www.rand.org/publications/MR/MR989/MR989.pdf> [January 30, 2004].

——and Ronfeldt, D. (eds) (1997) *In Athena's Camp: Preparing for Conflict in the Information Age*, MR-880-OSD/RC, Santa Monica, CA: Rand.

Baldas, B. (2000) "Indische Revolution in Deutschland," *Die Tageszeitung*, Tazmag, July 29–30, I–II.

Baldwin, D. (ed.) (1993) *Neorealism and Neoliberalism: The Contemporary Debate*, New York: Columbia University Press.

Bamford, J. (1983) *America's National Security Agency and its Special Relationship with Britain's GCHQ*, London: Sidgwick & Jackson.

Barlow, J.P. (1996) "A Declaration of Independence of Cyberspace," Davos, Switzerland, February 8, available from <www.eff.org/~barlow/Declaration-Final.html> [February 12, 2004].

Barnett T. (2004) *The Pentagon's New Map: War and Peace in the Twenty-First Century*, New York: Putnam & Sons.

Barth, R. and Smith, C. (1997) "International Regulation of Encryption: Technology Will Drive Policy," in B. Kahin and C. Nesson (eds), *Borders in Cyberspace: Information Policy and the Global Information Infrastructure*, Cambridge, MA: MIT Press, 283–99.

Barua, A. *et al.* (1999) "Measuring the Internet Economy: An Exploratory Study," Center for Research in Electronic Commerce, University of Texas, Austin, June, available from <http://cism.bus.utexas.edu/works/articles/internet_economy.pdf> [February 7, 2004].

BBC News (1999) "Olivetti Conquers Telecom Italia," May 22, available from <http://news.bbc.co.uk/1/hi/business/the_company_file/348931.stm> [January 8, 2004].

——(2000a) "French Anti-Racists Sue Yahoo," April 11, available from http://news.bbc.co.uk/1/hi/world/europe/710058.stm> [March 18, 2004].

——(2000b) "Vodafone v. Mannesmann," February 11, available from <http://news.bbc.co.uk/1/hi/business/621222.stm> [January 15, 2004].

——(2000c) "Net Snooping Bill 'Harms Business'," June 28, available from <http://news.bbc.co.uk/1/hi/uk_politics/810099.stm> [May 12, 2004].

——(2004a) "Italy 'Heads Piracy Shame League'," January 29, available from <http://news.bbc.co.uk/2/hi/entertainment/3441265.stm> [January 31, 2004].

——(2004b) "EU Agrees Anti-Terrorism Measures," March 25, available from <http://news.bbc.co.uk/1/hi/world/europe/3566845.stm.> [25 March, 2004].

——(20004c) "Q&A: EU 'Terror Tsan'," March 26, available from http://news.bbc.co.uk/1/hi/world/europe/3550543.stm> [March 26, 2004].

Bendrath, R. (2001) "The Cyberwar Debate: Perception and Politics in US Critical Infrastructure Protection," *Information and Security*, 7 special issue "The Internet and the Changing Face of International Relations and Security," 80–103.

——(2003) "The American Cyber-Angst and the Real World–Any Link?," in R. Latham (ed.), *Bombs and Bandwidth: The Emerging Relationship Between IT and Security*, New York: The New Press, 49–73.

Beniger, J. (1986) *The Control Revolution: Technological and Economic Origins of the Information Society*, Cambridge, MA: Harvard University Press.

Bennett, C. (1992) *Regulating Privacy: Data Protection and Public Policy in Europe and the United States*, Ithaca, NY and London: Cornell University Press.

Berners-Lee, T. (1999) *Weaving the Web: The Original Design and Ultimate Destiny of the World Wide Web by Its Inventor*, New York: Harper.

Bessette, R. and Haufler, V. (2001) "Against All Odds: Why There is No International Informational Regime," *International Studies Perspectives*, 2: 69–92.

Bonini, C. (2003) "Quel pugno di anarchici che inquieta il Viminale," Repubblica.it, November 5, available from <www.repubblica.it/2003/j/sezioni/cronaca/bombalavoro/bonini/bonini.html> [January 31, 2004].

Bowles, N. (1993) *The Government and Politics of the United States*, London: Macmillian.

Braman, S. (2004) "Introduction: The Process of Emergence" in S. Braman (ed.), *The Emergent Global Information Policy Regime*, Basingstoke, UK: Palgrave, 1–11.

Bronner, E. (2004) "Collateral Damage," *The New York Times Book Review*, February 22, 10–11.

Bruno, S. (2002) "CIIP Country Survey," in A. Wenger, J. Metzger and M. Dunn (eds), *International CIIP Handbook: An Inventory of Protection Policies in Eight Countries*, Zürich: Swiss Federal Institute of Technology, 12–110.

Buchner, B. (1988) "Social Control and the Diffusion of Modern Telecommunications Technologies: A Cross National Study," *American Sociological Review*, 53(3): 446–53.

Bull, H. (1995) *The Anarchical Society: A Study of Order in World Politics*, 2nd ed., New York: Columbia University Press.

Burton, D. (1997) "The Brave New Wired World," *Foreign Policy*, 106: 23–37.

Buzan, B., Waever, O., and de Wilde, J. (1998) *Security: A New Framework for Analysis*, Boulder, CO: Lynne Rienner.

Camilleri, J. and Falk, J. (1992) *The End of Sovereignty? The Politics of a Shrinking and Fragmenting World*, Aldershot, UK: Edward Elgar.

Cammarata, M. (2000) "Stavolta e' andata bene, ma la prossima?," Interlex.it, May 31, available from <www.interlex.it/attualit/sitipa.htm> [January 27, 2004].

——(2003) "Il problema è la vulnerabilità delle reti," Interlex.it, October 2, available from <www.interlex.it/attualit/blackout.htm> [February 2, 2004].

——(2004) "Società vulnerabile: lo scriviamo da otto anni," Interlex.it, June 12, available from <www.interlex.it/regole/bugbear.htm> [February 1, 2004].

Campbell D. (1999) *Interception Capabilities 2000*, Brussels and Strasboug: Scientific and Technological Options Assessment Panel of the European Parliament (STOA), available from <www.iptvreports.mcmail.com/interception_capabilities_2000.htm> [May 16, 2004].

Campen, A. (1992) *The First Information War: The Story of Communications, Computers, and Intelligence Systems in the Persian Gulf War*, Fairfax, VA: AFCEA International Press.

Caprara, C. and Picci, L. (2001) "Internet al governo," in P. Bonora (ed.), *Geografia Della Comunicazione*, Bologna: Baskerville.

Caravita, G. (2000) "Italia a due anni dal 'cyberboom'," *Il Sole 24 Ore* (New Economy Supplement), June 23, 1.

Cavazos, E. and Morin, G. (1995) *Cyberspace and the Law: Your Rights and Duties in the On-Line World*, Cambridge, MA: MIT Press.

Censis (2003) "Giovani & Media: Terzo rapporto sulla comunicazione in Italia," October 30, Milan.

Chamorel, P. (1994) "The Integration of the US Political System in Comparative Perspective," in R. Dahl (ed.), *The New American Political (Dis) Order*, Berkeley, CA: Institute of Governmental Studies Press (UCB), 49–86.

Chapman, G. (1998) "National Security and the Internet," Internet Society Annual Meeting, Geneva, Switzerland, July, available from <www.utexas.edu/lbj/21cp/isoc.htm> [March 18, 2004].

Chase, M. and Mulvenon, J. (2002) *You've Got Dissent! Chinese Dissident Use of the Internet and Beijing's Counter-Strategies*, Santa Monica, CA: Rand.

Chomsky, N. (1997) *Media Control: The Spectacular Achievements of Propaganda*, New York: Seven Stories Press.

Ciccarelli, S. and Monti, A. (1997) *Spaghetti Hacker*, Milan: Edizioni Apogeo.

CNN.com (2000) "Mideast 'Hacktivists' Take Conflict Online," November 3, available from <http://edition.cnn.com/2000/TECH/computing/11/03/israel.hacking.ap/index.html> [May 1, 2004].

——(2001a) "Encryption Advocates Resist Legal Limits," September 18, available from <http://edition.cnn.com/2001/TECH/industry/09/18/encryption.defense.idg/index.html> [May 13, 2004].

——(2001b) "France Toughens Anti-Terror Laws," November 1, available from <http://edition.cnn.com/2001/WORLD/europe/11/01/inv.france.measures/index.html> [March 24, 2004].

——(2002a) "Telecom Operators: Deutsche Telekom," December 2, available from <http://edition.cnn.com/2002/BUSINESS/11/14/bbtelecoms.dt/index.html> [January 20, 2004].

——(2002b) "Red Brigades Justify 'Execution'," March 21, available from <http://edition.cnn.com/2002/WORLD/europe/03/21/italy.march/index.html> [January 31, 2004].

Cogburn, D. (2004) "Elite Decision-Making and Epistemic Communities: Implications for Global Information Policy" in S. Braman (ed.), *The Emergent Global Information Policy Regime*, Basingstoke, UK: Palgrave, 154–78.

Committee on National Security Systems (2003) "National Information Assurance (IA) Glossary," May, CNSS Instruction No. 4009.

Corasaniti, G. (1998) "La tutela penale deisistemi informatici e telematici," in C. Parodi *et al.* (eds), *Informatica e Riservatezza*, Pisa: University of Pisa/Cnuce/IEI-CNR.

Corriere.it (2004) "Il 'cyber-razzismo' divide USA e Europa," June 16, available from <www.corriere.it/Primo_Piano/Esteri/2004/06_Giugno/16/razzismo.shtml> [June 17, 2004].

Cox, A. (1981) *Freedom of Expression*, Cambridge, MA: Harvard University Press.

Dahl, R. (1994) "The New American Political (Dis)Order," in R. Dahl (ed.), *The New American Political (Dis)Order*, Berkeley: Institute of Governmental Studies Press (UCB), 1–24.

Dam, K. (1996) "Preface," in K. Dam and H. Lin (eds), *Cryptography's Role in Securing the Information Society*, Computer Science and Telecommunications Board, National Research Council, Washington, DC: National Academic Press.

Delacourt, J. (1997) "The International Impact of Internet Regulation," *Harvard International Law Journal*, 38(1): 207–35.

Denning, D. (1997) "The Future of Cryptography," in B. Loader (ed.), *The Governance of Cyberspace: Politics, Technology and Global Restructuring*, London: Routledge, 175–89.

——(1999) "Activism, Hacktivism, and Cyberterrorism: The Internet as a Tool for Influencing Foreign Policy," paper presented at conference "The Internet and International Systems: Information Technology and American Foreign Policy Decision-making," December 10, Nautilus Institute, San Francisco, CA, available from <www.nautilus.org/info-policy/workshop/papers/denning.html> [May 24, 2004].

——(2001) "Is Cyber Terror Next?," in "After September 11," November 1, Social Science Research Council, New York, available from <www.ssrc.org/sept11/essays/denning.htm> [June 18, 2004].

Department of Commerce (1998) "A Proposal to Improve Technical Management of Internet Names and Addresses," US Department of Commerce, NTIA/OIA.

Deutsch, K. (1980) *Politics and Government: How People Decide Their Fate*, 3rd ed., Boston: Houghton Mifflin.

Diffie, W. and Landau, S. (1998) *Privacy on the Line: The Politics of Wiretapping and Encryption*, Cambridge MA: MIT Press.

Doh, J. and Teegen, H. (eds) (2003) *Globalization and NGOs: Transforming Business, Government and Society*, Westport, CT: Praeger.

Dugan, I.J. (2000) "Hackers Cause Costly Slowdown for E-Trade," Washingtonpost. com, February 10, available from <www.washingtonpost.com/ac2/wp-dyn?pagename=article&node=&contentId=A32515-2000Feb9&notFound= true> [February 10, 2004].

Dunn, M. and Wigert, I. (2004a) "Introduction," in A. Wenger and J. Metzger (eds), *International CIIP Handbook 2004*, Zürich: Federal Institute of Technology, 17–28.

——(2004b) "Overview Chapters," in A. Wenger and J. Metzger (eds), *International CIIP Handbook 2004*, Zürich: Federal Institute of Technology, 302–58.

Economist (The) (1997) "Hands Off the Internet," July 5, 13.

——(1998) "Privacy on the Internet," March 7, 18–19.

——(1999a) "Riding the Storm," November 6, 77–8.

——(1999b) "Walking on Air," October 23, 20.

——(2000a) "The World Beyond Deutsche Telekom," April 15, 67–8.

——(2000b) "The End of Privacy," May 1, 13–14.

——(2000c) "Vodafone's Folly," July 15, 16–17.

——(2000d) "Fighting Racism," August 5, 32.

——(2000e) "Germany's Neo-Nazi," August 12, 16–17.

——(2000f) "What the Internet Cannot Do," August 19, 9–10.

——(2000g) "A New Left Leader?," September 16, 34–9.

——(2000h) "Right Stuff," October 14, 41.

——(2000i) "Vive La Liberte!," November 25, 101–2.

——(2003a) "For Their Eyes Only," November 1, 51.

——(2003b) "Living with the Enemy," August 9, 49–50.

——(2004a) "Letters: Swipe at Swissness," March 20, 20.

——(2004b) "E-Commerce Takes Off," May 15, 9.

Electronic Frontiers Australia (2003) "Big Brother ISP Code Condemned," Media Release, August 19, available from <www.efa.org.au/Publish/PR030819.html> [March 26, 2004].

——(2004) "EFA Dismayed by IP Clauses of Free Trade Agreement," Media Release, February 12, available from <www.efa.org.au/Publish/PR040212.html> [March 26, 2004].

Electronic Privacy Information Center (EPIC) (1998) "Critical Infrastructure Protection and the Endangerment of Civil Liberties: An Assessment of the President's Commission on Critical Infrastructure Protection (PCCIP)," Washington, DC: Electronic Privacy Information Center.

——(1999a) *Privacy and Human Rights: An International Survey of Privacy Laws and Developments*, Washington, DC: EPIC.

——(1999b) "Advisory Group Urges Change in Crypto Policy," EPIC Alert, vol. 6.13, September 1, available from <www.epic.org/alert/alert_vol_6.html> [February 11, 2004].

——(1999c) "FCC Grants FBI Surveillance Standards Request," EPIC Alert, vol. 6.13, September 1, available from <www.epic.org/alert/alert_vol_6.html> [February 7, 2004].

——(1999d) "Appeals Court Rules Crypto Controls Unconstitutional," EPIC, Previous Crypto Policy News, available from <www.epic.org/crypto/news.html> [April 1, 2004].

——(2000) *Cryptography and Liberty: An International Survey of Encryption Policy 2000*, Washington, DC: Electronic Privacy Information Center, available from <www2.epic.org/reports/crypto2000/overview.html#Heading2> [March 10, 2004].

E-soft (2004) "Secure Server Survey," May 1, available from <www.securityspace.com/s_survey/sdata/> [May 11, 2004].

Evans, P., Jacobson, H., and Putnam, R. (eds) (1993) *Double-Edged Diplomacy*, Berkeley: University of California Press.

Everard, J. (2000) *Virtual States: The Internet and Boundaries of the Nation-State*, London: Routledge.

Evers, J. (2001) "Euro Civil Liberty Campaigners Urge Restraint," CNN.com, November 4, available from <http://edition.cnn.com/2001/TECH/industry/11/04/civil.liberties.idg/index.html> [March 22, 2004].

Fearon, J. and Wendt, A. (2002) "Rationalism and Constructivism: A Skeptical View," in Carlsnaes, W., Risse, T., and Simmons B. (eds), *Handbook of International Relations*, London: Sage, 52–72.

Ferguson, K. (1998) "World Information Flows and the Impact of Net Technology," *Social Science Computer Review*, 16(3): 252–67.

Ferguson, Y. and Mansbach, R. (2002) *The Elusive Quest Continues: Theory and Global Politics*, Upper Saddle River, NJ: Prentice-Hall.

Fischer, S. (2000) "Gute Nacht im Netz," *Der Spiegel*, March 27, 64–6.

Fox, S. *et al.* (2000) "Trust and Privacy Online: Why Americans Want to Rewrite the Rules," August 20, Washington, DC: The Pew Internet & American Life Project.

Frei, D. and Ruloff, D. (1989) *Handbook of Foreign Policy Analysis: Methods for Practical Application in Foreign Policy Planning, Strategic Planning and Business Risk Assessment*, Dordrecht: Martinus Nijhoff.

Fusani, C. (2003a) "L'FBI non 'legge' i palmari delle Br, sepolti nei Pc i segreti dei terorristi," Repubblica.it, April 26, available from <www.repubblica.it/online/cronaca/lioce/fbi/fbi.html> [January 31, 2004].

Fusani, C. (2003b) "Palmari, Palmari, telefoni, chiavi gli sbagli della compagna Lioce," Repubblica.it, October 25, available from <www.repubblica.it/2003/i/sezioni/cronaca/allarmeservizi/fusani/fusani.html> [January 31, 2004].

Gadrey, J. (2003) *New Economy, New Myth*, London: Routledge.

Gardner, F. (2004) "Europe's New Security Challenge," BBC News, March 15, available from <http://news.bbc.co.uk/1/hi/world/europe/3514398.stm> [March 23, 2004].

Gessler, P. (2000) "NPD Trifft auf Widerstand," *Die Tageszeitung*, Taz Berlin, August 7, 19.

Giacomello, G. (2003) "The Political 'Complications' of Digital Information Networks: A Reply to the Politics of Bandwidth," *Review of International Studies*, 29(1): 139–43.

——(2004) "Bangs for the Buck: A Cost-Benefit Analysis of Cyberterrorism," *Studies in Conflict and Terrorism*, 27(5), 195–212.

——and Picci, L. (2003) "My Scale or Your Meter? Evaluating Methods to Measure the Internet," *Information Economics and Policy*, 15(3): 363–83.

Gibbs, S. (2004) "Cuba Law Tightens Internet Access," BBC News, January 24, available from <http://news.bbc.co.uk/1/hi/world/americas/3425425.stm> [April 9, 2004].

Global Internet Liberties Campaign (GILC/EPIC) (1998) *Cryptography and Liberty: An International Survey of Encryption Policy 1998*, February, Washington, DC: Electronic Privacy Information Center (EPIC), available from <www.gilc.org/crypto/cryptosurvey.html> [March 10, 2004].

——(1999) *Cryptography and Liberty: An International Survey of Encryption Policy 1999*, Washington, DC: Electronic Privacy Information Center (EPIC), available from <www.gilc.org/crypto/crypto-survey-99.html> [March 10, 2004].

Government On-line (2002) "Annual Report on Canada's Progress – 2002," available from <www.gol-ged.gc.ca/pub/ica02/ica02-04_e.asp#_Toc24338138> [March 25, 2004].

Green, J. (2002) "The Myth of Cyberterrorism," *Washington Monthly*, November, available from <www.washingtonmonthly.com/features/2001/0211.green.html> [February 17, 2004].

Hafner, K. and Lyon, M. (1996) *Where Wizards Stay Up Late: The Origins of the Internet*, New York: Simon & Schuster.

——and Markoff, J. (1995) *Cyberpunk: Outlaws and Hackers on the Computer Frontier*, 2nd ed., New York: Touchstone.

Haiman, F. (1978) *Freedom of Speech*, Skokie, IL: National Textbook Company.

Haimes, Y. and Longstaff, T. (2002) "The Role of Risk Analysis in the Protection of Critical Infrastructures Against Terrorism," *Risk Analysis*, 22(3): 439–44.

Hamilton, A. (2000) "Online Shoppers Unfazed by Recent Hacks," ZDNet, February 11, available from < http://zdnet.com.com/2100-11-518485.html?legacy=zdnn> [February 10, 2004].

Harmon, A. (2004) "New Technology Loosens Controls over Images of War," *The New York Times*, May 14, A12.

Harrop, M. (2002) "Creating Trust in Critical Network Infrastructures: The Canadian Case Study," International Telecommunication Union Workshop on Creating Trust in Critical Network Infrastructures CN/07, May 20.

Heisenberg, D. and Fandel, M. (2004) "Protecting EU Regimes Abroad: The EU Data Protection Directive as Global Standard," in S. Braman (ed.), *The Emergent Global Information Policy Regime*, Basingstoke, UK: Palgrave, 109–29.

Henley, J. (2003) "Yahoo! Cleared in Nazi Case," *GuardianUnlimited*, February 12, available from <www.guardian.co.uk/international/story/0,3604,893642,00.html> [March 30, 2004].

Herrera, G. (2002) "The Politics of Bandwidth: International Political Implications of a Global Digital Information Network," *Review of International Studies*, 28: 93–122.

Hersh, S. (1999) "The Intelligence Gap: How the Digital Age Left Our Spies Out in the Cold," *The New Yorker*, December 6, 58–76.

Hershman, T. (2001) "Israel's Seminar on Cyberwar," Wired News, January 10, available from <www.wired.com/news/politics/0,1283,41048,00.html> [March 30, 2004].

Hillner, J. (2000) "Venture Capitals," *Wired Magazine*, July, available from <www.wired.com/wired/archive/8.07/silicon.html> [January 28, 2004].

Horowitz, A. (1990) *The Logic of Social Control*, New York and London: Plenum Press.

Hudson, D. (1998) "Germany's Internet Angst," Wired News, June 11, available from <http://www.wired.com/news/politics/0,1283,12884,00.html> [January 14, 2004].

Hulsink, W. (1998) *Privatization and Liberalization in European Telecommunications: Comparing Britain, the Netherlands and France*, London: Routledge.

Hundt, R. (2000) *You Say You Want a Revolution: A Story of Information Age Politics*, New Haven, CT: Yale University Press.

Hutchison, S. and Minton, S. (2002) "France," in G. Kirkman *et al.* (eds), *Global Information Technology Report 2001-2002: Readiness for the Networked World*, Center for International Development, Harvard University, available from <www.cid.harvard.edu/cr/profiles/France.pdf> [March 26, 2004].

Hutter, R. (2002) "Cyber Terror: eine realistische Gefahr?," March 8, Bereichsleiter Informationstechnik und Kommunikation Industrieanlagen-Betriebsgesellschaft mbH, available from <www.aksis.de/Hutter-Cyber-Terror.pdf> [January 30, 2004].

Interagency Director-Generals' Meeting (2000) "Action Plan for Building Foundations of Information Systems Protection from Hackers and Other Cyberthreats," Interagency Director-Generals' Meeting on IT Security, Provisional Translation, January 21, available from <www.kantei.go.jp/foreign/it/security/2000/0519action.html> [March 25, 2004].

International Press Institute (2003a) "World Press Freedom Review," available from <www.freemedia.at/wpfr/world.html> [March 26, 2004].

——(2003b) "World Press Freedom Review: Israel," available from <www.freemedia.at/wpfr/world.html> [March 30, 2004].

International Telecommunication Union (ITU) (1998) "General Trends in Telecommunication Reform 1998," Geneva: ITU.

——(1999) "Challenges to the Network. Internet for Development," Geneva: ITU.

——(2003a) "ITU Digital Access Index: World's First Global ICT Ranking," November 19, available from <www.itu.int/newsarchive/press_releases/2003/30.html> [March 18, 2004].

——(2003b) "World Telecommunication Development Report: Access Indicators for the Information Society," Geneva: ITU.

Johnston, D. and Purdum, T. (2004) "Missed Chances in a Long Hunt for bin Laden," *The New York Times*, March 25, A1.

Jonquieres, G. and Kehoe, L. (1998) "Regulators@Odds," *Financial Times*, October 8, 14.

Josselin, D. and Wallace, W. (eds) (2001) *Non-State Actors in World Politics*, Basingstoke, UK: Palgrave.

Kahin, B. and Nesson, C. (eds) (1997) *Borders in Cyberspace: Information Policy and the Global Information Infrastructure*, Cambridge, MA: MIT Press.

Kalathil, S. and Boas, T. (2003) *Open Network, Closed Regimes*, Washington, DC: Carnegie Endowment for International Peace.

Kaldor, M. (2001) "Beyond Militarism, Arms Races and Arms Control," essay prepared for the Nobel Peace Prize Centennial Symposium, December 6–8, available from <www.ssrc.org/sept11/essays/kaldor.htm> [March 18, 2004].

Katzenstein, P. (ed.) (1996) *The Culture of National Security: Norms and Identity in World Politics*, New York: Columbia University Press.

——(2003) "Same War – Different Views: Germany, Japan, and Counterterrorism," *International Organization*, 57: 731–60.

——Keohane, R., and Krasner, S. (1998) "*International Organization* and the Study of World Politics," *International Organization*, 52(4): 645–85.

Keck, M. and Sikkink, K. (1998) *Activists Beyond Borders*, Ithaca, NY: Cornell University Press.

Keohane, R. (ed.) (1986) *Neorealism and its Critics*, New York: Columbia University Press.

—— and Nye, J. (1998) "Power and Interdependence in the Information Age," *Foreign Affairs*, 77(5): 81–94.

——and ——(2000) "Introduction," in J. Nye and J. Donahue (eds), *Governance in a Globalizing World*, Washington, DC: Brookings Institution Press, 1–41.

Kidd, D. (2003) "Indymedia.org: A New Communications Commons," in M. McCaughey and M. Ayers (eds), *Cyberactivism*, London: Routledge, 47–69.

King, A. (2000) "Distrust of Government: Explaining American Exceptionalism," in S. Pharr and R. Putnam (eds), *Disaffected Democracies: What's Troubling the Trilateral Countries?*, Princeton, NJ: Princeton University Press, 74–98.

King, G., Keohane, R., and Verba, G. (1994) *Designing Social Inquiry: Scientific Inference in Qualitative Research*, Princeton, NJ: Princeton University Press.

Kirkman, G., Osorio, C., and Sachs, J. (2002a) "The Networked Readiness Index: Measuring the Preparedness of Nations for the Networked World," in G. Kirkman *et al.* (eds), *Global Information Technology Report 2001–2002: Readiness for the Networked World*, Center for International Development, Oxford: Oxford University Press, also available from <www.cid.harvard.edu/cr/gitrr_030202.html> [March 31, 2004].

Kirkman, G. *et al.* (eds) (2002b) *Global Information Technology Report 2001–2002: Readiness for the Networked World*, Center for International Development, Oxford: Oxford University Press, also available from <www.cid.harvard.edu/cr/gitrr_030202.html> [March 31, 2004].

Kizza, J. (1998) *Civilizing the Internet: Global Concerns and Efforts Toward Regulation*, Jefferson, NC: McFarland.

Kleffner, H. (2000) "Terroraufruf übers Internet," *Die Tageszeitung*, Taz Berlin, August 8, 19.

Koch, J. *et al.* (2000) "Ausfall im System," *Der Spiegel*, March 27, 40–64.

Koff, S. and Koff, S. (2000) *Italy: From the First to the Second Republic*, London: Routledge.

Kozak, D. and Keagle, J. (eds) (1988) *Bureaucratic Politics and National Security*, Boulder, CO: Lynne Rienner.

Krasner, S. (1995) "Power Politics: Institutions and Transnational Relations," in T. Risse-Kappen (ed.), *Bringing Transnational Relations Back In*, Cambridge: Cambridge University Press, 257–79.

Küblböck, K. (1999) "Austria," in I. Smillie and H. Helmich with T. German and J. Randel (eds), *Stakeholders: Government – NGO Partnership for International Development*, London: Earthscan Publications, 51–61.

Kurlantzick, J. (2004) "Dictatorship.com," *The New Republic*, April 5, 21.

Lake, A. (2000). *Six Nightmares: Real Threats in a Dangerous World and How America Can Meet Them*, Boston: Little Brown.

Lee, S. (2001) "IT Workers Chew over 'Carnivore' Bill," CNN.com, October 11, available from <http://edition.cnn.com/2001/TECH/industry/10/11/carnivore.resistance.idg/index.html> [February 14, 2004].

Lees, J. (1975) *The Political System of the United States*, 2nd ed., London: Faber & Faber.

Leiner, B. *et al.* (1998) "A Brief History of the Internet: Version 3.1," Washington, DC: The Internet Society, available from <www.isoc.org/internet/history/brief.html> [January 31, 2004].

Lessig, L. (1999) *Code and Other Laws of Cyberspace*, New York: Basic Books.

Levy, S. (2001) *Crypto: How the Code Rebels Beat the Government-Saving Privacy in the Digital Age*, New York: Viking.

Lewis, J. (2002) "Assessing the Risk of Cyber Terrorism, Cyber War and Other Cyber Threats," Washington, DC: Center for Strategic and International Studies, December, available from < www.csis.org/tech/0211_lewis.pdf> [February 17, 2004].

Libicki, M. (1997) *Defending Cyberspace and Other Metaphors*, Washington DC: National Defense University.

Lijphart, A. (1999) *Patterns of Democracy: Government Forms and Performance in Thirty-Six Countries*, New Haven, CT: Yale University Press.

Linde, E. van de, *et al.* (2002) "Quick Scan of Post 9/11 National Counter-terrorism Policymaking and Implementation in Selected European Countries," May, Leiden, The Netherlands: Rand Europe, available from <www.rand.org/publications/MR/MR1590/MR1590.pdf> [May 3, 2004].

Liptak, A. (2004) "Hate Speech and the American Way," *The New York Times*, January 11, 3.

Lukes, S. (1974) *Power: A Radical View*, London: Macmillan.

Mackenzie, D. (2003) "The Code War," February, Washington, DC: National Academy of Science, available from <www.beyonddiscovery.org/includes/DBFile.asp?ID=1097> [March 10, 2004].

Markoff, J. and Schwartz, J. (2002) "Bush Administration to Propose System for Wide Monitoring of Internet," *The New York Times*, December 20, A22.

Martirano, D. (2004) "Rodotà: no ai controlli su web e email," Corriere.it, March 21, available from <www.corriere.it/Primo_Piano/Cronache/2004/03_Marzo/21/rodota.shtml> [March 30, 2004].

Maschler, N. (2000) "Streit um Bannmeile," *Die Tageszeitung* Inland, August 8, 7.

Mates, M. (2001) "Report Technology and Terrorism," Science and Technology Sub-Committee on the Proliferation of Military Technology, NATO Parliamentary Assembly, October, Brussels, available from <www.nato-pa.int/archivedpub/comrep/2001/au-221-e.asp> [March 24, 2004].

Mayer-Schönberger, V. and Foster, T. (1997) "A Regulatory Web: Free Speech and the Global Information Infrastructure," in B. Kahin and C. Nesson (eds), *Borders in Cyberspace: Information Policy and the Global Information Infrastructure*, Cambridge, MA: MIT Press, 235–54.

Mayers, D. (1994) "Communication Technology and Social Movements: Contribution of Computer Networks to Activism," *Social Science Computer Review*, 12(2): 250–60.

McCaughey, M. and Ayers, M. (eds) (2003) *Cyberactivism*, London: Routledge.

McCullagh, D. (2001) "Bin Laden: Steganography Master?," Wired.com, February 7, available from <www.wired.com/news/politics/0,1283,41658,00.html> [May 16, 2004].

McMahon, P. (2002) *Global Control: Information Technology and Globalization since 1845*, Cheltenham, UK: Edward Elgar.

Metzl, J. (1996) "Information Technology and Human Rights," *Human Rights Quarterly*, 18, 705–46.

Milner, H. (1997) *Interests, Institutions, and Information: Domestic Politics and International Relations*, Princeton, NJ: Princeton University Press.

Mingers, M. (2003) "ITU Digital Access Index: World's First Global ICT Ranking," ITU Press Release, November 19, available from <www.itu.int/newsarchive/press_releases/2003/30.html> [March 31, 2004].

Ministero della Difesa (2002) *La Difesa: Libro Bianco 2002*, parts IV and IX, available from <www.difesa.it/librobianco/2002/indice.htm> [January 30, 2004].

Mitchell, R. (1997) "Eli Noam Wants to Disturb You," Wired.com, October, available from <http://hotwired.wired.com/collections/connectivity/5.10_eli_noam_pr.html> [February 16, 2004].

Miyashita, H. *et al.* (2000) "Three Regional/National Snapshots," in R. Hundley *et al.* (eds), *The Global Course of the Information Revolution: Political, Economic, and Social Consequences, Proceedings of an International Conference*, Santa Monica, CA: Rand, 43–56, available from <www.rand.org/publications/CF/CF154/CF154.pdf/> [March 25, 2004].

Mock, K. (2000) "Hate on the Internet," in S. Hick, E.F. Halpin, and E. Hoskins (eds), *Human Rights and the Internet*, New York: St Martin's Press, 141–52.

Mola, G. (2000), "Internet, al via le prime elezioni democratiche," Repubblica.it, July 27, available from <www.repubblica.it/online/tecnologie_internet/icann/icann/icann.html> [January 25, 2004]

Mowlana, H. (1997) *Global Information and World Communication: New Frontiers in International Relations*, 2nd ed., London: Sage.

MSNBC (1999) "Pentagon and Hackers in 'Cyberwar,'" ZDNet, March 4, available from <http://zdnet.com.com/2100-11-513930.html?legacy=zdnn> [March 30, 2004].

Mueller, M. (1999) "ICANN and Internet Governance: Sorting Through the Debris of 'Self-Regulation,'" *Info*, 1(6): 497–520.

——(2002) *Ruling the Root: Internet Governance and the Taming of Cyberspace*, Cambridge, MA: MIT Press.

Mulgan, G. (1991) *Communication and Control: Networks and the New Economies of Communication*, Cambridge, UK: Polity Press.

Murray, A. (2004) "The Lisbon Scorecard IV: The Status of Economic Reform in the Enlarging EU," March, Center for European Reform Working Paper, available from <www.cer.org.uk/publications/505.html> [March 18, 2004].

Murray, W. (1997) "Clausewitz Out, Computer In: Military Technology and the Technological Hubris," *The National Interest*, 48: 57–64.

Naisbitt, J. (1994) *Global Paradox*, New York: Avon Books.

Natalicchi, G. (1996) "Telecommunications Policy and Integration Processes in the European Union," unpublished Ph.D. dissertation, City University of New York.

——(2001) *Wiring Europe: Reshaping the European Telecommunications Regime*, Lanham, MD: Rowman & Littlefield.

National Telecommunication and Information Administration (NTIA) (1998) "Falling Through the Net II: New Data on the Digital Divide," US Department of Commerce, July 28, available from <www.ntia.doc.gov/ntiahome/net2/> [February 4, 2004].

Noam E. (1986) "Telecommunications Policy on Both Sides of the Atlantic: Divergence and Outlook," in S. Snow (ed.), *Marketplace for Telecommunications: Regulation and Deregulation in Industrialized Democracies*, New York: Longman, 255–74.

——(1990) "Preface," in I. de Sola Pool, *Technologies Without Boundaries*, Cambridge, MA: Harvard University Press, v–ix.

Nye, J. (2004) *Soft Power: The Means to Success in World Politics*, New York: Public Affairs.

O'Harrow, R. (2002), "Six Weeks in Autumn," *The Washington Post Sunday Magazine*, October 27, W06.

O'Neil, M. and Dempsey, J. (1999–2000) "Critical Infrastructure Protection: Threats to Privacy and Other Civil Liberties and Concerns with Government Mandate on Industry," *DePaul Business Law Journal*, vol. 12, available from <www.cdt.org/publications/lawreview/2000depaul.shtml#V> [February 11, 2004].

Organization for Economic Development and Cooperation (OECD) (1994) "Privacy and Data Protection: Issues and Challenges," Paris: OECD.

Oxman, J. (1999) "The FCC and the Unregulation of the Internet," Office of Plans and Policy Working Paper No. 31, July, Federal Communication Commission, Washington, DC, available from <www.fcc.gov/Bureaus/OPP/working_papers/oppwp31.txt> [February 7, 2004].

Pasquino, G. (2000) *La Transizione a Parole*, Bologna: Il Mulino.

Pearson, I. and Bikson, T. (2000) "Europe," in R. Hundley *et al.* (eds), *The Global Course of the Information Revolution: Political, Economic, and Social Consequences, Proceedings of an International Conference*, Santa Monica, CA: Rand, 65–74, available from <www.rand.org/publications/CF/CF154/CF154.pdf/CF154.chap9.pdf> [March 25, 2004].

Pew Internet & American Life Project (2000) "Trust and Privacy Online: Why Americans Want to Rewrite the Rules," August 20, available from <www.pewinternet.org/reports/toc.asp?Report=19> [February 6, 2004].

——(2001) "Fear of Online Crime," April 2, available from < www.pewinternet.org/reports/toc.asp?Report=32> [February 6, 2004].

Pharr, S. (2000) "Officials' Misconduct and Public Distrust: Japan and the Trilateral Democracies," in S. Pharr and R. Putnam (eds), *Disaffected Democracies: What's Troubling the Trilateral Countries?*, Princeton, NJ: Princeton University Press, 173–201.

Pool, I. de Sola (1983) *Technologies of Freedom*, Cambridge, MA: Belknap Press.

——(1990) *Technologies Without Boundaries: On Telecommunications in a Global Age*, Cambridge, MA: Harvard University Press.

Postel, J. (1994) "Domain Name System Structure and Delegation," Request for Comments No.1591, March, available from <www.isi.edu/in-notes/rfc1591.txt> [February 4, 2004].

Pound, R. (1997) *Social Control through Law*, New Brunswick, NJ: Transaction.

Bibliography 197

Provos, N. and Honeyman, P. (2002) "Detecting Steganographic Content on the Internet," paper presented at the Internet Society NDSS'02, San Diego, CA, available from <http://niels.xtdnet.nl/papers/detecting.pdf> [March 18, 2004].

Putnam, R. (1993). *Making Democracy Work: Civic Tradition in Modern Italy*, Princeton, NJ: Princeton University Press.

Rand Europe (2002a) "International Organizations and Dependability-Related Activities," Dependability Development Support Initiative (DDSI), May 31, available from <www.ddsi.org/DDSI-F/main-fs.htm> [March 27, 2004].

——(2002b) "National Dependability Policy Environments: Australia," Dependability Development Support Initiative (DDSI), November 1, available from <www.ddsi.org/Documents/final%20docs/DDSI_Country_Reports_Final_Australia.pdf> [March 28, 2004].

——(2002c) "National Dependability Policy Environments: Canada," Dependability Development Support Initiative (DDSI), November 1, available from <www.ddsi.org/Documents/final%20docs/DDSI_Country_Reports_Final_Canada.pdf> [March 28, 2004].

——(2002d) "National Dependability Policy Environments: Finland," Dependability Development Support Initiative (DDSI), November 1, available from <www.ddsi.org/Documents/final%20docs/DDSI_Country_Reports_Final_Finland.pdf> [March 28, 2004].

——(2002e) "National Dependability Policy Environments: France," Dependability Development Support Initiative (DDSI), November 1, available from <www.ddsi.org/Documents/final%20docs/DDSI_Country_Reports_Final_France.pdf> [March 29, 2004].

——(2002f) "National Dependability Policy Environments: Japan," Dependability Development Support Initiative (DDSI), November 1, available from <www.ddsi.org/DDSI-F/main-fs.htm> [March 29, 2004].

——(2002g) "National Dependability Policy Environments: The Netherlands," Dependability Development Support Initiative (DDSI), November 1, available from <www.ddsi.org/Documents/final%20docs/DDSI_Country_Reports_Final_Netherlands.pdf> [March 29, 2004].

——(2002h) "National Dependability Policy Environments: Spain," Dependability Development Support Initiative (DDSI), November 1, available from <www.ddsi.org/Documents/final%20docs/DDSI_Country_Reports_Final_Spain.pdf> [March 29, 2004].

——(2002i) "National Dependability Policy Environments: Switzerland," Development Support Initiative (DDSI), November 1, available from <www.ddsi.org/DDSI-F/main-fs.htm> [March 29, 2004].

——(2002j) "International Organizations and Dependability-Related Activities," Dependability Development Support Initiative (DDSI), May 31, available from www.ddsi.org/Documents/final%20docs/DDSI_Country_Reports_Final_Austria.pdf [March 27, 2004].

Ransom, H. (1970) *The Intelligence Establishment,* Cambridge, MA: Harvard University Press.

Rathmell, A. (2001) "Protecting Critical Information Infrastructures," *Computers and Security*, 20(1): 43–52.

"Remailer Geographical Mapping Project" (The), September 9, 2003, available from <http://riot.eu.org/anon/remap.html> [May 3, 2004].

Reporters Sans Frontières (2003) "The Internet under Surveillance: Obstacles to the Free Flow of Information Online," available from <www.rsf.fr/IMG/pdf/doc-2236.pdf> [March 31, 2004].

Risse-Kappen, T. (ed.) (1995a) *Bringing Transnational Relations Back In: Non-State Actors, Domestic Structures and International Institutions*, Cambridge: Cambridge University Press.

——(1995b) "Ideas Do Not Float Freely: Transnational Coalition, Domestic Structure, and the End of the Cold War," in R. Ned-Lebow and T. Risse-Kappen (eds), *International Relations Theory and the End of the Cold War*, New York: Columbia University Press, 187–222.

Rosenau, J. (2001) "The Information Revolution: Both Powerful and Neutral," paper presented at the 42nd Annual Convention of the International Studies Association (ISA), Chicago, February 22.

Rosenberg, R. (1998) "Privacy Protection on the Internet: The Marketplace Versus the State," Wiring the World: The Impact of Information Technology on Society, Proceedings of the 1998 International Symposium on Technology and Society, IEEE Society on Implications of Technology, June 12–13, Indiana University, 138–47 available from <www.ntia.doc.gov/ntiahome/privacy/files/5com.txt> [June 13, 2004].

Rosenzweig, R. (1998) "Wizards, Bureaucrats, Warriors and Hackers: Writing the History of the Internet," *American Historical Review*, 103(5): 1530–52.

Ruiz, B. (1997) *Privacy in Telecommunications: A European and an American Approach*, The Hague: Kluwer Law International.

Saich, T. (2001) *Governance and Politics of China*, Basingstoke, UK: Palgrave.

Sarzanini, F. (2003) "Acqua, elettricità, comunicazioni: gli obiettivi nel mirino di Al Qaeda," *Il Corriere della Sera*, December 16, 12.

Saurin, J. (1995) "The End of International Relations?," in J. MacMillan and A. Linklater (eds), *Boundaries in Question: New Directions in International Relations*, London: Pinter, 244–61.

Schneier, B. (1996) *Applied Cryptography*, 2nd ed., New York: John Wiley.

——(2000) *Secrets and Lies: Digital Security in a Networked World*, New York: John Wiley.

——(2003) *Beyond Fear: Thinking Sensibly About Security in an Uncertain World*, New York: Copernicus Books.

——(2004) "Toward Universal Surveillance," Crypto-Gram newsletter, February 15, from <schneier@counterpane.com>, available from <www.schneier.com/crypto-gram.html> [February 15, 2004].

Schut, M. and Essenberg, I. (2002) "Creating Trust in Critical Network Infrastructures: The Netherlands Case," International Telecommunication Union, ITU Workshop on Creating Trust in Critical Network Infrastructures, May 20, available from <www.itu.int/osg/spu/ni/security/docs/cni.08.doc> [March 27, 2004].

Segell, G. (2000) "French Cryptography Policy: The Turnabout of 1999," *International Journal of Intelligence and CounterIntelligence*, 13(3), 345–58.

Shapiro, A. (1999) *The Control Revolution: How the Internet is Putting Individuals in Charge and Changing the World We Know,* New York: Public Affairs/The Century Foundation.

Singer, P.W. (2003) *Corporate Warriors: The Rise of the Privatized Military Industry*, Ithaca, NY: Cornell University Press.

Singh, S. (1999) *The Code Book: The Science of Secrecy from Ancient Egypt to Quantum Cryptography*, London: Fourth Estate.

Siroli, G. *et al.* (1997) "Internet e World Wide Web," in P. Capiluppi (ed.), *Reti Informatiche*, Le Scienze Quaderni no. 95.

Smillie, I. (1999) "Australia," in I. Smillie and H. Helmich with T. German and J. Randel (eds), *Stakeholders: Government – NGO Partnership for International Development*, London: Earthscan Publications, 39–50.

Sole 24 Ore (Il) (2000a) "L'Italia maglia nera della New Economy," September 11, 1–2.

——(2000b) "E-commerce lontano per piccole imprese," May 9, 12.

Steeves, V. (2000) "Privacy, Free Speech and Community: Applying Human Rights Law to Cyberspace," in S. Hick, E. Halpin, and E. Hoskins (eds), *Human Rights and the Internet*, New York: St Martin's Press, 187–99.

Stoll, C. (1989) *The Cuckoo's Egg: Tracking a Spy Through the Maze of Computer Espionage*, New York: Doubleday.

Stone, A. (1997) *How America Got On-Line: Politics, Markets and the Revolution in Telecommunications*, Armonk, NY and London: M.E. Sharpe.

Strange, S. (1984) "What about International Relations?," in S. Strange (ed.), *Paths to International Political Economy*, London: Allen & Unwin, 183–97.

——(1988) *States and Markets*, New York: Basil Blackwell.

Strano, M. (2002) "Nuove tecnologie e nuove forme criminali," paper presented at the Cybercrime International Conference, Palermo, October 3–5, available from <www.poliziastato.it/pds/informatica/allegati/Cybercrime%20International %20Conference%20(STRANO).pdf> [January 28, 2004].

Supperstone, M. (1981) *Brownlie's Law of Public Order and National Security*, London: Butterworths.

Symonds, M. (2000) "The Next Revolution: A Survey of Government and the Internet," *The Economist*, June 24.

Szafran, E. (1998) "Regulatory Issues Raised by Cryptography on the Internet," *Communications Law*, 3(2): 38–49.

Taft, D.K. (2000) "Industry Group Tells Government to Keep Out," TechWeb, October 13, available from <www.techweb.com/wire/story/ TWB20001013S0008> [February 5, 2004].

Tageszeitung (2000) "Rechte Fliegen aus dem Internet," August 8, 19.

Tambini, D. (1998) "Civic Networking and Universal Rights to Connectivity: Bologna," in R. Tsagarousianou, D. Tambini, and C. Bryan (eds), *Cyberdemocracy: Technology, Cities and Civic Networks*, London: Routledge, 84–109.

Tengelin, V. (1981) "The Vulnerability of the Computerised Society," in H. Gassmann (ed.), *Information, Computer and Communication Policies for the '80s*, Amsterdam: North Holland, 205–13.

Trendle, G. (2002) "The e-Jihad against Western Business," it-analysis.com, April 5, available from <www.it-analysis.com/article_pf.php?articleid=2744> [March 30, 2004].

United Nations Development Program (UNDP) (2001) "Human Development Report 2001: Making New Technologies Work for Human Development," available from <http://hdr.undp.org/reports/global/2001/en/> [March 31, 2004].

US Department of Commerce (DOC) and Internet Corporation for Assigned Names and Numbers (ICANN) (1998) *Memorandum of Understanding*, Washington, DC.

US General Accounting Office (2004) "Data Mining: Federal Efforts Cover a Wide Range of Uses," Report to the Ranking Minority Member, Subcommittee on Financial Management, the Budget, and International Security, Committee on Governmental Affairs, US Senate, May, Washington, DC available from <www.epic.org/privacy/profiling/gao_dm_rpt.pdf> [May 28, 2004].

Van Evera, S. (1997) *Guide to Methods for Students of Political Science*, Ithaca, NY: Cornell University Press.

Vegh, S. (2003) "Classifying Forms of Online Activism: The Case of Cyberprotests Against the World Bank," in M. McCaughey and M. Ayers (eds), *Cyberactivism*, London: Routledge, 71–95.

Vise, D. (2001) "FBI Warns Infrastructure Vulnerable to Cyber-Attacks," Washingtonpost.com, March 20, available from < http://www.washingtonpost.com/ac2/wp-dyn?pagename=article&node=&contentId=A31203-2001Mar20&notFound=true> [February 15, 2004].

Vulpiani, D. (2002) "L'esperienza italiana nel contrasto al crimine informatico," Cybercrime International Conference, Palermo, October 3–5, available from <www.poliziastato.it/pds/informatica/allegati/Cybercrime%20international%20conference%20(VULPIANI).pdf> [January 28, 2004].

Warren, S. and Brandeis, L. (1890) "The Right to Privacy," *Harvard Law Review*, 4(5), December 15, available from <www.swiss.ai.mit.edu/classes/6.805/articles/privacy/Privacy_brand_warr2.html> [June 14, 2004].

Werle, R. (1999) "Liberalization of Telecommunications in Germany," in K. Eliassen and M. Sjovaag (eds), *European Telecommunications Liberalization*, London: Routledge, 110–127.

White House (The) (2000) "Defending America's Cyberspace: National Plan for Information Systems Protection Version 1.0," Washington, DC, available from <www.ciao.gov/resource/np1final.pdf> [February 10, 2004].

——(2002) "The National Strategy for Homeland Security," July, Office of Homeland Security, Washington, DC, available from <www.whitehouse.gov/homeland/book/nat_strat_hls.pdf> [February 16, 2004].

——(2003) "The National Strategy to Secure Cyberspace," February, Washington, DC, available from <www.dhs.gov/interweb/assetlibrary/National_Cyberspace_Strategy.pdf> [February 18, 2004].

Wigert, I. (2004a) "Australia," in A. Wenger and J. Metzger (eds), *International CIIP Handbook 2004*, Zürich: Federal Institute of Technology, 37–50.

——(2004b) "Austria," in A. Wenger and J. Metzger (eds), *International CIIP Handbook 2004*, Zürich: Federal Institute of Technology, 51–61.

——(2004c) "Canada," in A. Wenger and J. Metzger (eds), *International CIIP Handbook 2004*, Zürich: Federal Institute of Technology, 62–72.

——(2004d) "France," in A. Wenger and J. Metzger (eds), *International CIIP Handbook 2004*, Zürich: Federal Institute of Technology, 85–94.

——(2004e) "Germany," in A. Wenger and J. Metzger (eds), *International CIIP Handbook 2004*, Zürich: Federal Institute of Technology, 96–110.

——(2004f) "The Netherlands," in A. Wenger and J. Metzger (eds), *International CIIP Handbook 2004*, Zürich: Federal Institute of Technology, 123–34.

——(2004g) "Switzerland," in A. Wenger and J. Metzger (eds), *International CIIP Handbook 2004*, Zürich: Federal Institute of Technology, 172–82.

Wired News (1998) "German Net Porn Conviction," May 28, available from <http://www.wired.com/news/politics/0,1283,12571,00.html> [January 15, 2004].

Woodall, P. (2000) "Untangling E-Conomics: A Survey of the New Economy," *The Economist*, September 23.

Wooldridge, A. (1999) "The World in Your Pocket: A Survey of Telecommunications," *The Economist*, October 9.

Wright, S. (2000) "Political Control and the Internet," in S. Hick, E. Halpin, and E. Hoskins (eds), *Human Rights and the Internet*, New York: St Martin's Press, 200–10.

Zampaglione, A. (2000) "New Economy: Ecco Le 'Top Ten'. Dopo gli USA, Stoccolma e Israele," *La Repubblica*, July 3, 38.

Zittrain, J. (2004) "Internet Points of Control" in S. Braman (ed.), *The Emergent Global Information Policy Regime*, Basingstoke, UK: Palgrave, 203–27.

Index